GREEK TRAGEDY AND MODERNIST PERFORMANCE

Edinburgh Critical Studies in Modernism, Drama and Performance

Edinburgh Critical Studies in Modernism, Drama and Performance addresses the somewhat neglected areas of drama and performance within Modernist Studies, and is in many ways conceived of in response to a number of intellectual and institutional shifts that have taken place over the past 10 to 15 years. On the one hand, Modernist Studies has moved considerably from the strictly literary approaches, to encompass engagements with the everyday, the body, the political, while also extending its geopolitical reach. On the other hand, Performance Studies itself could be seen as acquiring a distinct epistemology and methodology within Modernism. Indeed, the autonomy of Performance as a distinct aesthetic trope is sometimes located at the exciting intersections between genres and media; intersections that this series sets out to explore within the more general modernist concerns about the relationships between textuality, visuality and embodiment. This series locates the theoretical, methodological and pedagogical contours of Performance Studies within the formal, aesthetic and political concerns of Modernism. It claims that the 'linguistic turn' within Modernism is always shadowed and accompanied by an equally formative 'performance/performative turn'. It aims to highlight the significance of performance for the general study of modernism by bringing together two fields of scholarly research which have traditionally remained quite distinct – performance/theatre studies and Modernism. In turn this emphasis will inflect and help to reconceptualise our understanding of both performance studies and modernist studies. And in doing so, the series will initiate new conversations between scholars, theatre and performance artists and students.

GREEK TRAGEDY AND MODERNIST PERFORMANCE

PERFORMANCE

Hellenism as Theatricality

Olga Taxidou

EDINBURGH
University Press

Edinburgh University Press is one of the leading university presses in the UK. We publish academic books and journals in our selected subject areas across the humanities and social sciences, combining cutting-edge scholarship with high editorial and production values to produce academic works of lasting importance. For more information visit our website: edinburghuniversitypress.com

© Olga Taxidou, 2021, 2023

Edinburgh University Press Ltd
The Tun – Holyrood Road
12(2f) Jackson's Entry
Edinburgh EH8 8PJ

First published in hardback by Edinburgh University Press 2021

Typeset in Sabon and Gill Sans by
Servis Filmsetting Ltd, Stockport, Cheshire,
printed and bound by CPI Group (UK) Ltd
Croydon, CR0 4YY

A CIP record for this book is available from the British Library

ISBN 978-1-4744-1556-9 (hardback)
ISBN 978-1-3995-1109-4 (paperback)
ISBN 978-1-4744-1557-6 (webready PDF)
ISBN 978-1-4744-1558-3 (epub)

CONTENTS

LIST OF ILLUSTRATIONS

ACKNOWLEDGEMENTS

One of the main themes of Greek tragedy is philia, friendship; its emotional, civic, political prominence occupies much of the drama, strife, but also compassion and empathy at the centre of many tragedies. What are the bonds that tie us beyond and above blood or even the law? Can philia help form civic society? Can it help construct, in the evocative words of Eve Kosofsky Sedgwick, 'extended, pretended families'? And 'pretended' in this context is not pitted against some fantastic notion of 'authenticity', but points towards the performative nature of all our bonds, parallel to the ways the term Hellenism in used in this book. I have been fortunate to have been carried through my life by such strong bonds of friendship, and this book has been informed and inspired by such friends, and families.

My primary thanks go to Jackie Jones at EUP. Editor extraordinaire and modernist scholar, she has provided direction, insight and support for this and many a project with EUP. I am indebted to her and her team, especially Ersev Ersoy and Camilla Rockwood. She took risks and chances with my modernist co-conspirator, Vassiliki Kolocotroni, and myself from the early stages of our careers, and we are grateful. Vassiliki Kolocotroni's deep knowledge of both modernism and Hellenism is everywhere in this book. Thank you.

Most of this book was written during several Visiting Professorships and Fellowships with New York University's Hellenic Studies Department. Thank you: to Liana Theodoratou for broadening the horizons of Hellenism for me, for seeing it in its most cosmopolitan and emancipatory dimensions, aspects that have shaped this book; to Laura Slatkin and Helene P. Foley for being the most welcoming classicists in the city; to Eduardo Cadava, Niki Kekos, Jasmine Presson, Risa Mickenberg and Vaia Trittas for giving me a second home, and for all the pizza; to Lee Breuer and Maude Mitchell for once again through your creative power and talent confirming how incredibly awesome these Greek plays are on the stage; to Benita Hoffstetter and Jim Martin for reaffirming that friendships do indeed span decades and continents. At Oxford, thank you to Fiona Macintosh, Oliver Taplin, Laura Marcus, Susan Jones, Sos Eltis and Barbara Kowalzig for the warm hospitality, for giving me a platform to share ideas, and for the insightful suggestions. At Edinburgh, thanks to my colleagues Roger Savage, Greg Walker, Douglas Cairns, Nicola McCartney, Carole Jones and Anouk Lang. Thank you to J. Michael Walton, whose work on both Craig and Greek drama has helped shape some of the foundations for this book. In Athens, thank you to Maria Lambraki at the NYU Global Research Institute, and to its formidable International Director, Jair Kessler, whose generous Fellowship allowed me to complete this book. I have been fortunate to live in two Athenses, the Athens of the South and the Athens of the North. The friends in the 'real' Athens, Athena Athanasiou, Elena Tzelepis and Gianna Stergiou, have always provided warmth and spirited debate. My thanks also to the anonymous readers of this book, who supplied helpful and instructive comments, ones that I have hopefully addressed.

This book could not have been written without the overwhelming support, emotional and physical sustenance of my extended family and friends: Katerina Taxidou, Kat Taxidou, Euan Hill, Sarah Zachs-Adam, Bill Zachs and Martin Adam.

The author and the publishers would like to thank the following for permission to use copyright material:

The Edward Gordon Craig Estate, with special thanks to Marie J. Taylor and Anthony Taylor for the use of the following images:

- *Hecuba*, from Edward Gordon Craig, *Black Figures: 105 Reproductions with an Unpublished Essay*, ed. L. M. Newman (Wellingborough: Christopher Skelton; Chalbury, Oxford: Senecio Press, 1989).
- Edward Gordon Craig, 'Isadora Duncan Dancing', *The Mask*, vol. 1, no. 6 (1908), p. 126b.
- Edward Gordon Craig, *Isadora Duncan: Sechs Bewegungsstudien von Edward Gordon Craig* (Leipzig: Insel Verlag, 1906).

The Archive of the Akedemie der Künste, Bertolt Brecht Archive/Hilda Hoffmann, Berlin, with special thanks to Mrs Hilda Hoffmann of the Ruth Berlau Estate and Anette Schubotz of the Bertolt Brecht Archive for the use of three photographs by Ruth Berlau from the Brecht-Neher *Antigone Modellbuch 1948*.

The Brooklyn Museum, for the use of Abraham Walkowitz (1878–1965), *Dancer – Five Line Drawings*. Pen and ink on paper, Sheet (a): 6 3/4 × 2 1/16 in. (17.1 × 5.2 cm). Brooklyn Museum, Gift of the artist, 39.644a–e (Photo: Brooklyn Museum, 39.644a-e_acetate_bw.jpg).

Every effort has been made to trace the copyright holders, but if any have been inadvertently overlooked the publishers will be pleased to make the necessary arrangement at the first opportunity.

For Liana
and
Kat and Euan

I

INTRODUCTION: 'WHAT'S HECUBA TO HIM, OR HE TO HECUBA?'

The image that graces the cover of this book does not come from a specific performance; it is not a prop, a costume or a piece of scenography. Yet it has a story to tell, which is why it was chosen as emblematic of the approach followed in this book, and of the kinds of projects it engages. Artefacts, designs, acting and dance theories, translations, reworkings and adaptations, all feature as experiments in modernist performance that exhibit a strong attachment to Greek tragedy and to Hellenism more generally. Sometimes these experiments may result in actual performance, but more often than not they are attempts, usually failed, that gesture towards a new, revived understanding and experience of both Greek tragedy and modernist performance. It is this sometimes difficult, sometimes fraught, but always passionate relationship that this book sets out to explore.

The image of Hecuba with hands elevated in a gesture of mourning was designed by Edward Gordon Craig and turned into one of his beautiful Black Figures, which start to appear around 1908.[1] It is a figure engraved onto wood, a woodcut, then dipped into ink to result in a type of stencil. Craig works on these figures while he is at the same time working with Stanislavsky on the notorious Moscow *Hamlet*[2] and formulating his manifesto on acting, 'The Actor and the Über-marionette' (1908). Craig would claim that he used these wondrous figures instead of notes to the actors for the production of *Hamlet*, as he thought they would be much more effective than words. And indeed they are. Both as prompts for the Russian actors and for theatre history, they speak volumes. For in mingling images from roles in *Hamlet* with images from classical Greek tragedy and locating them on his miniature model stages, Craig is also drawing a genealogy of modernist acting that goes through Shakespeare back to the Greeks.

'What's Hecuba to him, or he to Hecuba?', from Act 2 Scene 2, is pronounced by Hamlet as he addresses the Players in a pivotal metatheatrical moment for performance history, where he himself is portraying the role of an acting coach – or, we could even claim, a performance theorist. What he is interested in, as we know, is the ability of acting conventions themselves to reveal a kind of truth through affect, identification, but also through distance and estrangement. Interestingly, the above line is spoken while Hamlet is alone on the stage, once the Players and Rosencrantz and Guildenstern have left; it is one of his famous soliloquies, addressed to the audience, who in turn are invited to assess the efficacy of acting conventions themselves. In choosing to do this through recourse to anaphora in the figure of Hecuba, he is relying on the long-established historical link between rhetorical devices and acting conventions;[3] a history that the audience would presumably have recognised, or perhaps that they are invited to consider. We could claim that Craig is using a similar trope when he engraves Hecuba onto a Black Figure in his attempt to create a lineage for the Moscow actors in their approach to his modernist *Hamlet*, which was to be stylised, abstract and performed in the midst of his famous screens.

Aligning the images of Hecuba, Hamlet, Craig's screens and even Craig's Übermarionette together side by side in paratactic manner creates a constellation of ideas and images that is indicative of the approach taken in this book, where the role of Greek tragedy and Hellenism more generally is not deterministic, generative, or considered simply on the basis of influence and the possible anxieties that these discourses may entail. It is much more allusive, but no less present as a result. While it may fall within the broad and thick understanding of reception theory, this book is not focused on analysing specific performances. Rather, in ways that mirror both Hamlet's and Craig's quoting of Hecuba, it sets out to explore the kinds of experiments in performance that were facilitated, embodied, experienced and experimented with by such recourse and remobilisation of Greek tragedy. Sometimes these experiments reached performance and were successful, but usually they were failures – creative, constructive failures but failures nonetheless, all enacted through quotation and repetition of notions of Hellenism. They 'fail again' but possibly 'fail better', as Samuel Beckett would have it.[4]

These notions of Hellenism are traced as endemic to the experiments in modernist theatricality more generally. Theatricality in this sense is read as parallel to what in literary modernism, following the Russian formalists, we term as 'literariness': the attempt of the stage to form, delineate and articulate its own languages of representation. 'To make the stone stony' is Victor Schklovsky's famous adage when talking about the 'literariness' of poetic language and its ability to bring out a material and materialist truth.[5] In the same vein, modernist performance seeks to make the stage 'theatrical', to 'retheatricalise' theatre. And the prefix 're-' is crucial in this context, for this attempt is radical, 'new' and forward-looking, but also remobilises historical theatrical traditions. This quest for the autonomy of performance, and its many complex relationships to textuality examined in this book, is in many ways thought through in manifestos, embodied in theories of acting, puppetry and dance, conceptualised through the figure of the modernist director, through enlisting iconography, terminology, images, tropes and modes that are associated with Greek tragedy. In this sense at the heart of modernist performance we can trace a strong relationship to notions of Hellenism. This Hellenism is at times very close to modernist neo-classicism (as in the work of James Joyce or Virginia Woolf), but it is rarely strictly textual or based on specific readings/interpretations of the Greek play-texts themselves. As is the case with Craig's image, Hecuba certainly proposes a notion of Hellenism and Greek acting, but we are not certain whether it refers to the specific role in Euripides or whether it has been constructed through the various images of the role in its long history of reception in the performing, literary and visual arts. The point highlighted throughout this study is that this is perhaps the wrong question to ask. Rather the focus is on the ways versions of Greek acting, 'Greekness' and Hellenism more generally also construct proposals for modernist performance. So, not so much the ways these experiments try to reconstruct authentic versions of classical Greek acting or the stage, but more the kinds of licence that their understandings or misunderstandings of Greek drama gave modernists in their attempts, proposals, manifestos of modernist theatricality. This endeavour follows a double movement, one that at once looks towards the future in the modernist quest for the autonomy of performance, recreates the relationship with the past, and re-visions in radical ways our understanding of Greek tragedy itself. In this sense the reiterability of Hecuba follows a double movement: 'What's Hecuba to modernist performance, or modernist performance to Hecuba?'

'Hellenism' in this context is used as an umbrella term rather than 'classicism', which addresses mainly textual works and has traditionally had a primarily philological perspective. Rather Hellenism, from its initial coinage as referring to the Hellenistic period (323 BCE – 31 BCE), connotes both the attempt to copy, imitate, pay homage to classical Greek aesthetic models and ideals – formally and thematically – and the attempt to inflect these and inject them with local and contemporary elements. This is classical Greek culture, Hellas, stretching across the southern and eastern Mediterranean, and through the conquests of Alexander the Great (whose death in 323 BCE marks the notional starting point of this period) to West and Central Asia and parts of the Indian subcontinent. A crucial characteristic of Hellenism, one that also informs this analysis, is hybridity. Hellenism as a kind of classicism that is always informed and inflected by other cultural modes and traditions is an aspect that this book explores in its theatrical manifestations, as most of these modernist experiments approach the Greek model of theatre in conjunction with other performance traditions, sometimes non-European, sometimes deriving from local and popular traditions, or even Christianity. In this sense Hellenism is read as being in dialogue with the modernist legacies of primitivism. Like most hybrid fusions, these interactions are also sites of contestation, debate and struggle. An *agon* of sorts is staged between the Greek traditions of performance and traditions which are considered to derive from popular, oral legacies or are non-European. We could claim that this *agon* might be constitutive of Hellenism itself. It is certainly one that informs modernist theatricality.

This theatricality, in most cases addressed in this book, is focused on tragedy. This is due to the fact that the modernist theatre-makers explored here are themselves concerned with tragedy, rather than comedy or satyr plays. This is also in line with the prominence accorded to tragedy in the philosophical legacies of modernity from the Enlightenment onwards. Particularly in the traditions of German Idealism and Romanticism more generally, tragedy is expanded from a poetics to an all-encompassing philosophical discourse that addresses issues of ethics, politics and subjectivity.[6] The introduction of Hellenism as theatricality acts as both expansion and revision of this philosophical concept of tragedy.

This complex relationship with Greek tragedy, which features at the centre of modernist theatrical experimentation, also goes to the heart of modernism itself. It is now more or less a given within the broad field of modernist criticism that modernism does not simply refer to the anglophone, primarily textual traditions of so-called High Modernism; instead, as the New Modernist Studies has shown,[7] it is more critically enabling and historically accurate to view modernism as a series of networks and relationships that open up the field geopolitically, formally and aesthetically. This in many ways democratisation and radicalisation of modernist criticism results from the ways modernism had been reconstructed initially through the Frankfurt School of cultural criticism,[8] through postcolonial studies and through the more recent global take on modernism itself, and importantly through the shift in the hegemonical position occupied by modernist poetry and the modernist novel. In moving away from modernism as 'the revolution of the word', as Julia Kristeva would have it, and in turning towards more performative and geopolitical understandings of modernist practices, theatrical experimentation has more recently received more critical attention. The New Modernist Studies with its emphasis on networks, events rather than texts, encounters rather than textual reading, multiple, complex and fraught cultural exchanges, may be said to embody and enact a type of performative model of cultural production, one that may itself have a lot to gain from modernist experiments in theatricality.

This interesting interface between theatricality as an aesthetic mode and performativity as political-philosophical category might in some ways help to decentre the position of literary modernism and the emphasis its critical legacies have placed on the word, or the power of the logos (and its subversion, political debunking etc. mainly through the legacies of structuralism and poststructuralism). Reading theatricality in conjunction with literariness, and not necessarily in opposition to it, perhaps opens up the critical field of modernist studies in ways that allow us to read embodiment and textuality as performatively constitutive and not as binaries, for example. These experiments in modernist performance allow us to rethink the whole paradigm of modernism.[9] In turn, at the centre of these experiments is a radical reconceptualisation and re-experience of the Greek model of theatre and performance. For it is in dialogue with, debate against, homage to the Greek paradigm that most modernist theatre sets out to redefine itself.

Certainly, this is not the only theatrical tradition that modernist performance engages, but it is a crucial one. Usually the encounter with Greek tragedy is also inflected by recourse to the classical theatres and performance traditions of India, China, South-East Asia and Japan. In this context this book is also concerned with the interactions between Hellenism and orientalism and the aesthetic and ideological/political challenges that such interactions involve. To return to the Black Figure of Hecuba, Craig may also have been influenced by the stencil paintings of Indian dance from Ananda Coomaraswamy's book on the same subject,[10] the first in English, which he himself reviewed in his journal *The Mask*. This interface between Hellenism and orientalism – evidenced in the theatrical works of Ezra Pound, W. B. Yeats and T. S. Eliot through the very significant contributions of the dancer Michio Ito, as well as in the work of Bertolt Brecht through his encounter with the Chinese actor Mei Lanfang – creates a network of relationships and events that open up modernism to the East/West encounter and that may result in a non-Eurocentric understanding of Hellenism itself, or at least gesture towards one. And in this way these experiments in theatrical modernism might also propose a more radical reading of Hellenism and classicism, one that is more clearly and deliberately articulated in later twentieth-century multicultural and intercultural performances.[11]

It is in this very broad sense that multiple relationships between Greek tragedy, Hellenism and modernist performance partake in the general concerns and experiments of the modernist project more generally, but may also help in their re-visioning. When Ezra Pound, for example, proclaims 'Make it New', surely he is also saying 'Make it new, again.' If we take into account his interest in the classics (both Greek and Latin), his studies of Chinese and Japanese poetic and visual traditions, and his own translations of Sophoclean drama, his aphoristic slogan acquires a citability and reiterability. In this sense, his and other modernists' relationships to Greek tragedy challenge both the absolute 'newness' of modernism and the 'datedness' of tradition. For it is not simply a case of the dominant anglophone figures of modernism attempting to translate or adapt Greek tragedies; in doing so they also enact the complex relationships between tradition and innovation, between tradition and 'individual talent'. The theatrical paradigm also to some extent helps redefine understandings of authorship, influence and its various anxieties, and understandings of readership, spectatorship and reception more generally. It helps to reconfigure the relationships between textuality and embodiment, between the word and the body.

The body in this context isn't simply read in opposition to the word, but through the specific body in performance the tensions and possibilities of that historically difficult relationship is experimented with, sometimes with recourse, as this study hopes to show, to classical theories of acting or perceptions of these. Placing the body as a methodological and theoretical unit does not necessarily negate or oppose the poetic word, but is read in conjunction with it, approaching the notion of embodiment as a dialectic between body and word that perhaps shapes our understanding of both. It is in this context that acting theories form a foundational aspect of the overall framework. Within modernist performance acting theories become a dominant discourse; in conjunction with theories of the director they become formalised for the first time in theatre history with such systematic rigour. And within all these crucial experiments from Stanislavsky to Craig, from Isadora Duncan to H.D., from Brecht to Eisenstein, there features an ongoing dialogue with classical theories of acting. And this dynamic tension between the body of the performer and the poetic word is nowhere more intense than in the encounter with the 'word' that carries possibly the most cultural currency in the Western European and Eurocentric tradition: the word of the classics. For in articulating experimental and innovative ideas about stage presence, movement and acting in its broadest sense, many modernist performers and theatre-makers, by recourse to 'the Greeks', are also revising the very dominant position of the classical, literary play-text within classical studies more generally.

The impact of Friedrich Nietzsche and of the charismatic group of anglophone classicists grouped as the 'Cambridge Ritualists' (although one of their most influential figures, Gilbert Murray, was Australian and held the chairs of Classics at the universities of Glasgow and Oxford) is vital in the move away from the predominantly German Romantic legacies of classicism towards the more modernist and radical ones. This shift is one that this book attempts to chart; it is not always straightforward, and poses its own methodological challenges. Still, this study claims that the modernist performing body is given shape and language through this sometimes counterintuitive recourse to the classical body. One way, for example, that this encounter may be counterintuitive is the fact that the classical body of the actor was male, whereas modernist performance is marked by the significant presence of the 'New Woman' on the stage and by discourses of queer performance.[12] However, modernist performance might also help construct a more ambivalent or queer understanding of that very classical body. The intricate ways in which Isadora Duncan and H.D., for example, decode and interpret vase images and Greek statues for their own purposes, or the ways that the men-playing-women convention may allow for experimentation with biological and essentialist notions of gender, are tropes that inform the modernist constructions of the classical body through performance.

Gender is another way in which the image of Craig's Hecuba speaks to the complex interactions between Hellenism and modernist performance. Craig praised the Greek model precisely because it did not feature women performers on its stage. He considered the arrival of the actress as one of the main reasons for the downfall of the modern stage from the Restoration and the arrival of the first English actresses onwards. However, as contemporary classical scholarship has shown,[13] the physical absence of women from the stage was more than made up for by their 'enacted' presence through the narratives of the plays themselves and through the bodies of the male performers. In a similar trope, Craig's vehement proclaiming that women should be banned from the stage, or that 'female nature' is not suited to any form of artistic endeavour, is paralleled by his strong creative and personal attachment to Isadora Duncan and by the designs of his Black Figures, inspired by Duncan and the great Italian actress Eleonora Duse.

This Hecuba is not a standalone work of visual art, but a visual image in this case meant to be 'read' by a performing body. It may be Eleonora Duse, or it may be the actors of the Moscow *Hamlet*. Either way, through recourse to a role from Greek tragedy and perhaps also an interpretation of classical Greek acting (the gesture, the pose, the *cheironomia*), it brings together discourses of visuality, textuality and embodiment, perhaps again allowing us to approach the performing body as one – not necessarily in hierarchical order – of the analytical and methodological units of modernism; one that, in addition to enacting the difficult relationship between tradition and innovation, also enacts the equally tense relationships between gender and representation.

This attempt to read these encounters through the performing body with a version of Hellenism at its centre also raises further issues about *how* to read modernism *in and through* performance. The use of *and* here, as I have indicated in previous work, is paratactic, creating a broad constellation of ideas and a network of encounters that aims to avoid the issue of belated modernity (expressed in the list) or the power dynamics of hypotaxis (because, after, therefore, etc.). For modernism's linguistic turn is surely also and always its performative turn, evidenced clearly at that crucial interface where performativity, as a philosophical/linguistic concept, encounters actual experimentation in performance. In this sense the performing body within modernist experimentation becomes a kind of ekphrastic machine, mediating between genres, disciplines and artforms, and remobilising another classical rhetorical but also performative trope. The term *machine* here is borrowed from Friedrich Hölderlin's writings on Greek tragedy, where the binary between *techne* and *mechane* is elided, reworking the Greek term *polymechanos*, which expresses a kind of embodied critical/practical thinking. Indeed, reading the modernist performing body this way – what in contemporary critical terms might be termed 'intermediality' – might help shift our understanding of modernism as being premised solely on the revolutions of the 'word'. The referencing of Hölderlin's writings on tragedy also traces a thread within the German Romantic tradition itself that follows its more radical strand, against the more classical and primarily textual readings of Schiller and Goethe. Hölderlin's work is approached in the ways it in turn inspired the radical and visionary traditions of German Romanticism, from Nietzsche to modernist thinkers like Bertolt Brecht and Walter Benjamin, to Hans-Thies Lehmann and his contemporary theories of the postdramatic.

Furthermore, almost despite its modernity, this emphasis on the performing body also rehearses the longue durée of the anti-theatrical legacy, always projected (from Plato onwards) and enacted through the performer. This ekphrastic use of the performing body (what some scholars have conceptualised as the *hieroglyph*, citing H.D. and in contrast to Pound's *ideogram*), exhibits the intricate and sometimes contradictory ways the anti-theatricality debate is staged within modernism. And in this way the most modern of experiments may be read as reviving the most ancient of debates. Could we in turn suggest that modernism itself (what Susan Stanford Friedman broadly calls 'the aesthetic domain of modernity') has a longue durée,[14] reviving, inflecting, and reworking older aesthetic debates? Susan Stanford Friedman seems to think so, and theatrical modernism attests to this and, we could also claim, enacts this principle.

The modernist encounter with Greek tragedy unearths what could be considered the oldest debate in the history of aesthetics, what Plato in *The Republic* calls 'the ancient quarrel between poetry and philosophy', interestingly, already termed 'ancient'.[15] And this 'unearthing', sometimes literal (through its reliance on the period's archaeological discoveries and anthropological theories), sometimes successful (in actual productions), others less so as in utopian designs and manifestos of a modernist/Greek stage, throws up and problematises the terms of this quarrel itself. Bodies posited against ideas, ideas against forms, corporealism against textuality, catharsis against estrangement, empathy against abstraction are all binaries that can be said to derive from the old debate; and they are all binaries that get confused, substituted, experimented with, both on the physical stages of modernist performance and in the theoretical writings about theatre of the period. The argument claims that it is partly the encounter with Greek tragedy that provides both a springboard for physically manifesting these debates and a new critical language, which helps to place theatre centre stage, again activating the old debate between theatricality and anti-theatricality. Is there a modernist aesthetic of performative Hellenism? Is there a politics to this aesthetic? How does it impact on the ways the relationships between the main protagonists of theatre practice – the playwright, the director, the performer, the audience – are radically reworked within the experiments in modernist performance? These questions are approached not with the aspiration of providing definitive answers, but more in an attempt to tease out the ways in which the encounter with Greek tragedy as a vehicle for performance has helped to reconfigure the questions themselves.

Many of the themes and tropes that form the reception of Greek tragedy within modernism were thought through, particularly from the eighteenth century onwards, within the context of the so-called 'German cast' of Greek tragedy. This is the philosophical tradition that initiates a split between tragedy as a literary form – a poetics, in the legacy of Aristotle – and tragedy as a philosophical category, as something that pertains to life in general; an 'idea of the tragic'. This Kant-inspired philosophical tradition, part of the German legacy of idealism and romanticism, with its list of impressive protagonists (Schelling, Hegel, Winckelmann in the fine arts and archaeology, and Lessing, Schlegel, Goethe, Schiller, Hölderlin, Heine amongst others in the literary arts and criticism) approaches the tragic as part of a metaphysical, ethical and universal quest where the ideal of aesthetic judgement occupies a privileged position. In the words of Peter Szondi: 'Since Aristotle we have a poetics of tragedy, only since Schelling a philosophy of the tragic.'[16] This split is further fractured by the introduction within modernism of a performance imperative. The philological and the philosophical versions of tragedy also confront the notion of tragedy as embodied performance and the potential of theatricality itself.

However, it would be unfair to the 'German cast' itself not to acknowledge a certain complexity beyond this split, as I would claim that the principle of theatricality is already located within the somewhat schematic binary of the idea versus the aesthetic form of the tragic. From Friedrich Hölderlin (1770–1843) onwards the return to the Greeks and specifically to tragedy was not a form of nostalgia but, as Philippe Lacoue-Labarthe claims, a quest 'for the grounds of theatricality'.[17] So this 'idea of the tragic' also engages the *praxis* of tragedy (Hölderlin's *mechane*,[18] Schiller's introduction to *The Bride of Messina*, 'On the Uses of the Chorus in Tragedy' of 1803, Nietzsche's championing of ritual and music; the list could also encompass the whole of the modernist experiment in theatre). In turn this 'idea of the tragic' is heavily inflected by this revived theatricality. This more radical and performative strand of German Romanticism and Idealism informs modernist performance practice and theory, especially in the epic traditions of Brecht. At the same time, the interface between this mostly German tradition and the anglophone one of the Cambridge Ritualists (Gilbert Murray's collaboration with Reinhardt, Craig's failed collaboration with Reinhardt, for example) also informs the anglophone modernist experiments in performing Hellenism.

Interestingly enough, this strand can be seen to follow a Platonic legacy rather than an Aristotelian one. Although Aristotle provides us with a formal and, as some scholars claim, formalist definition of tragedy,[19] it is Plato who is more concerned with the political, ethical and, to use his own term, 'muddy' aspects of tragedy.[20] In his repudiation of tragedy, in *Laws* and *The Republic* but also in *The Symposium*, Plato provides us with one of the first and most insightful accounts of the impact of theatricality both on the body of the actor *and* on the *body politic*. Through a kind of negative critique, it is Plato and not Aristotle who is concerned with the fundamental issues of theatricality: its supplementarity, its falseness, its distortion of the divine, its power to distort the truth and our perception of it. In terms that eerily pre-echo twentieth-century critiques of the spectacle and spectacularisation,[21] Plato seems to provide us not with the redemptive, socially constructive powers of tragedy, but is somewhat graphically and 'dramatically' concerned with the power of tragedy to mislead the audience and demagogically influence the *polis* itself. His notorious term *theatrocracy*, where the discourses of theatricality and spectacularisation spill over into the public sphere, making the political assembly appear as a mere parody of the theatrical audience, are confronted head-on and, I would claim, embraced body and soul in the modernist encounter with Greek tragedy. In this sense, modernist performance may define itself against Aristotle, but it seems that Plato and Platonism help to create some of its main conceptual, analytical and formal theatrical tools. This positing of Platonic thinking as a constitutive frame of the encounter with Hellenism as performance and theatricality seems to be in line with the work of contemporary classical scholars like Barbara Kowalzig and Leslie Kurke, who view Plato, and not Aristotle, as the first performance theorist.[22] Where Aristotle seems to be mainly concerned with the textual and poetic aspects of tragedy, it is Plato with his writings on the rhapsode of epic who is more concerned with theatricality and the ethico-political dimension of the performative more generally.

This modernist encounter with Greek tragedy can be read as Platonic in a number of ways: in the ways it deals directly with the truth claim of the 'tragic ideas'; in the ways it mobilises the power of theatricality for both performers and audiences; in the ways it unashamedly confronts both the distorting but also the enabling political dimension of that theatricality; and sometimes in the sheer utopian and unperformable aspects of some of these projects. From Wagner and Nietzsche, the Cambridge Ritualists, Gordon Craig and anglophone poetic drama, through to Brecht, the modernist stagings of Greek tragedy also propose ways of staging the dialogue or *agon* between tragedy and philosophy. In doing so they not only mobilise the discourses of Aristotelianism, but also those of Platonism. And they do so not only by reintroducing the notion of the theatre of ideas, but also by positing the idea of performance itself centre stage.

The ethico-political dimension of theatricality, so crucial for Platonic thinking, can also be said to be revived in the debates about engagement and autonomy voiced in the 1930s in the shadow of the rise of fascism and Nazism. These discussions between Ernest Bloch, Georg Lukács, Bertolt Brecht, Walter Benjamin and Theodor Adorno about the relationships between aesthetics and politics, about the political efficacy of aesthetic form itself, include a model of theatre as their paradigm (whether it be Benjamin championing Brecht and engaged art, or Adorno proposing Beckett as the paradigm of autonomous art that is more politically impactful precisely because of its autonomy). These debates have come to define the later Frankfurt School of criticism, so formative for modernist studies and for the whole category of ideological critique.[23] The point I would like to tentatively raise in this context is that these debates themselves could perhaps be read as a revival, or a modernist reiteration of the 'ancient quarrel'. For we could claim that one of the earliest attempts at an ideological reading of theatrical form and convention appears in Plato. As stated above, this would be in line with reading Plato as a performance theorist, but also in line with the more recent attempts by philosophers like Alain Badiou to reclaim Plato as both a performance theorist and a radical thinker.[24]

It is Plato that Walter Benjamin quotes in his writings on Brecht, *Understanding Brecht*,[25] which he posits as his thesis on engaged art in the above debate (indeed he analyses the notorious *theatrokratia*). And Edward Gordon Craig, who might even be read as occupying the opposite end of that political spectrum due to his fascination with Mussolini, also quotes Plato's famous denouncement of the rhapsode, in his manifesto 'The Actor and the Über-marionette'. As in Plato, it is mainly the body of the performer that throughout modernist performance becomes the main site where the *agon* about the political and philosophical efficacy of theatre is fought. In this sense, the so-called man or marionette debate, the modernist fascination with the mechanical body, especially the female robot, can also be said to have a long and primarily a classical, Hellenic lineage.

At one extreme we can posit the complete banishment of the human form and at the other the absolute validation of its presence. Edward Gordon Craig could be said to form one bookend of this notional spectrum and the visionary Russian director Vsevolod Meyerhold (1874–1940) the other. However, and parallel to the work of Jane Goodall on stage presence,[26] these two *poses* need not be read in opposition, where one is viewed in terms of metaphysical/ idealist, anti-somatic discourses and the other in terms of corporealism and spatialisation (i.e., one extreme in terms of a reactionary/conservative anti-theatricality and the other in terms of a materialist/radical theatricality). The *locus classicus* of this debate within modernist acting theories, as previously mentioned, is Edward Gordon Craig's 'The Actor and the Über-marionette', an essay/manifesto published in 1908 in Craig's journal *The Mask*.[27] This essay continues today to ignite responses equal in passion, vehemence and sometimes misunderstanding to those that met its original publication. Chapter 2 of this book, on Craig and Isadora Duncan, revisits the essay in an attempt to both take away some of its glamour of newness by placing it within a historical and theoretical genealogy, and also possibly revive some of its radical potential in the ways it reads the binaries of presence/absence, human/automaton, director/ actor. These binaries are problematised throughout the essay, almost despite Craig's intentions, by the rhetorical and dramatic tropes employed. The shock effect of the newness of the essay itself is somewhat diminished if we read it in dialogue with Heinrich von Kleist's (1777–1811) important essay of almost a century earlier, echoed in its title, *Über das Marionettentheater*.[28] Craig himself, utilising the many editorial masks he wears in his journal (sixty-five in total), unashamedly uses the tropes of theatricality to display his sources (or, we could equally claim, to hide them, straddling the double bind of deception/revelation that is enacted in the essay itself). He publishes the first English-language translation of the Kleist essay in the journal that was to be the foil of *The Mask*, the aptly named *The Marionette* (1917–18), also edited and published by Craig. In ways similar to Plato, Craig utilises the rhetorical tropes of theatricality (the use of the philosophical dialogue, the creation of characters, etc.) to denounce the art of the actor. This reading also draws on the epigraphs and footnotes that help to stage this essay. Interestingly, Craig frames his manifesto with two iconic quotations: one from Aristotle regarding the function of *opsis*, and the other from Plato – the famous quotation about the rhapsode from *The Republic*.[29] Again, this most radical and aphoristic of essays about the role of the actor engages the old debate and restages it within a modernist context.

Rather than a literal negation of the presence of the actor, Craig's essay resurfaces as more ambivalent and contradictory. In fact, it could be seen as inhabiting almost in a *classical* manner the tropes of modernist anti-theatricality itself, where the negation of theatre helps to create a new theatre. That this trope, too, in the work of Craig appears with a Greek mask is significant. For Craig it offers a critical language to express his views about acting, to help forge the new role of the director, but equally it could be argued that it also feeds into the nostalgic and utopian aspects of his work. For Craig's notoriety relies as much on his passionate writing about theatre as it does on the fact that he didn't actually make much theatre. Personal and biographical reasons aside, it could be argued that Craig's main concern is with creating a body of work where the writing and the doing are not seen as binaries, but form part of the quest for a language of the new theatre – 'the Theatre of the Future', to use Craig's favourite phrase. Rather than see Craig's small output in theatre production as a shortcoming deriving from his personality traits (his inability to work collaboratively, etc.), it might be equally interesting to see that his commitment was to theorising performance itself. He didn't want to 'waste time' producing plays, as he claimed. However, he did spend much time designing, writing about and discussing possible productions. And this utopian aspect of his work can also be read within the framework of modernist Hellenism, where the relationship with the Greeks helps to create a vision of a theatre that is at once imaginable but practically unrealisable and unperformable. This principle of 'unperformability', so central to many of the modernist experiments in the theatre, pushes the limits of theatricality itself, but also proposes a relationship with the Greek 'model' that can be seen as both enabling and binding. Craig's beautiful *Black Figures*, mostly designs for roles from Greek tragedies and the Moscow *Hamlet*, begun as early as 1907 and extending throughout his life, can be read as studies in the creation of presence for the human form; equally, they can be seen as figuratively enacting this double and ambivalent quality of his relationship with the Greek model.

Another attraction of the Greek model for Craig was the absence of female performers. The 'decline' of the modern theatre for Craig was at least partly due to the introduction of the female performer. Associated with supplementarity and falseness itself, the female figure only added to the phantasmic *and* phantasmagoric quality of theatre. If the actor himself was seen as inappropriate raw material for art, the actress only served to double the inability of the stage to access a sense of truth for Craig. And in as much as the 'new theatre' was seen as providing a platform for the 'new woman', then it too was seen as lacking. However, again these aphoristic proclamations need to be read in conjunction with Craig's longstanding association with Isadora Duncan and Eleonora Duse and, of course, in relation to his ambivalent relationship with his mother, Ellen Terry. For despite his objections, many of Craig's ideas were given shape and form through his association with female performers. Isadora Duncan's Hellenism plays a significant role in proposing new theories of presence for the female performer. And its impact can be felt on Craig's ideas, in his designs for the stage and in his designs for these performers themselves.

Isadora Duncan Dancing is the title of an etching by Craig that appears in *The Mask* in 1908, the same year that features his essay/manifesto against the art of the live actor. Interestingly, an article on 'Madame Eleonora Duse' appears in the same year.[30] Far from being antithetical, these works can be read, as indeed they had initially appeared, side by side. Modernist dance, which was undergoing radical changes partly due to female dancers and choreographers, can be viewed as representing liveness and embodiment – the ultimate stage presence infused with the radical gender politics of modernism. Rather than read this in opposition to Craig's Übermarionette, it could be read as part of the period's experimentation with the presence *and* the absence of the stage performer. Both for Craig and Duncan the modernist fascination with the dancing female body helps to revive the ancient debate about the efficacy of the performer; and in this case it is *her* presence. Equally at the opposite extreme, from Kleist's essay onwards the evocation of the marionette, the puppet, the doll, the automaton, the robot, need not necessarily be read as advocating absence alone, but possibly gesturing towards creating a new type of presence on the stage, one where *techne* and *mechane* co-exist, and one that in some cases helps to manifest the ghostly presence of a Hellenic past.

As much as this project is concerned with the performing body, it is also concerned with the poetic word. Indeed, one of the binaries that theatricality itself examines, problematises and perhaps sets out to negate is that between the body and the word. Both the textuality of the performing body and the physicality of the poetic word are experimented with in modernist performance; and this principle of performativity that we have been utilising allows us to read enactment itself as an event that is both textual/linguistic and physical/bodily, that is both material and materialist in the ideological sense. And this dialectic, dynamic dialogue is nowhere more prevalent than in the modernist translations of the classics. Chapter 3 looks at the translations of Greek tragedies by very canonical anglophone modernists, T. S. Eliot, Ezra Pound and W. B. Yeats, and tries to sketch out the ways that their encounter with the Greek model of drama impacted their overall poetic projects and modernist poetic drama more generally. It looks at the ways modernist anxieties about influence, tradition and individuality and authorship are negotiated through their projects of translating the Greeks. More often than not concerns about translation, or translatability, as Walter Benjamin would phrase it (whose seminal essay of 1918 helps frame this chapter), are echoed by equally demanding questions about performability. These translations, especially Pound's, do not readily lend themselves to performance. In many ways they enact another modernist aesthetic principle, that of difficulty. This chapter addresses the ways these translations also engage modernist formal experimentation more broadly, and heighten the concept of difficulty, not necessarily as an exclusive, elitist mode but as a mode of experimental, formal critique. And the challenges that some of these translations pose for performance are ones that are not simply 'belated' or due to the fact that they are 'ahead' of their own historical time.

Sometimes, we may claim that we now have the technology to construct an Übermarionette, or we can begin to transfer Ezra Pound's astonishing translations to the stage, because somehow stage technologies and technologies of the body have caught up with these visionary projects, as it were. In other ways, however, we may claim that the difficulty of these projects, one that makes us confront and experiment with the whole edifice of theatricality, perhaps is not contingent on historical, linear time but adds to their futurity, making these projects more utopian. And part of that utopia revives a sense of pastness which is populated by a Hellenism that is ghostly and fantasmic.

In his introduction to Pound's version of *Elektra*, Richard Reid claims that Pound addresses 'the operative deception at the core of translating from ancient Greek: the living play dead, so that the dead may be quickened' and cites Pound's translation of Orestes' lines 'Haven't you ever learned/that the DEAD don't DIE' as 'Pound's heartfelt assertion of the translator's credo'.[31] As in his other 'stab' at Greek tragedy, his version of *Women of Trachis*, Pound's act of reviving the Greeks, like Hölderlin's, also involves reburying them. These translations not only raise questions of how to relate to a 'dead' past, but also pose demands on theatricality, which always locates itself in an embodied, living present and sometimes points towards a utopian future. Interestingly, in the case of *Women of Trachis*, Pound proposes the model of the Noh theatre as a way of addressing the issues of performability raised by his difficult and strange translations.[32] In a familiar trope of the period, once again we come across the creative fusions of Hellenism, orientalism and primitivism. It is primarily the demands placed by performability itself that allow these fusions to take place, and in the case of Pound's translations, not necessarily during his lifetime or on the theatrical stage as such; his *Elektra* was not performed until 1987 by Carey Perloff's Classic Stage Company in New York, and his *Women of Trachis* was first performed on radio on the BBC's Third Programme in 1954.

The fact that Greek tragedy provides a springboard/reference point/medium for modernist theatrical experimentation makes sense in a genealogy of theatre history but also performance theory. Cinema might sit uncomfortably within this context and its inclusion might imply a hasty and reductive conflation of the two media. However, during this early period of cinema there is a structural overlap between the two forms, with artists working in both media, transferring experiments from one form to the other. For H.D., the cinema could possibly also offer a channel for her particular brand of modernist Hellenism, one that the stage was unable to provide at the time. It has been claimed of many of the modernist experiments on the stage that in some ways they were ahead of their time, suggesting a stage technology that was not yet available.[33] H.D.'s turn to the cinema could on one level be read as part of the general modernist anti-theatricality that views the stage itself as limited, too traditional and stifling. On another level the cinema could also be seen as the quintessential medium that embodies the utopian dimensions of modernist Hellenism. In combining the miraculous with the mechanical, the cinema itself could be read as a form that helps to create *presence* or to revive the Greeks in a more fundamental way, that fuses the physical with the metaphysical and provides form for the Greek ghost in the machine. This Greek ghost that H.D.'s writing on the cinema evokes could be said to haunt many of the utopian aspects of modernist experiments in theatre and cinema.

Arguably the most radical reconfiguration of *mechane* and *techne* occurs in this newly formed art of the cinema, where the art of the 'stage machinist' comes fully into its own. In her pamphlet on the film *Borderline* in 1930, H.D. presents an evocative image of the director Kenneth Macpherson, claiming that he is 'like the Perseus who snatched the EYE from the clutch of the slobbering and malign Monsters ... Kenneth Macpherson, at work, is a hard-boiled mechanic, as if he himself were all camera, bone and sinew and steel-glint of rapacious grey eyes.'[34] We could read this image as a radical reworking and validating of the art of the stage machinist and as a direct reference to Aristotle's ambivalence about *opsis*. Such a reading is possible because H.D. was an imagist poet, actress and cinema-maker who by the 1930s had a considerable body of work behind her that involved essays on Greek tragedy and, significantly, translations of Euripides. Her engagement with Greek tragedy in many ways forms the backbone of all her intellectual and artistic endeavours. H.D.'s Hellenism and the parallels it bears with the work of the Cambridge Ritualists have been documented.[35] However, her writing about cinema and her filmmaking could also be read within a similar context of modernist Hellenism. Like her theatrical counterparts, the encounter with Greek tragedy formed part of her search for an autonomous language of performance. For H.D., many of her theoretical and aesthetic concerns find a form and outlet in the newly established art of the cinema. It is surprising that this quintessentially modern medium also needs to be interpreted and articulated in terms of its relationship to the classics. In *Close Up* (1927–33), a small radical journal very much within the modernist little magazine tradition, H.D. presents a series of articles entitled 'Cinema and the Classics',[36] where the ultra-modern meets the ultra-classic. These are written in the manifesto style of the period and appear as a 'defense' of cinema itself. 'Here is our medium', she proclaims, 'as I say here is the thing that the Eleusinians would have been glad of; a subtle device for portraying of the miraculous.'[37] And for her it is this combination of the miraculous and the mechanical that finds its true form in the art of the cinema.

For H.D. too this Hellenism is inflected by an equal fascination with primitivism. What Pound finds in his reworking of the Chinese and Japanese ideogram, H.D. finds in the Egyptian hieroglyph, with cinematic form as its modernist counterpart. However, for H.D. the discourses of Hellenism and primitivism are much more interlocked and interdependent, as her Hellas is not located in Athens but in Alexandria. Discussing the forms of the 'new Hellenism' in a letter published in *The Little Review* in 1917, Pound assesses the Hellenism of 'Alexandria' as 'Not so good'.[38] His own version of the new Hellenism, as his translations clearly show, was to be hard, virile, clear and masculine. The model of Hellenism that finds its *topos* in Alexandria is Hellenistic, relying on diffusion, diaspora and influence, and is considered by Pound to be decadent, nostalgic and effeminate. However, these are the very qualities that prove attractive for H.D. and, like the poet C. P. Cavafy, she makes Alexandria the home of her particular brand of modernist Hellenism. Corrupt and nostalgic it may be, but it helps forge an alternative genealogy of Hellenism, one that she explores in her poetry and in her translations throughout her life. In many ways this culminates in her long lyric poem *Helen in Egypt*, composed in the early 1950s. Her parallel writing on cinema and her practical involvement in making films also provide her with a form where her particular brand of modernist Hellenism can manifest itself, a form where the mechanical meets the miraculous. In the process, H.D.'s work also makes a case for reinterpreting the notion of nostalgia. Anathema to many of the modernists, castigated as effeminate, sentimental and in extreme cases pathological, H.D.'s reworking of nostalgia, particularly after her period of psychoanalysis with Freud (1933–4, a period that many scholars see as a turning point in her work) proposes a revised relationship with the Greeks, one where nostalgia is not viewed simply through the lens of trauma and loss, but itself helps to create formal and experimental languages of representation. Some of these can be traced in H.D.'s own acting style (as in her appearance in the film *Borderline*) and in her essays on cinema.

Chapter 4 sets out to examine H.D.'s translations of Euripides in conjunction with her theories of cinema *and* her own acting style in *Borderline*. It makes a case for her acting that parallels her translation techniques. Again the idea of the poetic, translated word as embodied practice is read both in H.D.'s highly literary translations of Euripides and in her own acting style. Furthermore, this approach makes a case for reading H.D. as a dramaturg in conjunction to her function as a translator. And in reading her translations as dramaturgical reworkings, we can also draw parallels with the notion of the 'landscape play' as theorised and exemplified in the theatrical works of Gertrude Stein. The two major modernists had never met. However, we could perhaps read them in tandem, as examples of Sapphic modernism, where the stage itself is reworked as a reproduction machine (as an *ur*-mother trope), and the principle of the *theatrum mundi* is reworked as the landscape play. Reading H.D.'s translations this way, together with Gertrude Stein's plays and phenomenological theories on performance, places H.D. in the midst of theatrical modernism and somewhat reinvents her as a dramaturg/ playwright.

Brecht or the Brechtian project more generally is crucial in any study about the encounter between Hellenism, Greek tragedy and modernism. Probably more so than any other modernist theatre-maker or theorist, Brecht sets out to define the whole edifice of epic theatre against what he terms dramatic theatre, which in this instance he also identifies with Aristotelianism. Brecht in many ways continues the formal and political concerns of the Russian formalists and their theatrical counterparts Vsevolod Meyerhold and Sergei Tretyakov. Epic theatre throughout all the debates within modernism about the relationships between aesthetics and politics becomes the paradigmatic engaged artform. In the midst of all the political upheavals of the early twentieth century, Brecht's epic theatre is presented as a solution of sorts in the quest for an artistic medium that is at once formally innovative, experimental, but also accessible while being politically engaged. And in all these sometimes heated debates and discussions (indeed debates that sometimes were a matter of life and death, as in the Moscow show trials of the 1930s), Brecht comes to formulate his theories on epic in opposition to Greek tragedy. Rightly or wrongly, his project somewhat reductively identifies the Greek model of drama as a type of bourgeois aesthetic and in his attempt to create a forceful and convincing manifesto in a classic modernist vein he outlines his programmatic lists, which appear in the *Short Organum* (1949), and constructs these in binary opposition: epic vs dramatic theatre. Chapter 5 revisits those notorious lists in an attempt to contextualise them and to re-read them not so much in the ways that the Brechtian project misreads the dramatic and the tragic theatre, but in the ways it reconstructs versions of classical epic.

In this sense the Brechtian epic is read in conjunction with other modernist attempts to revitalise, rewrite and reclaim epic. In a similar way to Sergei Eisenstein's (who was Meyerhold's student) rewriting of epic in his theories on montage, Brecht is read as also finding in the form aspects that are both experimental and politically critical. In this context Brecht's schema for epic theatre is read as parallel to Eisenstein's 'Montage of Attractions' (1923), which becomes the manifesto for a modern cinema. Contrary to the so-called dramatic and primarily literary tradition of representation in the performing arts, the epic tradition is seen as tapping into the popular and oral traditions of storytelling, which, in an almost Bakhtinian sense, are emblematic of the 'voice of the people'. Epic offers a narrative that is not linear, that is episodic, fragmented, that has multiple authors and, importantly, is viewed as connected with a performing tradition that is irreverent and non-literary. This chapter examines the ways Brecht reconceptualises epic and repoliticises it for the purposes of modernity.

Brecht's somewhat fraught relationship with German Romanticism and Idealism is approached in the ways his work initially mimics the debate of 'epic versus drama', between Goethe and Schiller (1794–1805), but by the 1930s no longer sees these as opposites. In a recent study by Fiona Macintosh and Justine McConnell that looks at contemporary revivals of epic as performance and insightfully re-examines the longstanding opposition between epic and drama, they claim that 'the theoretical interplay between narrative and theatre, which has often been agonistically (mis)cast as epic *versus* drama, begins with Plato and Aristotle',[39] once again locating this debate within the ancient quarrel where 'Epic poetry is always there in the mix of these aesthetic debates; and is usually cast as an earlier, more primitive, art form in comparison with the new tragic ideal.'[40] In this theoretical context, Brecht's revitalisation of epic unearths it from its 'primitive' status and gives it a modernist gloss, in ways that echo relationships between modernist theories of acting and popular traditions of puppetry. So epic is no longer associated with discourses of empire, with dubious gender politics and with formal conservatism. Rather it is associated with what Walter Benjamin calls the 'overgrown stalking track' of European theatre,[41] which gives voice to an irreverent and blasphemous popular tradition.

This blurring of the binary between epic and tragic, which is already present in Aristotle, allows us to create a genealogy for Brechtian theories of acting that may possibly be read in conjunction with Plato's theories on acting, as these appear in his writings on the epic rhapsode. This in turn may also offer some insight into the classical tragic actor, following both the double movement of this analysis and the reading of Plato himself as a performance theorist. In this context Chapter 5 also engages with the contemporary phenomenological and emotional turn in approaching Greek tragedy as a performance practice, and draws parallels between Brechtian epic theories of acting and contemporary approaches. These approaches in many ways result from contemporary performance reception of Greek plays, which attempt to portray the many visceral but no less political emotions of the tragedies, and in many cases the Brechtian epic take offers a valid way of presenting tragic emotion on stage. What transpires from this weaving together of the different epic legacies is possibly an approach that, rather than negating the tragic, reconceptualises it in terms of this modernist understanding of epic. This chapter stages a fantastical dialogue between the monstrous mother of Greek tragedy, Medea, and Brecht's epic mothers in its attempt to seek out parallels between epic and tragic constructions of character and role, again stressing the significance of theories of acting. It also presents a reading of Brecht's *Antigone-Model 1948*, as Brecht's experiment in fusing epic and tragic modes. In turn this encounter has facilitated the creation of new modes of performance, especially in relation to the portrayal of emotion and the idea of character on stage. And in this sense both the Brechtian epic project and its love/hate relationship with tragedy (as expressed through the dramatic theatre) are seen to partake in the modernist phenomenological approach to performance.

This folding over of epic and dramatic theatre reassesses Brecht's relationship with Greek tragedy, but also possibly looks forward to the concept of the postdramatic and its relationship to the tragic. Coined by Hans-Thies Lehmann, 'postdramatic' has proved to be a very enabling term in describing the radical performance practices of the late twentieth century and beyond. Interestingly, Lehmann's recent book, *Tragedy and Dramatic Theatre*,[42] also addresses the full edifice of tragedy in relation to his initial formulation of the postdramatic. In some ways, Lehmann's binary between dramatic and postdramatic theatre revisits and continues in the tradition of that original binary articulated by Schiller and Goethe of epic versus drama. Indeed, I feel the use of the term 'drama' associates it with this specific, predominantly literary legacy, and not necessarily with the Greek sense of the term, which already contains ideas about enactment and embodiment. And, of course, the postdramatic appears as an epigone of Brecht and Benjamin's writing on theatre. This is the legacy perhaps that Lehmann occupies and furthers in his attempt to theorise tragedy as well.

However, the reliance on the notions of rupture, crisis and subversion, indicated by the 'post' in the postdramatic, which mirrors the 'post' of the 'postmodern', I feel may miss some of the complexities and nuances already and ever present within the dramatic-as-tragic itself. Indicatively, this seems to both undervalue and overvalue the relationships between bodies and words, between textuality and literariness on the stage. On the one hand, the absence of a clear, linear narrative or indeed of language altogether from the theatres that are hailed as postdramatic does not necessarily imply that textuality and discourse are absent. Indeed, in the work of Sarah Kane, for example, the cruelty and seeming absence of narrative may imply an equally strong attachment to morality and ethics, in an almost Old Testament mode, somewhat reminiscent of the staging of saints' lives in the medieval mysteries or the cruelty of Greek tragedies themselves (one of which she deliberately rewrites as *Phaedra's Love*). This may be a matter of interpretation, but the point raised here is that the literary word and the performing body are locked in dialectical embrace; the conspicuous presence of the performing body does not mean that it automatically allows for an 'escape' from individuation and identity (as implied in some of the work of radical directors of Greek tragedy that are celebrated under the umbrella of the postdramatic, like Jan Fabre and Theodoros Terzopoulos). The simple point raised here is that the shift from modernist understanding and experimentation in Greek tragedy to contemporary notions of the postdramatic may be one of degree rather than of kind, or even genre. The ways that these modernist experiments engage with Greek drama and Hellenism more generally could possibly be read as 'unearthing' a postdramatic quality in the tragedies themselves. And perhaps this constructs a reading of the postdramatic as always shadowing the dramatic, as its double in the ways that both Artaud and Plato understand the 'doubleness' of theatre; as the condition of the possibility of both deception and critique. This is perhaps the 'secret smugglers' path' of theatre history that Benjamin saw epic theatre following. In turn, rather than rely on rifts and ruptures, primarily between the modern and the postmodern, this reading of the postdramatic sees it as part of the longue durée of the debates between epic and drama, and as part of the ancient quarrel itself.

As stated throughout this Introduction and throughout this book, this project does not offer an exhaustive account of specific performances of Greek tragedy during the modernist period. Rather, it sets out to look at a group of instances that may connote performance events, but more often than not refer to projects that remained unrealised, projects that have nevertheless left traces of their creative and theoretical process. Indeed, the emphasis on process that was to be formalised by late twentieth-century performance, and performance studies as both an aesthetic and pedagogical ideal, begins to take shape and form through these experiments. These projects not only challenge the whole idea of performance as an end result, but also help create the idea of performability itself, as parallel to the critical categories of translatability, readability and reproducibility that were to mark the reception of literary modernism, and the literary theory that followed it. Within this context, the Greek model of theatre is called upon less as an evocation of romantic Hellenism to perhaps add nostalgia and cultural capital, and more as a licence for radical experimentation. Rather than being located on a specific stage, this experimental Hellenism contributes to a utopian aspect of modernist performance, where the non-topos is the absence of the stage itself, the *skene*. What does it mean to have a drama without a stage, or to have projects that were not written to be performed at all, or when the stage is a manifesto, a dancer's body, a model stage or the page itself? And it is in this sense that Hellenism contributes to the idea of theatricality and performability, as both part of the quest for autonomy of the stage and possibly *from* the stage, and as critical/theoretical categories.

This study tries to read these experiments as constellations of ideas, of practices and sometimes of theatre artists themselves. Another way of approaching them might be as *poses*, underlining the emphasis placed on acting theories and especially on the significance of the pose. From Delsarte to Meyerhold, from Balinese dance to Chinese acting, from the *commedia dell'arte* to Wayang puppetry, theories of acting and stage presence more generally are obsessed with the political, expressive and overall aesthetic power of the pose or the *gestus*. H.D.'s hieroglyph and Ezra Pound's ideogram might also be read as attempts to transfer the vitalism of the pose onto the linguistic text. It is the power of the pose, the *gestus*, the *étude*, to crystallise both a specific image in the moment and to create a world-view that extends beyond the stage. The poses for the theatres of the future that these experiments strike all exhibit a passionate attachment to Greek drama and to Hellenism more generally. In embodying these poses, as physical presence and as theoretical studies (*gestus* and *études*), they urge and inspire us to rethink and re-experience both modernist theatre and classical Greek drama.

NOTES

1. See Newman (ed.), *Edward Gordon Craig, Black Figures*.
2. See Senelick, *Gordon Craig's Moscow Hamlet*.
3. For an insightful analysis of these connections see Wiles, *The Players' Advice to Hamlet*.
4. Beckett, *Worstward Ho*.
5. See Erlich, *Russian Formalism*. Also see Entry on FORMALISM by Alexandra Smith, in Kolocotroni and Taxidou (eds), *The Edinburgh Dictionary of Modernism*.
6. See Leonard, *Tragic Modernities*; Billings and Leonard, *Tragedy and the Idea of Modernity*; Billings, *Genealogy of the Tragic*.
7. Mao (ed.), *The New Modernist Studies*. Also see the journal *Modernism/modernity*.
8. See Miller, *Modernism and the Frankfurt School*.
9. See Kastleman, Riordan and Warden (eds), *Modernism on the World Stage*.
10. Coomaraswamy, *The Dance of Shiva*.
11. As evidenced in the 1984 Kabuki-inspired *Medea* directed by Yukio Ninagawa, and the 1983 production of *The Gospel at Colonus* directed by Lee Breuer, inspired by the African American traditions of Gospel.
12. See Farfan, *Performing Queer Modernism*.
13. Indicatively see Foley, *Female Acts in Greek Tragedy*.
14. Friedman, *Planetary Modernisms*.
15. Plato, *The Republic*, Book X, 1211, 607b, in *The Collected Dialogues*, pp. 575–844. Also see Gould, *The Ancient Quarrel between Poetry and Philosophy* and Levin, *The Ancient Quarrel between Poetry and Philosophy Revisited*.
16. Szondi, *An Essay on the Tragic*, p. 1. For an early twentieth-century study of the centrality of 'the tragic' for German Idealism see Butler, *The Tyranny of Greece Over Germany*.
17. Lacoue-Labarthe, 'Hölderlin's Theatre', pp. 118–19.
18. See Hölderlin, *Essays and Letters on Theory*, p. 101.
19. See Edith Hall, 'Is there a *Polis* in Aristotle's *Poetics*?' in Silk (ed.), *Tragedy and the Tragic*, pp. 295–309. For Plato's repudiation of the tragic see *Laws*, trans. A. E. Taylor, 1225–1513; *The Republic*, trans. Paul Shorey, 575–844; *Symposium*, trans. A. E Taylor, 526–74, in Hamilton and Cairns (eds), *The Collected Dialogues*.
20. For an analysis of Aristotle's term *catharsis* and its relation to what Nussbaum calls the '*katharsis* . . . word-family', where it is described as 'clearing up' and 'clarification', 'as the removal of some obstacle (dirt or blot, or obscurity, or admixture', 'as clearing up of the vision of the soul of [bodily] obstacles', see Nussbaum, *The Fragility of Goodness*, pp. 389–93.
21. In its most radical and aphoristic mode this critique appears in Debord, *The Society of the Spectacle*. Written in 1967, it came to act as the manifesto of Situationism, expressing the repudiation of the spectacle as the quintessential political tool of capitalism. For a recent insightful contemplation of the relationships between

philosophy and media culture – from Aristotle to modernity – see Weber, *Theatricality as Medium.*

22. See Kowalzig, 'Broken Rhythms in Plato's *Laws*', and Kurke, 'Imagining Chorality'.
23. See Jameson (ed.), *Aesthetics and Politics.*
24. See Badiou, *Plato's Republic.*
25. Benjamin, *Understanding Brecht.*
26. Goodall, *Stage Presence*, pp. 5–7.
27. Craig, 'The Actor and the Über-marionette'.
28. Heinrich von Kleist, *Über das Marionettentheater*, *Berliner Abendblatter*, c. 1810. Craig presents his readers with the first English translation of Kleist's essay, by Amedeo Foresti, in *The Marionette* no. 4 (1918). Subsequent English translations include those by Dorothea B. McCollester in *Theatre Arts Monthly* (July 1928); Eugene Jolas in his volume *Vertical* (1941); and Beryl de Zoete in *Ballet* magazine (June 1946), rpt in the journal *The Puppet Master* (BPMTG, October 1946).
29. 'And therefore when anyone of these pantomimic gentlemen, who are so clever that they can imitate anything comes to us, and makes a proposal to exhibit himself and his poetry, we will fall down and worship him as a sweet and holy and wonderful being; but we must also inform him that in our state such as he are not permitted to exist; the law will not allow them. And so, when we have anointed him with myrrh, and set a garland of wool upon his head, we shall lead him away to another city. For we mean to employ for our soul's health the rougher and severer poet or story-teller, who will imitate the style of virtuous only, and will follow those models which we prescribed at first when we began the education of soldiers', 'the whole passage being too long to print here, we refer te [sic] reader to *The Republic*, Book III, 395', *The Mask*, vol. 1, no. 2, p. 5. Craig uses Benjamin Jowett's (1817–1893) translation. The Oxford classicist's translations of Plato were to have a huge impact on the next generation of 'Oxford Platonists' like Walter Pater and Oscar Wilde and the generation of aesthetes, who were instrumental for the development of Craigian thought and are quoted throughout *The Mask*.
30. Edward Gordon Craig, *Isadora Duncan Dancing*, in *The Mask*, vol. 1, no. 6, p. 126b.
31. Pound and Flemming, *Elektra*, p. xix.
32. For a fascinating reading of Pound's translation as a performance text that fuses Greek tragedy with Japanese and Chinese modes of performance and the practical implications for the performer herself see Harrop, 'Ezra Pound's *Women of Trachis*'.
33. A characteristic quotation from Stanislavski about Craig reads: 'May a time come, when the newly discovered rays will paint in the air shadows of colour, tones and combinations of lives. May other rays light the body of man, give it the indefiniteness of outline, that disembodiment, that ghostliness which we know in our waking and sleeping dreams. Then with a hardly seen ghost in the image of a woman we will be able to realise Craig's conception of Hamlet's "To be or not to be". But with the use of ordinary theatrical means, instead forced to work with disgusting glue, paint, papier mâché and projector, the interpretation suggested by Craig looked like a piece of hokum.' Stanislavski, *My Life in Art*, p. 520.
34. Quoted in Marcus, *The Tenth Muse*; see chapter 'The Moment of *Close Up*', p. 226.
35. See Gregory, *H.D. and Hellenism.*
36. H.D., 'The Cinema and the Classics', in Donald, Friedberg and Marcus (eds), *Close Up, 1927–1933*, pp. 105–20.
37. Ibid. p. 112.
38. D. D. Page, 'Letter to Margaret C. Anderson' (January 1917), in Pound, *Selected Letters*, p. 107.

39. Macintosh and McConnell, *Performing Epic or Telling Tales*, p. 22.
40. Ibid. p. 29.
41. Benjamin, 'What is Epic Theatre?' [First Version], in *Understanding Brecht*, p. 6.
42. Lehmann, *Tragedy and Dramatic Theatre*.

2

ISADORA DUNCAN, EDWARD GORDON CRAIG AND THE DREAM OF AN IMPOSSIBLE THEATRE

On 16 March, 1900, at the New Gallery in London, Isadora Duncan gave her first recital in Europe. It was hosted by the artist and gallery owner Charles Hallé, who orchestrated Isadora's London début.[1] Hallé was very much aware that the introduction of Isadora Duncan's art to a London audience needed careful planning and contextualisation, particularly after the mixed reception of her work in New York. The distinguished list of guests/patrons included Princess Christine of Schleswig-Holstein, the artists Holman Hunt, Walter Crane and Sir William Richmond, the novelist Henry James, the playwright J. Comyns Carr, the composer Sir Hubert Parry, the music critic J. Fuller Maitland and the classical scholar, anthropologist and poet Andrew Lang. But perhaps Hallé's coup was to cast Jane Harrison as the narrator of the event, reciting extracts from Homer and Theocritus to accompany Duncan's dance. In hindsight this grouping of these two formidable women seems too good to be true, utterly staged and theatrical, acting as a constellation of a moment in time: a moment that brings together the visionary scholar/theorist and the equally visionary dancer/practitioner.

Harrison was yet to write her monumental *Themis* (1912) and Duncan herself would deliver her manifesto *The Dance of the Future* (1903) a few years later, in Berlin. The presence of Andrew Lang, pioneer of the so-called British School of Anthropology, is also crucial. Part of a group of charismatic and radical thinkers, he 'made possible the work of Frazer and the Cambridge Ritualists'.[2] And this was a project that merged classicism, sociology and anthropology in a heady cocktail that proposed an evolutionary model for the study of human culture. This evolutionary model, eclectic in its approach, shifted the focus from a philological perspective based on narrative and text to one that highlighted the significance of ritual and performance in the study of myth and religion. Indeed, it was these very principles that seem to have been embodied by Isadora Duncan's dance and punctuated by Jane Harrison's text. This fusion of textuality, visuality and movement through the figures of two iconic women brings together the scholarly and the aesthetic in a manner that at once pays homage to the past and points towards the future.

This 'past' for both scholar and dancer is, of course, Greek. In the words of a reviewer of that emblematic performance:

> Ropes of roses wind about the body and the feet are shod with golden sandals. Not a single stock step is taken, and the whole dance seems like something that might have happened in ancient Greece . . .
>
> Most of the time she has spent in the British Museum, analysing and memorising the steps and attitudes of the classic nymphs of antique art. Her work is thus the result of the application of poetic intelligence to the art of dancing, and her aim is to study nature and the classics and abjure the conventional.[3]

Duncan's art at this stage was fuelled more by 'poetic intelligence' than museum-style authenticity. However, this 'Greek' aspect of her quest becomes a type of shorthand throughout her life, work and writing. From her account of her own family drama – 'Like the family of the Atrides'[4] – through her early training in the Delsarte system, to her later stay in and engagement with modern and ancient Greece, this Hellenic dimension of her art and her identity as a dancer is at once historicising and radical. It helps to 'free' her as a dancing woman, but also to ground her in a tradition that she sees as ancient. It fuses romance, archaeology, travel narratives, philosophy and gender politics in a gesture that could have come straight from her choreographies, remaining elusive and contradictory, almost impossible to notate.

This chapter is less concerned with defining the type of Hellenism that informed Isadora Duncan's work – its philological or archaeological correctness or accuracy – and more interested in the 'licence' that her view of 'the Greeks' gave her as a female performer to radically rework her medium – her aphorism 'Do not call me a dancer' comes to mind[5] – and prepare the ground for the revolution of modern dance. This 'licence' could be read as at once part of the New Woman movement in the performing arts of the period, where the female performer is given presence and validated, changing the discourses of representation in the process, but also part and parcel of the period's anthropological and philosophical take on performance. Isadora Duncan's presence in London was possibly more successful than it had been in New

York, as there was already a context that could accommodate her work. The staging of Greek plays at Oxford and Cambridge, E. W. Godwin's productions influenced primarily by Schliemann's archaeological discoveries, and the work of the Cambridge scholars themselves all provided Duncan's experiments with an aesthetic context and with a critical language that could engage with her work. More often than not, that language had recourse to models of Hellenic art and sensibility which both provided the authenticating stamp of classicism and also, crucially, created an evolutionary trajectory that could conceptualise her work, making it simultaneously 'Greek' and modern.

A few nights after her début performance at the New Gallery, Hallé took Duncan to Henry Irving's Lyceum Theatre, where she was impressed by Irving's performance in *The Bells* and also saw him and Ellen Terry in *Cymbeline*. She also saw a young man in the performance whom she would later meet in Berlin. This was Ellen Terry's son, Edward Gordon Craig. Duncan and Craig's relationship has been well documented. Creatively, this was an odd coupling, as the two figures epitomise opposing strands in the experiments of the period regarding the presence of the performer. On the one extreme, Duncan's experiments in dance and movement are concerned with embodiment, the breaking of convention, the re-enforcing of primal femininity, laying the foundations of what was to be termed 'modern dance'; at the other, Craig, who was soon to formulate his manifesto on acting, 'The Actor and the Über-marionette' (1908), was advocating the complete absence of the human form and its substitution by his hyper-marionette. Interestingly and somewhat incongruously, they influenced each other. And both approaches in this presence/absence nexus of the human performer draw on notions of Hellenic traditions to help conceptualise and materialise their aspirations. Sometimes these aspirations take specific form; at other times they remain unrealised and unrealisable, utopian dreams of a modern Hellenic theatre.

The figure of the performer becomes central in the quest for the 'Theatre of the Future', as Craig was soon to term it, somewhat paraphrasing Duncan's lecture of 1903. In locating this revival of the theatre on the performing body, in many ways both Duncan's and Craig's experiments also revive the ancient quarrel. This at once partakes in the general anti-theatricality of much of modernist theatre, *and* in the period's quest for a language that would create presence for the human form on stage: a presence that was beyond psychological expressivism, an actor who could also be a prophet, a dancer or even a marionette. Duncan's and Craig's work could be said to occupy opposite and extreme points along this notional axis of presence/absence. In line with the overall aesthetics of catastrophe that characterises many modernist stage experiments, Craig advocates the total banishment of the human form from the stage; meanwhile, Duncan's work is concerned with creating embodiment, physicalisation, i.e. presence – and female presence at that, rewriting and revising the historically difficult relationship between the female performer and the stage. Whereas for Craig, the downfall of the modern theatre was at least partly due to the appearance of the female performer, for Duncan the quest for the female performer was quintessentially part of the quest for modern dance. The gender politics of these two projects could not be more different and oppositional. Despite this, or perhaps because of it, their work is intertwined, concerned with the same problematics of creating presence for the performer. For both projects, versions of Hellenic theatre and art act as inspiration and template for their experiments. Craig finds in the Greek model a theatre without female performers and Duncan is inspired by both archaeological objects (the Tanagra vases) and archaeological sites in her quest for a primal femininity that will create her modern dancer. Importantly, both were also influenced by Nietzsche's reworking of Greek drama in *The Birth of Tragedy*. This was the book Duncan was reading throughout her first tour of Europe; and from the very term 'Übermarionette' onwards, the impact of Nietzsche reverberates throughout Craig's work.

However, to return to the talismanic figure of the performer, it might be helpful to revisit the case of Henry Irving, who somewhat surprisingly features heavily in most of Craig's writing about acting. Irving is said to perform a transitional role between the acting styles of late Victorian theatre and the more radical traditions of the modernists. This is also a return to that initial visit of Isadora Duncan's to London, which we are reading as heralding much of hers and Craig's later development as artists and theorists of performance. One of the performances that Hallé took Duncan to see at the Lyceum was *The Bells*. This was, of course, a legendary performance, centred round Irving himself, and has more recently been read by performance theorists like Jane Goodall as an exercise in mesmerism.[6] Based loosely on the work of the German physician Franz Anton Mesmer (1734–1815), who propagated the existence of a type of 'animal magnetism' that connects all living beings, acting itself becomes an aspect of mesmerism based both on a quasi-scientific notion of vitalism and on the actor's supernatural power to hypnotise, transfix and carry us to another world. Goodall comments on Irving's performance technique together with that of the French actress Rachel Félix:

> If there was something of the supernatural, and especially of the demonic supernatural, about the presence of both Henry Irving and Rachel Félix this is because they were mesmerists who also operated as trance mediums, appearing to channel forces too powerful for human containment. What were they channelling? One answer might be: all the passions, ideals and intensities Herzen found wanting in 'modern man' . . .
>
> Perhaps the metaphysical and mystical dimensions of human imagination that science had tried to excise were coming back with a vengeance,

answering to a need for the greater energies to be manifested not just in technological spheres but also as part of individual life experience.[7]

This is a tall order for the performer to fulfil, but one nevertheless that both Duncan and Craig aspired to. And the figure of Irving looms large for both artists. Continuing the trope of mesmerism, we could claim that they both wanted to *be* a modern Irving: Duncan a female version and Craig a marionette version. Despite all his aphoristic proclamations about banning the human form from the stage, Craig continuously returns to the figure of Irving, hailing him in the end as the epitome of all he is striving for in acting: the Masked-Marionette. Here is how Craig later described that legendary performance in *The Bells*:

> He moves his head slowly from us – the eyes still somehow with us – and moves it to the right – taking as long as a long journey to discover a truth takes. He looks to the faces on the right – nothing. Slowly the head revolves back again, down along the tunnels of thought and sorrow, and at the end the face and eyes are bent upon those to the left of him . . . utter stillness.[8]

Interestingly, Craig calls Irving's acting here 'a dance', no doubt influenced by Duncan. However, whereas Irving's mesmeric power is mostly concentrated on the face, albeit on the face as mask, Duncan's is concentrated on the body, and on the female body at that. Here is how early critics of Duncan responded to her dances:

> When she stood still, she was like a Greek statue in grace of classic outline. But she had neither the colour nor the immobility of marble. Her arms were bare to the shoulders . . . Her pose and movements were often eloquent with the ideas which were being read and in delightful unison with the music which was being played.[9]

The pioneering modern dancer Helen Tamiris recalls having witnessed an early performance of Duncan's in Paris:

> She was dancing the *Pathétique*. She started on the ground, lying close to the floor – it took a long time – the only physical action was the very slow movement which carried her from prone to erect with arms outstretched. At the finish everyone was crying and I was crying too.[10]

It is this very impact of her dance that Craig possibly was simultaneously drawn to and repulsed by. (The above dance was created by Duncan using the so-called 'Tanagra figures', a series of gestures and movements arrived at by creatively reading figures on Greek vases from Tanagra). It would at once have reminded him of Irving, but at the same time possibly repulsed him, as what he experienced in Duncan's version of mesmerism would have been the impact of the female form in performance: its power to conjure up desire and fear, to connect the past with the present and to transfix its audience.

This fusion of the physical – the actor's body – and the metaphysical – its power to induce spiritual conditions, to sway and influence us – is precisely what is being experimented with at the time, and always with a Hellenic slant. Sometimes this Hellenism is material, drawing its inspiration from actual archaeological finds, and at other times it appears in its purely idealist/Romantic modes. In its more intriguing guises, however, the Hellenic aspect of these experiments in stage presence elides this separation and fuses the material and materialist with the spiritual and the metaphysical. The work of both Craig and Duncan in many ways represents attempts to overcome that binary and create a presence for the performing body within a genealogy of historical conventions located in theatre's past, but also within its present moment; and this present moment within the aesthetics of modernism also points towards a future to come.

Tales of Troy/Tales of Hellenism

Jane Harrison's contribution to Isadora Duncan's New Gallery performance was certainly not that of a novice or even simply a fan. By 1900, she herself had considerable experience in performing the 'Greek' plays, from her first attempt to stage Euripides' *Electra* in 1877 at Cambridge (which was called off by the college principal as it featured women acting as men, performing with bare arms and legs)[11] to her appearance as Penelope in *Tales of Troy*. This consisted of four performances in May 1883 in a specially built private Greek theatre at Cromwell House, the London home of Sir Charles and Lady Freake, with a distinguished cast that included Herbert Beerbohm Tree and his wife Maude. Indeed, this production gained notoriety amongst classical scholars and lovers of so-called 'aesthetic Hellenism' for its combination of antiquarianism and 1880s aestheticism. Again, visits to the British Museum were seen as a prerequisite and although 'the actual Pelian spear' was impossible to obtain, it was rumoured that Eugénie Sellers, who played both Helen (in English) and Cassandra (in Greek) was lent her golden jewellery by Charles Newton, probably borrowed directly from the British Museum.

A few years later, in 1886, the architect and stage designer E. W. Godwin (Craig's father) staged John Todhunter's *Helena in Troas* at Hengler's Circus in London. This venture went even further, recreating an Attic theatre in the huge arena space, what was considered at the time to be an archaeologically correct Greek arrangement of proscenium, orchestra and thymele.[12] The audience was assembled in semi-circular tiers modelled on the Theatre of Dionysus next to the Acropolis, and in the centre of the orchestra was an altar to Dionysus with burning incense. This event was praised both for its authenticity and its aesthetic quality. In his review of the performance, Oscar Wilde wrote:

> As an artistic whole, however, the performance was undoubtedly a great success. It has been much praised for its archaeology, but Mr Godwin is something more than a mere antiquarian. He takes the facts of archaeology and converts them into artistic and dramatic effects and the historical accuracy that underlies the visible shapes of beauty that he presents to us is not by any means the distinguishing quality of the complete work of art. This quality is the absolute unity and harmony of the entire presentation, the presence of one mind controlling the most minute details, and revealing itself only in that true perfection which hides personality.[13]

It is interesting that Oscar Wilde should praise Godwin for his unity of vision, a theatrical aesthetic that his son, Craig, would later theorise as that of the modernist director.

Archaeology as a discipline was undergoing drastic changes at this time, in many ways defining itself within the contours of modernity, empire and nationhood. The discoveries of Heinrich Schliemann (1822–1890) had a huge impact on the staging of 'Greek' plays during this period and prompted a re-evaluation of the function of the historical artefact and its relation to modern theatrical practice. Rather than archaeology as the purveyor of a lost unity or beauty, in the tradition of Johann Joachim Winckelmann (1717–1768), Schliemann's excavations and the narratives that surrounded them proposed a version of archaeology that was in many ways more far-reaching and open to metaphorical and aesthetic application. This was archaeology as purveyor of eternal primal truths; the excavated object it prioritised was not necessarily the harmonious object of beauty, but the ruin. The excavation of ruins, often prompted by actual visits, tied in almost seamlessly with the search for origins and ritual within an evolutionary model of development. Thus, the act of excavating the past also became for theatre-makers a way of thinking about the future. This allowed them to be at once antiquarian and innovative, Greek and modern. And Wilde, the Oxford classicist, comments on the uses of archaeology as establishing a genealogical link in terms of performance, as he connects the medieval masques and pageants to the romantic uses of archaeology that he witnessed in the Godwin designs. Here is Wilde writing in *The Dramatic Review* in 1886:

> The performance was not intended to be an absolute reproduction of the Greek stage in the fifth century before Christ: it was simply the presentation in Greek form of a poem conceived in the Greek spirit; and the secret of its beauty was the perfect correspondence of form and matter, the delicate equilibrium of spirit and sense.[14]

However, despite this new and somewhat modernist conception of archae-ology, the legacy of aestheticist Hellenism, closely linked with the British Museum and with university productions at the end of the nineteenth century, was already in Harrison's terms becoming somewhat clichéd. She writes in a letter to John Todhunter's wife Dora in 1886, the same year as the production of *Helen in Troas*:

> Anyone who has watched the modern restoration of a Greek play has, if he is honest, been conscious of a sense of extreme discomfort . . . The whole is artificial, conventionalised, utterly unlike the simple, large, straightforward freedom that would naturally be expected of a Greek representation . . . How absurd Agamemnon and his chariot look, shot half through a side door on a modern Greek stage . . . It is only the humble and touching conviction that the effect is 'Greek' that enables a modern audience to support the sight without laughter.[15]

Both Craig and Duncan intervene in this tradition of aestheticist Hellenism but also in many ways derive from it. The combination of pseudo-archaeology and late nineteenth-century aestheticism had created a legacy that, as Harrison's quotation above claims, quickly became conventionalised and stilted.[16]

This was not the kind of 'Greekness' that Harrison saw as authentic and true. For Harrison, what conceptualised these productions as 'Greek' were simply the conventions of spectatorship as understood by the audience. In the end, for her, despite the references to Schliemann, the use of artefacts from the British Museum and all the will of the audience to support these performances, they became what was anathema to her: a parody of 'Greekness'.

Isadora Duncan added a totally different conception and practice of Greekness to these experiments. Gone were the cluttered costumes, the props and the antiquarianism. For Harrison, Duncan's vitalist, non-decorous dances chimed well with her own research into the relationships between religion and ritual, movement and rhythm. The fact that Duncan's work had a spe-cific feminine perspective was also attractive to Harrison, whose reading of Dionysus and the *eniautos daimon* too has been read by contemporary critics as partaking in both the late nineteenth-century Bachofen-inspired vitalist quest for a primal matriarchy and in the more radical discourses of Sapphic modernism.

Isadora Duncan and Jane Harrison established their connection at that first night of Duncan's dance in London. This study has been drawing on the influence of the so-called Cambridge Ritualists, on the ways that modernist performance, particularly in its anglophone guise, had been engaging with classical Greek theatre. Unlike Duncan, Craig was not so keen on establishing collaborations and links with other artists, let alone academics. Still, I believe that this group of modernist classicists had some impact on him. Indeed, we can claim that this impact was reciprocal. Francis Cornford, who had yet to write his groundbreaking *The Origin of Attic Comedy* (1914) and who was very involved with the Cambridge Triennial Greek Play, wrote a letter to his wife Frances in 1909 expressing his disappointment about the staging of the play, which that year was *The Wasps*. Although unable to express his views about it in public as a member of the play's committee, he states in the letter that he loathed everything about it apart from the music of Vaughan Williams. He writes:

> I have had a long empty day without you – mostly making an index and reading Gordon Craig's book which I bought yesterday. It has some wonderful things in it & makes me think a lot more of him and also how awful is the Greek play and other things we do.[17]

This is quite an admission from a prominent classicist. The book was *On the Art of the Theatre*, and Cornford soon wrote directly to Craig to express his admiration. Craig responded from Berlin, where he was with Isadora Duncan, saying that he was on his way to Moscow to work on *Hamlet*. This correspondence continued, as there is another response from Craig a few years later:

> 27 Nov 1913: Arena Goldoni – That's very strange that my book should have brought you near anything Greek. How I studied – groping my way – to keep off the old & to move *only* towards new times, and sights, & loves. But what you write me of your new book is suggestive, and if you've managed to say at length what you say in your letter it will be a book I shall like. As you say 'it is a strange story' & that phrase might stand as prelude to your book.[18]

It is fascinating that Craig's ideas and designs about the New Theatre proved inspirational for Cornford in writing his book about Attic comedy. Like Harrison, he was becoming weary of the 'sham-Greek' aesthetic of the late nineteenth century, as Craig would call it in *The Mask*. He, too, would look towards the more recent modernist developments in theatre experimentation, developments that relied more on stagecraft and modernist theories of acting than on classicism, translation or textuality more broadly. Here is Cornford, writing about the notion of dramatic character in Attic comedy in tones that are distinctly Craigian:

> A character created by a great dramatist is a permanent possibility of human nature, independent of its accidental trappings of time and country. It is only the vulgar and corrupt realism of the modern stage that could ever disguise this fact for a moment. The ancient drama wisely preserved the mask, which . . . represented in a conventional language of signs what the poet wished to be represented – the universal character.

The masks . . . were retained . . . because the Greek spectator was trained in a tradition of art which taught him, when he went to the theatre, to look for something more important than the damnable faces [*Hamlet* III.ii.242] of Mr So-and-So. It is no pedantic archaism, but a profound understanding of drama that leads the greatest artist now in the production of plays to revive the use of masks, and even to hanker after substituting the marionette for the living actor.* [FMC's note: '*E. Gordon Craig, *The Art of the Theatre* [sic], London, 1911.'] It might be well if the revival of Greek plays in the modern theatre could be prohibited until the public had learned to tolerate nothing more realistic than the masked and stylised, puppet-like, figures that trod, with stilted gait, the stage of Aeschylus and Euripides.[19]

Cornford, like Harrison with Duncan, finds correspondences in Craig's experiments that at once look towards the new Theatre of the Future, but also help to revise received understanding about classical Greek drama. Cornford here reinterprets the classical Greek actor through Craig's Übermarionette. And it is this double motion, both forward and backward, that is quintessentially modernist.

'CAN THE DANCING MAENAD DANCE?'

Duncan's ideas came together in a pamphlet that she wrote during the Berlin leg of her European tour. This was *The Dance of the Future* (1903), which was to become the first manifesto of modern dance. It was at least partly inspired by a statue of a dancing Maenad that she saw in the Berlin Museum. Equally important is the way she integrates her reading of this statue into her overall argument. In response to an article in the *Berlin Morgen Post* which claimed that the 'American' had no technique and subsequently her 'dance' was not an artform, she proposed a reading of the dancing Maenad that was in direct opposition to the strict style of classical ballet. To the accusation 'Can Miss Duncan Dance?' of the paper, she responded with the equally provocative 'Can the Dancing Maenad Dance?'[20] Again she backed her claims with her interpretation of Greek dance; claims that provided her both with historical genealogy and with modernist radicalism. For her, the engagement with the Greeks was less a 'return', a backward-looking antiquarianism, and more of a gesture towards the theatre to come. 'To return to the dances of the Greeks would be as impossible as it is unnecessary,' she writes in her manifesto.[21] From the Greeks she borrowed the notion that the 'dance of the future will have to become again a high religious art', a form of religious art that, like Harrison, also carried with it an utterly modern sense of gender politics. She writes:

It is not only a question of true art, it is a question of . . . the development of the female sex to beauty and health, of the return to the original strength and to natural movements of woman's body. It is a question of the development of perfect mothers and the birth of beautiful children. The dancing school of the future is to develop and show the ideal form of woman. [. . .]

O, she is coming, the dancer of the future: the free spirit who will inhabit the body of the new woman . . . the highest intelligence in the freest body.[22]

So, for Duncan, the *locus* of the modern 'New Woman' is the dance that at once presents itself as part of the evolutionary trajectory of religious/ritualist art and points towards a utopian future.

Duncan's visit to Berlin familiarised her not only with the monumental Hellenism of the museum, but crucially exposed her to the work of Friedrich Nietzsche. More recently, dance theorists and even theologians[23] have analysed Duncan's encounter with the work of Nietzsche not simply as one of influence and inspiration, but as formative for both the dance and the philosophical tradition of modernity. Duncan, in many ways, is seen as embodying Nietzsche's critique of the dualisms of Christianity, particularly those concerning the body/spirit divide. Interestingly, Nietzsche's emphasis on the power of ritual, rhythm and collectivity is derived from his specific reading of Greek tragedy: a reading that prioritises ritual over narrative and the chorus over the protagonist. In *The Birth of Tragedy* Duncan finds not simply the theory for her practice, but a way of overriding the division between the two. Her statement that she 'never once danced solo'[24] expresses her attempt to dance *as* a chorus, a Dionysian chorus that brings together the individual dancer and the collective. She called Nietzsche's first book 'my bible',[25] and in her early essays on dance wrote in terms that reverberated with echoes from that book.

To give back to the dance its place as the Chorus, that is the ideal. When I have danced I have tried always to be the Chorus . . . I have never once danced a solo.[26]

Of course, she *did* dance solo – and, possibly more than any other modern dancer, her dances were charged with the mesmeric quality that Craig found problematic in live performers. However, the fact that she desired and attempted to dance as a chorus is crucial. Her almost impossible task gestures towards a form of embodiment that was experimented with in many a modernist school of acting: that of the performer as emblematic symbol and laboratory for the creation of collective identity. This collective identity, for Duncan, both via Nietzsche and via her own studies and experiments, had a distinctly Greek inflection. Marc Franko calls this process *disindividuation*, and rightly, I believe, links it to the broader attempts of literary modernism at impersonality and *loss* of individual character. The convention of the Greek chorus, quite appropriately for a dancer, becomes that trope through which the individual and the collective is constantly negotiated. Franko writes that for Duncan, 'the experience of a multiple and divided self joined her body to a hallucinated and intoxicating community . . . The chorus represented the loss of self in community, a desubjectification in the interest of *Gemeinschaft* as presence.'[27] Again in a quasi-evolutionary trope, the dance both connects with a glorious past and points towards a utopian future. Franko even posits the possibility that this past/future nexus of ideas and practices also connects Duncan's Hellenism to a type of socialism:

> Duncan's Hellenism pictures socialist community as located between the private and the public spheres whose most provocative moment is the 'post': the demystification of loss is produced on the outside as a social experience rather than on the inside as a religious allegory.[28]

This political reading of Duncan's experiments is fascinating as it echoes her later fascination with the USSR and at the same time strikingly differentiates her from Craig, who would later exhibit a similar political fascination with Mussolini. Central to Duncan's utopian thinking is also the feminine. This feminine dimension led to her vision of a collective chorus that belonged not necessarily to the superman, but to the superwoman. Nevertheless, this prefix *über-*, the same one that Craig was to use for his marionette, continues to plague that utopian relationship between the individual and the collective that both Craig and Duncan tried to radically renegotiate through their experiments.

In this context we can further understand Harrison's attraction to Duncan. She too was fuelled by her reading of Nietzsche; and what Nietzsche did – and Harrison was soon to do – to the so-called 'German' tradition of classical philology, Duncan was proposing to do to its aesthetic. For all her references to and admiration of Greek monuments and artefacts in London and Berlin, her performances could not have been further removed from the kind of aesthetic Hellenism that Harrison was already tiring of in the 1890s. This was Hellenism that was fluid, embodied, modern and feminine. Its chief exponent for Duncan was not the philosopher, the archaeologist or the classicist, but the dancer. Indeed, Duncan found in her reading of 'the Greeks' a vitalist organicism that could give form to all those categories and previous modes of engagement with the past. For her that form was the female dancer, primarily embodied in herself.

This prioritising of the dancer could be read against Craig's and theatrical modernism's all-dominant director figure. If according to Alain Badiou the director figure is also a philosophical figure (a thinker of mediation), then the dancer as such a trope opens up further possibilities for the whole issue of theatricality. Indeed, positing the dancer as the central figure round whom all the issues of performability and theatricality hinge makes for a very radical reading of the theatrical event, one that does not necessarily define itself against philosophy and the word, but rather attempts to embody these categories. In opposition to Craig's all-powerful but absent Director, Duncan's dancer is ever-present and vulnerable. For Duncan, Craig's 'Artist of the Theatre of the Future' is the dancer. Badiou writes about the significance of Duncan in this hypostasising of dance:

> In the wake of Russian ballets and Isadora Duncan, dance is a crucial art precisely because it is only act. The paradigm of a vanishing art, dance does not produce works in the ordinary sense of the term. But what is its trace, where does it circumscribe the thinking of its own singularity? Is there only ever a trace of its repetition, and never of its act? Art would then amount to the unrepeatable within a repetition. It would have no other destiny than that of giving form to this unrepeatable.[29]

Interestingly, Badiou groups Duncan's work with the Russian ballets, and much recent scholarship has been devoted to tracing the impact of Duncan's tours of Russia and how they influenced the aesthetics and the ethos of what would later become the phenomenal Ballets Russes. Importantly, too, this claim of dance to provide the *meta-language* for theatrical presence within the modernist experiments also has its roots in Isadora Duncan. The ways Badiou theorises dance are pre-echoed in much of Duncan's own writing. Interestingly, though, Badiou somewhat neglects the presence of the dancer's body and the ways that presence rubs against the 'paradigm of a vanishing art'. For Duncan, the female dancer's body becomes the ultimate ekphrastic trope on the stage that is capable of giving presence to that 'vanishing art', of bridging the word and the flesh and the past and the future; that past, for Duncan's dancer, was Greek.

This Hellenic dimension, again, takes many forms: it can be aesthetic, vitalist, archaeological, geopolitical, but it is also Greek in the ways it revises the ancient quarrel. To posit the female dancer at the centre of performance is to engage the ancient quarrel between tragedy – theatricality – and philosophy in very challenging ways. Duncan's embodied, physicalised and feminised version of theatrical presence blatantly goes against everything that Plato abhorred about the power of the theatrical, particularly the power of the chorus. The fact that Duncan herself claimed to always dance as a chorus only compounds her vision. Duncan's dancer in many ways comes to enact Plato's fear of those 'poets' who were 'ignorant of what is right and legitimate in the realm of the Muses', and 'raging like Bacchanals and possessed with inordinate delights, they mingled lamentations with hymns and paeans with dithyrambs'.[30] This for Plato creates the ultimate anathema: the 'universal confusion of forms'. And it is this 'universal confusion of forms' that Duncan may be said to strive for through the ekphrastic use of her dancing body. It becomes a mechanism to explore this confusion, its modernist aesthetics, but also its politics and its metaphysics. For Plato this confusion of forms spills out into the audience and through its particular modes of spectatorship has dire political implications, substituting the assembly for the audience and aristocracy for the notorious theatrocracy.

In positing the notion of a female dancer as chorus, we can claim that Duncan was embracing this view of theatrocracy, where the body was both its agent and its medium of production. The fact that she herself saw her work as part of the emancipatory project of modernity is telling. For Duncan this has a politics, but significantly it also has a metaphysics, and the two are not necessarily read in opposition. Kimerer L. LaMothe writes:

> When Duncan describes her dance as a 'prayer' or a 'revelation', or when she describes a dancer as a 'priest', she is gesturing toward this function of dancing: its ability to exercise a creative capacity – not a capacity of our minds or even imaginations per se, but a capacity of our bodily becoming that finds expression in thinking and imagining . . . Dancing is so by enacting the inherent creativity of our bodily existence. As bodies we are always already bringing into being (kinetic images of) ourselves, world, gods, and thus, our relationships to what these images represent. Acknowledging and exercising this creative capacity, for both Duncan and Nietzsche, is a moral responsibility.[31]

This is the dancer not distinctly as artist or philosopher, but as a type or merging of those categories; we could say that it proposes the dancer as a type of demiurge.

Nietzsche's phrase from *Thus Spoke Zarathustra* – 'I would believe only in a God who could dance'[32] – comes to mind. And, indeed, it stresses the degree to which Isadora Duncan was not simply influenced by Nietzsche, but in many ways proposed a spatial and physicalised version of his philosophy. The two projects can be read as analogous. We could even possibly claim that the ways in which Nietzsche and subsequently the Cambridge Ritualists – and particularly Harrison – revised and radically reworked the German tradition in classicism find an aesthetic equivalent in Duncan's dances.

This aesthetic for Duncan encompasses a totality, one that also brings with it a philosophical and, crucially, a pedagogical dimension. 'To dance is to live. What I want is a *School of life*.'[33] In line with the modernist legacy of creating schools of training performers, Duncan's work had a strong pedagogical dimension, although the more traditional dance theorists have accused her of not having a technique. However, equating dance with life places demands on the pedagogy that does not see itself simply as imparting technique and concrete knowledge, but as passing on a style that becomes an attitude towards life itself. For Duncan was not simply interested in training new dancers; hers was a more ambitious project. Deborah Jowitt writes:

> Duncan's interpretations of Nietzsche and Darwin led her to a vision of the 'dance of the future' as an emblem of an improved human species. Jean-Jacques Rousseau's *Emile* filled her with ideas about education through nature. It's no wonder that she thought her mission to found schools. Certainly she made no money from them.[34]

In a connecting thread that both links and rewrites Nietzsche's *übermensch* and Craig's Übermarionette with Duncan's experiments, for her that 'improved human species' is the dancer, whose body can act as a lightning rod, connecting it both to the earth and to the sky, to the past and to the future. Further on in the above quotation, Jowitt claims that Duncan 'thought of herself as a dynamo' and draws analogies with much of the thinking about electricity at the time. Indeed, this is a fascinating image, one that brings together the spiritual/metaphysical aspect of her dance with the purely mechanical and even technological. For Duncan was as much interested in the dancer's body as a locus of primal (female) energies as she was in the body as a 'natural machine', governed by the rhythms and movement of nature itself. Her fascination with Nietzsche was matched by a fascination with Darwin. This blending of evolutionary theory with the rhythms of primal ritual has clear parallels in the work of Harrison and the Cambridge School and it also bears clear parallels with Craig's mechanical but phantasmic Übermarionette. The idea that the body itself is transformed into a type of physicalised ekphrasis, able to shift between artistic forms and the spheres of the earthly and the divine, could be said to find two opposing but complimentary paradigms in the work of Duncan and Craig.

Craig's Übermarionette was never materialised, remaining a ghost in a machine, whereas Duncan was able to turn her body into the thing she strived for. However, the issue of notation and reproduction remains. In some ways Craig resolved this by never actually creating his vision and locating all its power, creative, phantasmic or otherwise, within the agent who controls his Übermarionette: the Director. Duncan, on the other hand, in effect turned her body into such a laboratory for the presence of the dancer. LaMothe calls this enterprise 'kinetic imaging', a process through which the dancer creates her own presence:

> As Duncan confirms, her goal in dancing was never to become a professional dancer. Nor was dance one activity among others she could take or leave. Dance, for Duncan, was *the* activity capable of exercising and educating the medium through which women and men live in ways that help them develop the physical consciousness needed to generate values

that nourish and affirm life. As she avers, 'To dance is to live. What I want is a *School of Life*.' Her dancing exercises faith in the body and its great reason.[35]

Like her classicist counterpart Jane Harrison, Duncan is here read not solely as inspiring a particular discipline or artform but as partaking in and helping create a specifically feminist sensibility (albeit not always aligned with the socio-historical movements of feminism itself) that formulates its own aesthetics and philosophy.

Duncan's various schools of life were not interested in creating reproductions, or even training in particular techniques. More interested in creating a particular *attitude* towards physicality and the art of dance in general, her methods and indeed her choreographies themselves placed demands on notation.

The notation of dance, like the formalising of the pedagogy of acting, becomes significant within the experiments of modernism. In some ways, Duncan's experiments at once undo the previous, more traditional modes of teaching and notation, but they pose new demands themselves. In creating work that was not meant to be reproduced – that substituted the paradigm for the example – her work may have inspired many artists, visual and otherwise, but was almost impossible to notate. Her early tours of Russia (between 1904 and 1909) inspired prominent visual artists like Léon Bakst, and indeed more recent scholarship sees her work as a precursor to that of the Ballets Russes (which would have delighted Craig, who claimed that the Russian company had merely plagiarised 'the American', as he referred to her in *The Mask*).[36] Indeed, in a manner this was true, for what Bakst and later the Ballets Russes inherited from Duncan was a pose, an attitude towards dance, not necessarily a system. Bakst himself drew several images of Isadora Duncan after her performances in St Petersburg, but tellingly, as Michelle Potter states, she also had a huge impact on Bakst's own designs for the theatre. Bakst himself prior to Isadora's tours had had a formative 'Greek period' in designing for three tragedies in the period 1902–4 (*Hippolytus*, *Oedipus at Colonus* and *Antigone*). The impact on him was also to change his concept of Hellenism. After Duncan's tours his aesthetic changed, becoming more organic and fluid, less cluttered with the aestheticist Hellenism of the museum references (Bakst visited Greece prior to designing the tragedies) and more 'pregnant with the future', as he wrote in a letter to Benois describing Duncan's dancing. Benois himself wrote a passionate defence of Duncan entitled 'Music and Plastic Art. (A Propos of Isadora Duncan)'.[37] Insightfully, both these images of her – as that which contains the possibility (sometimes utopian) of the future, and as that which translates and morphs into another medium – seem to be appropriate.

It is in this sense that the dancer's body becomes a type of ekphrastic machine, exploring the form of ekphrasis itself. Interestingly, the metaphor used above by Bakst is one of female fecundity ('pregnant'), where the bringing into presence of one artistic medium through another is read through the metaphorical rendition of the female body and its reproductive function. Perhaps Duncan's insistence on the gendered nature of her enterprise could be read as at once partaking in the long genealogy of employing the female body as aesthetic trope and also attempting to rewrite, revise and possibly reclaim it. And it is also in this sense that her work could be read – again in conjunction with Harrison's – as part of a broader feminist aesthetics of modernism. This does not simply posit the eternal female body as the locus of critique against a dominant patriarchy, in yet another metaphorical rendition. Rather, this dancing body could be read as exploring the mechanics, the forms, the economies of representation that have shaped and facilitated these uses of the female body in the first place, in literature, in the plastic arts and especially in classical dance. This helps create a mode of expression, embodiment and movement *and* writing in the broadest sense that is very appealing to the literary Sapphic tradition of modernism, in some ways equally concerned with exposing and sometimes enacting the gendered aspects of representation itself. Here is how Gertrude Stein writes about Isadora Duncan:

> This one is the one being dancing. This one is one thinking in believing in dancing having meaning. This one is one believing in thinking. This one is one thinking in dancing having meaning. This one is one believing in dancing having meaning. This one is one dancing. This one is one being that one. This one is one being in being one being dancing. This one is one being in being one who is dancing. This one is one being one. This one is one being in being one.[38]

Indeed, one can here see Stein's writing as a dance while reading it, again enacting the principle of modernist ekphrasis. This is almost a type of writing *as* dancing notation, where the words and the ideas surrounding them – thinking, believing, meaning, dancing, being – are engaged not simply syntactically or semantically, but in a dance. Characteristically, the agent of this dance is not marked with a gendered pronoun but with the all-encompassing 'one'. It might not be coincidental that while Duncan's dances proved very difficult to notate, they nevertheless acted as a source of inspiration for literary and visual modernism. Craig himself could not resist drawing Duncan. And perhaps the most famous drawings of her are those by fellow American Abraham Walkowitz, who drew over five thousand versions of Duncan in an attempt to visually capture her dance.

The fascination that Duncan inspired in her fellow modernists, particularly in the plastic and visual arts, was immense. In many ways, this fascination could also be read as an attempt to capture and notate her experiments. Drawing as it did on a variety of sources and filtering them through the female body, Isadora Duncan's dance placed demands on systems of notation, demands that could perhaps only be addressed by recourse to other artistic media. And this crucial impact that she had on these other modernist arts, textual and visual, need not necessarily be read as a shortcoming or a failure of her artform – its inability to have its own meta-language – but can be seen as part of its radical potential. Its ability to transform, to morph into other forms, again underlines its ekphrastic dimension, at once located but permeable and utopian. The dance critic Walter Terry writes about this quality of her dance:

> Although her dance inarguably sprang from her inner sources and resources of motor power and emotional desire, the overt aspects of her dance were clearly coloured by Greek art and the sculptor's concept of the body in arrested gesture promising further action. These influences may be seen clearly in photographs of her and in the art works she inspired.[39]

Interestingly, Terry's phrase 'arrested gesture promising further action' and his fusion 'of motor power and emotional desire' points towards this utopian quality of Duncan's dance, but also somewhat incongruously can be read as drawing parallels with the phantasmic qualities of Craig's Übermarionette. Again the mechanical and the vitalist seem to morph into each other. And recording, being inspired by, attempting to notate Duncan's dances almost invariably creates that 'confusion of forms' that Plato so abhorred in the power of theatre. The image and imagistic trope that transpires throughout most of these attempts is probably most clearly exemplified in Walkowitz's many sketches of Duncan: and that is the trope of the *hieroglyph*. Used throughout modernist experiment as that mode that attempts to graphically notate a particular kind of kinetic and poetic sensibility, the hieroglyph becomes a type of *gestus* of writing that brings together movement and stasis, writing and image, the present and the future. And, of course, the hieroglyph, as we shall later explore in the work of H.D., also inflects the model of Hellenism, making it no longer pure and classical, but hybrid and Alexandrian.

THE DANCER, THE ÜBERMARIONETTE AND SOME BLACK FIGURES

In some ways the image of the dancer as hieroglyph could not be further removed from the image of the actor as Übermarionette. Although Isadora Duncan's impact on modern and contemporary dance is undoubtable, the impact of Craig might initially appear to be incongruous. However, if we approach their work as intricately linked – both in their attempts to address the issue of the presence of the performer and in their multiple excursions in creating a pedagogy and a terminology for such a presence – then we may begin to approach the issue of their impact not only on their contemporaries,

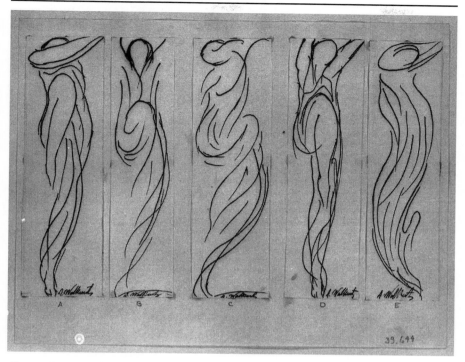

Figure 2.1 Abraham Walkowitz, from *Dancer – Five Line Drawings*. Pen and ink on paper (1943). Reproduced courtesy of the Brooklyn Museum.

but primarily on the performers of the future. This concept of the future can be read in its immediate historical trajectory (Duncan's and Craig's seminal influence on contemporary performance), but crucially it also engages the utopian dimension of their work, in a sense addressing *all* the futures to come. It is in this context that the specifically Hellenic dimension of their work also features, as a trope that at once creates the aura of lineage and authenticity but also points towards an always unrealisable, phantasmic future to come.

Craig's and Duncan's conceptions of the performing body have sometimes been read in opposition: a complete absence of physical and psychological embodiment at one extreme, and absolute expressiveness at the other. Where Craig's Übermarionette might be read as a mechanised puppet, Duncan's experiments could be said to lack technique or even form. However, throughout this chapter we have tried to problematise these binaries and the ways that they have respectively been read as undiluted anti-theatricality at one extreme, and pure theatricality at the other. Reading them as folding into each other, as addressing similar issues in the ways they present themselves

Figure 2.2 Edward Gordon Craig, 'Isadora Duncan Dancing', *The Mask*, vol. 1, no. 6, p. 126b (1908). Reproduced courtesy of the Edward Gordon Craig Estate.

as both Greek and modern, may again help us to see them as doubles rather than opposites.

I would like to propose possibly another ekphrastic use or application of Duncan's dancing. And that is in the way it may have inspired Craig to create possibly his most evocative creatures: the Black Figures. The initial period during which Craig worked on these figures was between 1907 and 1914, a period when Duncan's experiments in movement were very much on his mind. Indeed, they may provide us with yet another way of reading this interface between the dancer and the Übermarionette. This is also the period when Craig's manifesto for the art of acting appears. Rather than attempt to make or even design a template for his phantasmic creature, Craig focuses on these beautiful figures that bring together his interests in engraving, acting and dance, all contributing in a sense to his attempt at reviving the classical Greek stage as a type of total theatre.

This revival could not be more different than the existing ones he had experienced in England before his self-imposed exile to Italy. He writes in the first issue of *The Mask*, under one of his pseudonyms, John Balance:

Dancing, Pantomime, Marionettes, Masks; these things so vital to the ancients, all parts of their respected Art of the Theatre at one time or another, have been all turned into a Jest.[40]

Proceeding to quote Anatole France, who 'writes of these strange and wonderful beings, the Marionettes' as 'resemblent à des hiérogliphes Egyptiens', he then accuses the English 'revivalists' of being 'sham-Greek in idea' and 'sham-Greek in their manufacture'.[41] It is noteworthy that in this very first issue of *The Mask*, Craig already presents us with a very different and I would claim modernist notion of Greek theatre, and employs his manifesto rhetoric through his signature tropes, which themselves are voiced through the mask of the pseudonym. His seminal essay 'The Actor and the Über-marionette' appears in the following issue of the journal.

While Craig is busy formulating his fiery manifestos he is also heavily involved with Isadora Duncan, and when he refers to 'the dancer' in his writings of this period, it is impossible not to think of Duncan. He writes:

The father of the dramatist was the dancer . . . the dramatist made his first piece by using action, words, line, colour, and rhythm, and making his appeal to our eyes and ears by a dexterous use of these five factors. The first dramatists were children of the theatre. The modern dramatists are not. The first dramatists understood what the modern dramatist does not yet understand. He knew that when he and his fellows appeared in front of them the audience would be more eager to see what he would do than to *hear* what he might say . . . he spoke either in poetry or prose, but always in action: in poetic action which is dance, or in prose action which is gesture.[42]

At the same time, all these ideas about movement, revivalism, marionettes über- or not, could be seen to become crystallised through his Black Figures, which appeared on his model stages. These marionette/woodcuts would later function as models for the actors in the Moscow *Hamlet*. They bring together his skills as an engraver, a theatre theorist and, we can claim through Isadora Duncan, a dance theorist as well, with a particular Greek inflection including figures from classical drama, Helen, Hecuba and Iphigenia among them. As Michael Walton claims:

This enthusiasm for the theatre of the mask, looking forward not back, became concentrated in these solid forms . . . here was a vision of Greek drama which, probably for the first time since the Hellenistic period, addressed the way in which Greek tragedy was created as a masked performance with all that implies for the chorus and for *cheironomia*, the language of stage gesture. Emotion was crystalized, as in Greek sculpture and in the composite vase paintings with theatrical subjects from the fifth and fourth centuries BCE.[43]

These were the same vase paintings that had inspired Duncan. This fusion of the statue, or the phantasy of the moving statue, the composite vase paintings and the living body of the dancer, present us with a very modernist idea of the actor, one that comes together in Craig's theories of the Übermarionette. Also significant is the fact that Craig felt the need to design model stages for his Black Figures. In the absence of a real stage that could accommodate his vision of the Theatre of the Future, and in the absence of real actors, these stages with their beautiful figurines could function as Craig's utopian theatre. Count Harry Kessler writes:

> The effects which Craig showed on his [model] stage were diverse and grand. Magnificent, however, and truly inspired were the drawings and figurines which he produced afterwards. He has made prints on paper from his wooden figures, which can take their place beside the most beautiful woodcuts of the quattro-cento, so perfect is their balance between line and meaning, between inner fire and thrilling decorative effect.[44]

These Black Figures located on Craig's model stages bring together in an inspiring constellation ideas and images, actors and marionettes, real stages and model stages, again underlining the fact that embodiment and presence in these modernist experiments was at once physical, fleshly, but also always facilitated and thought through with the help of inanimate creatures and architectural settings. Daniel Albright has written convincingly about 'the strange reciprocity of dancers and décor' and about the 'intimacy of ballet and architecture'.[45] These model stages populated by Craig's Black Figures also gesture towards the constitutive relationships between modernist theories of acting and theories of puppetry. And these theories also come with their own scenography, where scenography is no longer a simple backdrop but also helps to create these wonderful creatures, is formative of their very construction. This 'strange reciprocity' between actor and décor, or rather between actor/puppet and décor, that these model stages propose highlights Albright's claim. In addition, we could claim that they foreshadow Gertrude Stein's idea of the 'landscape play',[46] where décor/scenography, movement and performers (and, crucially for Stein, the word as well) all are semiotically symbiotic on the stage and contribute to the 'landscape' of the play. This 'landscape' is not mimetic of an outside world, but creates its own *topos*. It does not represent the world, but creates its own. It is not coincidental that Stein, too, was fascinated with Duncan and her use of space.

Craig's use of space and the relationship of theatrical space to the moving figure in his work has sometimes been labelled 'architectural'. However, to call Craig's designs for the stage architectural would not simply be somewhat schematic, but also would accord architecture a discursive privilege that in many ways his work deliberately resists. Of course, he was influenced by his father, E. W. Godwin (featured throughout *The Mask*); he had seen Todhunter's *Helena in Troas* as a young man; and he was aware of the recent monumental archaeological findings. But Craig's 'sham-Greek' referred to the Wagnerian playhouse (whose architect, Gottfried Semper, was influenced by the ancient theatre of Epidaurus) as much as it did to Reinhardt's monumental staging. His idea of scenography was instead small-scale and populated by his Black Figures. More often than not, these designs for the stage appeared on model stages and in books rather than on theatrical stages. Or rather, while they may have looked monumental on paper other than in a few instances (the Moscow *Hamlet* and W. B. Yeats' *The Hour Glass*), their more permanent home was the book and the miniature stage rather than the Wagnerian or Appian real stage.

These figurines, nevertheless, were also composite, bringing together Craig's knowledge of Greek acting and choral movement as presented by Duncan with his extensive knowledge of puppets from around the world. At the Arena Goldoni, Craig had possibly the most formidable collection of puppets of his day.[47] Indeed, had he wanted to actually construct an Übermarionette, he certainly had the means and the know-how to do so. Instead, he chose to design and make his Black Figures. Although they are very deliberately not statuesque, they share some of the qualities of the dancers of the period. As Daniel Albright writes:

> But most importantly perhaps is that these 'statuesque' figures are truly composite: after Frazer and early anthropology, Shiva informs perception of the Greek at this time no less than St Denis's Isis intermingles in her practice with contemporary ideas about, say Athene.[48]

Craig's figures can be read as following a similar trajectory, but on a smaller scale. Rather than pose or perform in ancient temples, his Black Figures appear on his small model stages. Carved in whitewood, inked and pressed on paper, these Black Figures bring together his interest in the woodcut and the marionette, but also in the art of the actor. Indeed, very early on in his career, which he started as an actor, he claims that 'By 1900, I felt I had served a sufficiently long woodcutting apprenticeship to produce a play. You do not see the connection between chopping wood and theatricals, and yet there is one.'[49] This is a connection that he would pursue throughout his life, one that finds an outlet in the Black Figures. And this is another way in which these figures can be read as composite and ekphrastic. Jennifer Buckley has written convincingly about the constitutive and complex relationships between print culture and modernist theatre, with Craig as a prime force:

> Craig's career provides an early and exceptionally influential example of how modern artists seeking to dissociate theater and literature have

combined anti-textual polemics with extensive and innovative print production. His published engravings reveal with particular clarity that 'writing', 'text', 'dramatic literature', and 'print' are not the synonyms they are too often taken to be.[50]

And she insightfully asserts that:

> In at least one respect, modern xylography had already become what Craig hoped the modern theater would someday be: a medium that expressed a single artist's singular vision.[51]

The issue of pressing on paper and impression more generally has a particular cadence in this context in the ways that the figures themselves create impressions, but also perhaps in the ways that they were created through impressions: impressions of Greek dances mediated through Duncan; impressions of ancient puppets, especially the Javanese Wayang from Craig's personal collection; impressions of Godwin's architectural designs, but also of Irving's 'impressionist' acting style. Sophie Aymes states that Craig's work facilitates the transition from 'the symbolist realm of suggestion and evocation to that of the modernist imprint'.[52] I would claim that it probably does both, maintaining its symbolist aura and its modernist materiality. The figures appeared in books and on Craig's model stages, but were also meant to provide prototypes for approaches to acting. Craig writes about the ways these figures could facilitate the actors for the Moscow *Hamlet*:

> Into each engraving of each character in the play I have put what I saw in my mind's eye, not to *exhibit* as woodcuts, but to *show* the actor what I had seen . . . I think it is much better that an actor should have designs to look at, rather than he should be annoyed by a great deal of *talk*.[53]

So, rather than analyse the character for the benefit of the actors, Craig opted to engrave what he had seen in his mind's eye. This is a wonderfully layered and complex understanding of character and one that I would claim is at once very classical and Greek, and quintessentially modernist. It crosses and transgresses the binary between expressive psychology and stylisation, and it does this by consciously or perhaps unconsciously reviving the classical Greek understanding and etymology of character: as that which is engraved on a mask ($\chi\alpha\rho\dot{\alpha}\sigma\sigma\omega$ – $\chi\alpha\rho\alpha\kappa\tau\dot{\eta}\rho$). Whether or not Craig was aware that the word 'character' has a genealogy that started with the Greek word for 'engrave' is almost irrelevant, as the terms and especially the theatrical conventions that he is evoking partake in their own intertextuality. In a sense, it would be impossible to engage with masks and engraving in the ways that Craig does without reviving the etymological links between masks, engraving and notions of character. This is especially pertinent in this case as Craig is working with

Stanislavsky, whose whole approach to acting could not be more diametrically opposed to Craig's, based as it was on emotional interiority and expressiveness (at least at this stage in Stanislavsky's experiments). Against this Craig might be read as positing a notion of acting and 'character creating' that is based on craftsmanship and skill, where impression follows the opposite direction, from the outside rather than springing from an interiority. Still, Craig did work with Stanislavsky, and we can assume that the men were aware of each other's approaches to acting. As Mark Franko claims about Duncan's experiments in dance, much of the thinking about embodiment in this period is focused on the inner/outer binary.[54] And this may be another way in which what he calls a 'culture of feeling' and a 'philosophy of mechanism' is, if not completely elided, at least bridged. Of course, it was Isadora Duncan who introduced Craig to Stanislavsky, perhaps creating another bridge through her dancing body.

The issue of the mechanical is central to understanding both projects. This may be obvious in regard to Craig's Übermarionette. It is, however, of no less significance in discussions about Duncan. While the mechanical might be associated with the quintessentially modern, and the ethereal with the Hellenic and ancient, both these artists experiment with these categories in challenging ways. The concept of the body itself as an automaton is prominent in the work of both. The idea of the automaton, dominant in late nineteenth-century and early twentieth-century thinking, transpires as a *topos*, where mimesis itself is experimented with and challenged. The binaries of internal/external, free will/control, material/metaphysical, anthropomorphism/abstraction are all experimented with during this period. Craig's Übermarionette could also be seen within the context of the turn-of-the-century fascination with automata and the challenges they pose to notions of originality, interiority, artistic agency and artistic expression. Interestingly, many early modernist automata presented themselves as copies of ancient, mostly Greek statues. Equally fascinating is the fact that Duncan's poses, influenced by her training in the Delsarte system, can be read as attempts to copy Greek statues. These statues, however, are at once material and ethereal, the result of archaeological endeavour but also the locus of desire. It is this idea of the statue not simply as moving but also as fluctuating between materiality and idealism that provides the prototype for Craig's Übermarionette as a type of desiring machine.

Indeed, Craig very deliberately writes against the type of archaeology that is based on reviving the relic; the artist, he states, must not 'dig in the ground'.[55] And in a polemical tone that is aimed at both private and museum collections, he writes: 'Sculpture! Quick, fly to Greece! Now's the time! Nobody's looking – occupied with affairs – no money in the country, a lot of money in the ground; dig it all up; let sculpture go to the dogs, and let the old remains come back from Athens to fill our collections.'[56] Here Craig, in a conflation of the statue with the mask, is proving himself not only a sophisticated performance theorist or philosopher – conceptualising what Franko might call a 'philosophy of mechanism' – but also an astute political analyst. For him, in a tone that is almost postcolonial, this idea of the private collection and the museum is quintessentially 'sham-Greek'. He pours scorn on theatrical productions that draw their inspiration from the museum and calls for the return of the statue and the mask 'to the stage to restore – expression – the visible expression of the mind – and must be a creation, not a copy'.[57]

Anxieties about reproduction/reproducibility, authenticity/copy permeate the writing of both Craig and Duncan. The notion of sham-Greek is shared by both. Duncan's relationships to Greek statues and the Tanagra vases, in a similar vein to Craig, cannot be read as mere reproductions. Embedded in this kind of thinking for both artists might be a kind of neo-Platonic fear of the copy as that which distorts reality and distracts from the truth. For Craig this becomes the crux of his theories on the art of the actor, as he expresses and mediates these through the figure of the Übermarionette; an Übermarionette, however, that has been thought through and experimented with through the figure of Duncan's dancer and his own Black Figures. These Black Figures, through the 'characters' they represent and through the ways these characters are engraved and then pressed on paper, come to form a very nuanced 'model' for actors that may also be read as a double for the Übermarionette.

The evocation of Plato in this context is not coincidental, as Craig's famous manifesto for the art of the actor also quotes Plato in his attempt to theorise the aesthetics and, I would claim, the politics and ethics of acting. As in Plato, theories of embodiment carry within them theories of ethics and politics; or rather, as Craig does when talking about the Theatre of the Future, thinking and theory about representation and mimesis is enabled through the notion of embodiment.

This idea of embodiment in Plato, as Leslie Kurke has insightfully explored, is also thought through the figure of the puppet. Interestingly, she also underlines Plato's 'lurking fantasy of choruses of dancing puppets'. Kurke writes:

> I suggest that there is a significant nexus of ideas that links the imagery of puppets to Plato's theorisation of choral habituation, while this image also participates in the complex superimposition of the levels of individual, community, and cosmos in Plato's modelling of *choreia*. At the same time, Plato's lurking fantasy of choruses of dancing puppets will allow us in turn to make out the lineaments of a much older set of Greek cultural associations that imagines choruses as moving statues and statues as frozen choreuts, all bound together under the sway of wonder (*thauma*) and desire (*eros*).[58]

This is a bold claim, one that Kurke analyses convincingly and one that chimes well with this reading of the constitutive links between the dancer and the Übermarionette. Duncan's dancer and Craig's mechanical puppet seem to have a long genealogy in theories not only of acting but of the politics and ethics of representation more generally. And in deliberately quoting Plato in his manifesto 'The Actor and the Über-marionette', Craig himself might be read as participating in a long genealogy of thought that scrutinises the political and ethical efficacy of mimesis as enacted through the double figures of the dancer and the puppet.

As Kurke states, this *choreia* is also collective, bringing to mind Duncan's notion that she 'never danced solo'. This relationship between the performing body and the body politic is also crucial for many modernist schools of acting. The whole idea of a school is, of course, central to both Duncan and Craig. The impact of Duncan's schools and their multiple contributions to the pedagogy of modern dance has been well documented. Craig's School of the Arts of the Theatre at the Arena Goldoni has received less attention as a serious attempt at a theatre pedagogy. Still, the concept of *paideia* is central to both. And this concept is theorised, as Kurke claims is also the case in Plato, through the benefits of *choreia*, a chorality that brings together the dancer, the actor and the marionette. Kurke writes:

> *Choreia* is a machine for the production of pure presence, which, through mimesis links together and merges the gods, the dancers, and the human spectators. This is what makes it a *thauma*. The engine or motor of this mimetic chain is *eros*.[59]

Indeed, this reading of Plato's use of puppets can be seen to parallel the notion put forward here of the Übermarionette as a desiring machine. Again Craig proves to be an insightful reader of Plato and a modernist reinterpreter of the role of puppets in reviving the anti-theatricality debate. If we trace the uses he makes of references to 'ancient puppets', as he calls them in his manifesto but also throughout the whole of *The Mask*, we can see quite a few parallels with the interpretation proposed by Kurke, where puppets are seen as central to Platonic thinking about education, politics and ethics. Far from mere playthings, they are called *thaumata* by Plato, in a fusion of the earthly and the divine. Craig himself, citing Xenophon's reference to *neurospasta* ('moved by means of a string') in his *Symposium* (in 'A Note on Marionettes' in *The Mask*, in the same issue that carried his manifesto), claims that these small figurines also were accompanied by 'life-size figures or even larger than life, each of which contained a manipulator, and my reason for holding this view is that I do not find the Greeks lacking in a sense of proportion . . . Not so unlike Mr. Craig's übermarionette, this.'[60] Here Craig is following a thought process that almost mirrors Plato's conceptualisation of the puppet as not merely a plaything but a *thauma*, a miraculous creature/creation. Kurke writes that in Plato, 'this collapse or uneasy fusion of three normally mutually exclusive categories – divine, mortal human, and artifice or object of skilled crafting – is indeed a "wonder" that is also, I suggest, very much at the core of the Greek imagination of chorality'.[61] It is also at the core of Craig's conceptualisation of his Übermarionette. In claiming this Greek lineage for his life-size puppet, Craig is again being both modern and classical.

The article referenced here is written under the guise of yet another Craig pseudonym. In all these dialogues with himself where his own voice is being refracted and echoed, Craig might be seen to be practising the type of impersonality (rather than aggrandising himself, as he has been accused of) he claimed for his creation. If character is seen as something that can be engraved on a figure or projected onto an Übermarionette, it becomes more pliable, flexible and accountable, i.e. it becomes the appropriate material for art. Having accused the live actor of having 'too much personality' and being 'too unreliable', his phantasmic creature expresses an attempt to fuse this 'too much' of life that the actor carries with a kind of nothingness. As Adolf Furst (Craig) writes of this puppet, 'it is doing nothing, this saying nothing, this meaning nothing which raises [the puppet] to an altitude that is limitless'.[62]

This wondrous aspect of the puppet, this thaumaturgical function, raises it upwards towards the gods but simultaneously lowers it towards the earth, the grave and death itself. This is the closing paragraph of 'The Actor and the Über-marionette':

> I pray earnestly for the return of the Image ... the über-marionette to the theatre; and when he comes again and is but seen, he will be loved so well that once more will it be possible for the people to return to their ancient joy in ceremonies ... once more will ... creation be celebrated ... homage rendered to existence ... and divine and happy intercession made to Death.[63]

So this phantasmic creature creates links between ideas of interiority and exteriority, but also between life and death. This is a 'happy intercession', as Craig mentions; nevertheless it is one that adds *thanatos* to the idea of the Übermarionette as a desiring machine. The *eros* that provides the motor for the creation of the *thauma* of pure presence in Platonic thinking, according to Kurke, here also becomes death-driven, making it *thanato-erotic*. This might be linked at once to its modernist pose (the lost innocence to which Kleist refers in his comparable essay), but also might be linked to that constitutive structure of theatre itself: birth/death/resurrection. This is something that is central to the thinking about theatre in the work of the Cambridge Ritualists, and in modernist anthropology more generally. Ideas of death but also of resurrection permeate Craig's writing, and his influential essay carries Eleonora Duse's famous aphorism as its epigraph:

To save the Theatre, the Theatre must be destroyed, the actors and actresses must all die of the plague . . . They make art impossible.[64]

Epigraph in this context might also be read in conjunction with the classical Greek *epitaph*, as that inscription that appears on a funerary monument. And it appears by means of engraving. As mentioned earlier in this chapter, this connection between engraving and ideas of death has also been explored by Sophie Aymes in her work on Craig's book *Woodcuts and Some Words*, where she writes 'of the woodblock [as] being both a medium and a grave'.[65] So this miraculous work of the Übermarionette, mediated through the engraving of character on Black Figures but also through the dancing body of Isadora Duncan, will contribute to the death of the old theatre and the birth of the Theatre of the Future. The inclusion of the dancer through the figure of Duncan in this context is challenging, particularly as Craig connects the death of the ancient puppets with the appearance of the female performer on the stage. Here is how he conflates the two images:

> The figure of the Divine Puppet attracted fewer and fewer lovers, and the women were quite the latest thing. With the fading of the Puppet and the advance of these women who exhibited themselves on the stage in his place, came that darker spirit which is called chaos, and in its wake the triumph of the riotous Personality.[66]

This is an astonishing quotation. The *thanatoerotic* attraction of the puppet is clearly read as homosocial (if not directly homosexual), and the audience are cast as its lovers. This flow of desire is interrupted with the appearance of women on the stage. This itself is seen as part of the fall from grace (or heaven, even). A similar trope is also present in the figure of the young male dancer in Kleist's essay, who tries to emulate the puppet by narcissistically observing himself in the mirror. As the infamous Personality or Consciousness creeps in, the dancer/puppet is no longer able to maintain the state of innocence. Fascinating that Craig should quite deliberately rework this idea through the figure of the female performer. The presence of the female interrupts the flow of homosocial and narcissistic desire. And the female performer herself is viewed through classic misogynist tropes of exhibitionism, 'riotous Personality', and 'chaos'. So according to Craig one of the reasons, and possibly the main one, for the demise of the great ancient theatres is the appearance of women on the stage. It is this very absence of women from the classical Greek stage that was one of its main attractions for him.

This also expresses another way in which Craig might be read as neo-Platonist, for part of Plato's castigating of the stage and a central tenet of his anti-theatricality was that the theatrical experience was seen as feminising. It had the potential to turn men into women, quite literally through the acting convention of men playing women, but also by arousing the emotions of the all-male audience. It is this longstanding structural connection between the discourses of anti-theatricality and misogyny that Craig is reviving and inflecting in the above quotation. This raises the question of whether his Übermarionette has a gender.

Sometimes these phantasmic/wondrous automata of the modernist stage are read as being genderless. However, as the longue durée of anti-theatricality clearly attests, they also enact the difficult and fraught relationships between gender and representation as these are manifested on the stages of classicism. In many ways, the Übermarionette also partakes in the responses to the arrival of the New Woman on the stage of modernity. At the same time, the figure of the female automaton has a distinct modernist pedigree, and this is not one that Craig embraces, nor is it necessarily feminist. From E. T. A. Hoffman's Olympia in 'The Sandman' tale (1816), which Sigmund Freud interprets in his 1919 essay 'The Uncanny', to Auguste Villiers de l'Isle-Adam's Alicia Clary in *The Future Eve* (1885–6) and the 'false' Maria in Thea von Harbou and Fritz Lang's *Metropolis* (1925 novel; 1927 film), the figure embodies anxieties about sexuality, gender and reproduction. Closer to Craig, F. T. Marinetti's early play *La donna è mobile* (*Electric Puppets*), which appears in 1909, the same year as *The Mask*, features living actors and automata together, combining Marinetti's adoration of technology with his strident misogyny. Although Craig publishes the first English translation of the Futurist Manifesto in *The Mask* in 1909, he is not in the least interested in Marinetti's experiments with automata on the stage.

Contrary to Craig, Marinetti thought that women made good actresses due to their 'highly strung' nervous system, which meant they could be manipulated like puppets. This idea is very similar to Craig's notion of 'riotous Personality'. This exuberance of emotion for Marinetti compounded the puppet-like nature of women, but for Craig made them unsuitable for the stage and for partaking in his ideas about the Übermarionette. Either way, these modernist puppets and automata clearly exhibit anxieties about gender, which begs the question of the gender of the Übermarionette itself. This analysis claims – in many ways following the pioneering work of Jennifer Buckley on the relationships between print culture and modernist performance[67] – that despite Craig's declared intentions, his Übermarionette, all the better for not having actually been constructed, finds many other modes through which it is thought and expressed: the woodcut, the Black Figure and the figure of Isadora Duncan dancing.

THE DANCER, THE DANCE AND THE PUPPET-MASTER

In the above drawing of Duncan by Craig from 1906, her pose is significantly different from the ones presented in Walkowitz's many drawings of her, where she herself appears like a hieroglyph of sorts. Here Craig depicts Duncan in a characteristically unclassical pose, and indeed she is presented so as somewhat to resemble a puppet.[68] Her hands and one of her feet seem to be held up by strings, while the other foot, barely touching the ground, seems also to be propelled by some external/internal force, which is creating a dizzying whirl. Rather, I would claim that this pose is only 'unclassical' if we associate classicism with its romantic and aestheticst renditions. In other ways it may appear as quintessentially classical, even Platonic in presenting movement as a result of a perfectly wound-up mechanism. This Platonic notion of movement as a type of clockwork resurfaces in all the writing about puppets and automata from Kleist and romanticism onwards. Here is Schopenhauer, who is frequently quoted in *The Mask*:

Figure 2.3 Edward Gordon Craig, 'Beethoven', from *Isadora Duncan; Sechs Bewegungsstudien* (Insel Verlag, 1906). Reproduced courtesy of the Edward Gordon Craig Estate.

> The human race presents itself as puppets that are set in motion by an internal clockwork. I have said that those puppets are not pulled from outside, but that each of them bears in itself the clockwork from which its movements result. This is the *will-to-live* manifesting itself as an untiring mechanism, as an irrational impulse, which does not have its sufficient ground or reason in the external world.[69]

This is a similar *will-to-live* to that which characterises Duncan's vitalism. It is at the same time Platonic in presenting the idea of the mechanical as almost metaphysical. This quotation could be one of many from Schopenhauer that feature in *The Mask*. The same idea is present in both Kleist's and Craig's *über*- essays. It does raise the question of who or what controls this smoothly wound-up clock that is the marionette or the dancer. From where does its vital force derive? Duncan famously locates the source of her movement in the solar plexus:

> For hours I would stand quite still, my two hands folded between my breasts, covering the solar plexus . . . I was seeking and finally discovered the central spring of all movement.[70]

So in this sense Duncan is both the dancer and the dance. Her movement derives from herself; it is a self, however, that has been distilled of all personality, has been disindividuated (Franko) and turned into a type of chorus. Still the issue of agency remains pertinent. Is there a model of authorship at work in this construction, and what kind of authority does it entail? These modernist theories of puppetry and dance also partake in the thinking of the period about textuality and authorship. In this sense they can be said to contribute to all the debates about the autonomy of performance itself, and to the thinking about the newly formed figure of the director.

Interestingly, in the above drawing and perhaps despite Craig's attempt to portray Duncan's movement as externally controlled, the image remains ambivalent. She appears to be both the dancer and the dance; the force compelling her to move is at once following two opposing directions. Could the same be said of Craig's Übermarionette – is it an automaton in the Greek sense, i.e. self-motored, through a smooth, well-wound-up internal force, or is it controlled by a puppet-master? For both approaches will also construct an equivalent model for the modernist director.

Craig's hailing of the Übermarionette can be read as constructing a modernist theory of acting, but also a modernist theory of the director. The figure of the director himself (and it is a him in this context) is seen to derive from all the changes brought about by the New Movements in the theatre. The debates about authorship, the claims to impersonality, the relationships between autobiography and artistic practice are all issues that are theorised, experimented with and contested through these New Movements in modernist theatre. In renegotiating the relationship between the actor and the playwright, the text and the stage, the rise of the director can also be read as comment – or a proposal – on more general thinking at the time about the concept of authorship. Indeed, the theatre might be seen as the most appropriate *locus* for such an exploration. Its synaesthetic quality, coupled with its civic/political dimension, makes it ideal for both the discourse that sees the director as the embodiment of individual genius and the one that sees him as a channel through which the various artforms and performing artists are filtered.

This notion of the director as a 'mediating' figure – or a thinker of mediation itself, as Badiou would have it – has been well charted in terms of theatre history. However, as I have analysed elsewhere,[71] the rise of the modernist director needs to be thought through and theorised in terms of the relationships between directors and actors, especially female performers. The New Woman of the New Movements in the theatre helps to carve out a space, political and aesthetic, that also constructs the modernist director. Rather than viewing these female performers as simply and unproblematically mediating the thoughts of these modernist directors, it might be more useful and historically more accurate to assume that the performers themselves had a considerable and formative input in the creation of the performance aesthetic of modernist theatre. August Strindberg worked with both his actress wives, Siri

Wrangel and Harriet Bosse, and towards the end of his life with the seventeen-year-old actress Fanny Falkner; Ibsen was served by a number of influential actresses; Craig designed for Eleonora Duse and Isadora Duncan and directed his mother, Ellen Terry; Meyerhold worked with Zinaida Reich; Stanislavsky with Olga Kipper; Harley Granville-Barker with Lillah McCarthy; Brecht with Helene Weigel.

It is commonly accepted that while the New Movements in the theatre helped to shape the figure of the mostly male director, modern dance resulted from the experiments of pioneering women dancers. Ramsay Burt writes in *The Male Dancer*:

> The label 'modern dance' generally refers to the work of the pioneer dance reformers (nearly all of whom were women) who developed styles other than ballet, including Ruth St Denis (1879–1968), Isadora Duncan (1877–1927), Doris Humphrey (1895–1958), Martha Graham (1894–1991), Rudolph Laban (1879–1958), Ted Shawn (1891–1972) and Mary Wigman (1886–1973) during the first half of the twentieth century.[72]

It would be interesting to analyse how this dynamic is inflected in the Craig/Duncan coupling, especially in the ways that this is mediated through the figures of the Übermarionette and the dancer. What propels both into movement, and is this movement automatic? Are agency and authorship one and the same in this context? Kurke very helpfully talks of 'mimetic chains'. Indeed, the idea of mimesis is crucial here. The dancer might be mimetically and rhythmically[73] imitating the movement of the 'life-force', the same life-force that may be propelling the automaton into motion. Is there an author that creates the artwork that results from such a movement? For Kleist's dancer this author may be God, and for Duncan it may be Dionysus. Is Craig the ultimate God/puppet-master of his Übermarionette? It is through this analogy that Craig might be read also as proposing the figure of the all-powerful modernist director through his theories of acting. Parallel to this reading, if we continue the analogy with Duncan's dancer, who practises a type of modernist impersonality and disindividuation (Franko), we may be able to claim a similar impersonality for Craig's puppet-master. This is the puppet-master as craftsman, as modest impersonal manipulator, rather than as tyrannical figure. In some ways, in this framework it is the puppet-master who also mimics the movements of the puppet, rather than externally imposing them. Kurke claims that this aspect of puppetry also has a Platonic lineage. She writes:

> We can see this clearly once we realise that properly to manipulate a puppet on strings, the puppet master has to mime the same movements

he wants to cause in the puppet with the corresponding sides of his body – only his motions are more subtle. That is to say, the tendons or cords that make the puppet move and dance are literally mimetic chains.[74]

This reading presents an image of puppet and puppet-master smoothly integrated through the work that is at once mechanical, aesthetic and human. So, far from being a tyrannical figure, the puppet-master emerges as a figure constructed through the 'mimetic cords of reason and sympathy', as Kurke insightfully states.[75] This is another sense in which it may be helpful to read Duncan's dancer and Craig's Übermarionette as linked. These mimetic cords form a fundamental aspect of theatricality itself, one that confuses the boundaries between actor and puppet and, crucially, between actor and director.

Souls and Machines: Discipline and Freedom

The dance historian Arnold Rood claims that 'Craig expected the actor to be an Isadora Duncan *with* discipline,'[76] repeating an assumption that has plagued Duncan's reception by the more traditional dance theorists. However, if we look at the ways that Duncan herself spoke about her technique, it is clear that the language she uses is saturated with images of motors and machines. 'Emotion works like a motor. It must be warmed up to run well,' she writes in *Art of the Dance*.[77] Carrie Preston writes convincingly about Isadora Duncan's use of the image of the motor to describe the relationship between independent artistic will and its expression:

> The motor's ability to move several objects simultaneously offers an image of a 'multiplied body', an interest that was shared by F. T. Marinetti (who was also cheering 'Hurrah' for motors) and influenced Futurist Dance. The power of motorised propulsion to channel forces and move a foreign object offered the ideal of dance movements that appear to be executed effortlessly in a self-abandonment that Duncan associated with classical rituals. Finally, the motor's endless repetition inspired Duncan's desire to simulate spontaneity in her dances.[78]

Preston helpfully calls this Duncan's 'deliberate choreography of spontaneity', and locates it within a 'tension in anti-modern performances' where 'a soloist attempts to assert agency and freedom but through preformulated mythic construct that inevitably confines'. However, it might be equally interesting not to read this tension as a constraint on individual artistic expression but rather, as Preston's own analysis implies, to see it as enacting a dialectic between humanism and abstraction, between indeed 'pure' expression and form. Repeating a familiar trope, the move towards abstraction is seen as a classicising impulse. Rather than being anti-modern, this impulse and the tensions and contradictions it entails might be at the heart of the modern. It also might be part of the ways the modern and contemporary gestures – or poses, to use Preston's evocative term – towards the future.

Where Preston reads this turn towards Hellenism as 'anti-modern', on the contrary, I think, it is constitutive of modernist experimentation and Duncan's attitude towards the Greeks is emblematic of this. Rather I would agree with Jacques Rancière, who claims that this 'archaeomodern turn . . . is located at the core of the modern project' and 'sets up two categories: that of figurative reason or of sleeping meaning, and the temporal category of anticipation'.[79] So this attitude towards the Greeks is possibly about the past, but probably has more to say about the aesthetics of utopia. And we know how often the term 'future' features in the writing of both Duncan and Craig.

The tension between the animate and the inanimate, between the 'soul' and the 'motor', also haunts Craig's writing, especially when it comes to his manifestos about acting. Although we associate him with the banishing of live actors from the stage, in 1921 in *The Theatre – Advancing* he writes: 'I ask only for the liberation of the actor that he may develop *his* own powers and cease from being the Marionette of the playwright.'[80] In this sense the Übermarionette, rather than replacing the actor, becomes an über-actor. This type of actor would be free from emotion, from personality, from psychology and primarily free from the dominating power of the playwright. This critique of the dominating power of the playwright has traditionally been read as heralding the era of the dominating director; in a sense, the actor substitutes one form of agency for another. However, to do justice to Craig himself and to further forge the incongruous links with Duncan's project, it might be useful to complicate this binary further by locating Craig's writing within the manifesto fervour of the avant-garde (its modernist pose) while simultaneously reading it as part of modernism's classical turn.

Craig's famous aphoristic call for the banishing of the actor from the stage can be read as part of modernist theatre's resuscitation of the anti-theatricality debate: a debate that uses the discourses of theatre at once to attack it and to herald the Theatre of the Future. Craig's essay, hugely influential since it first appeared, can be seen to partake in the manifesto writing of the period; apocalyptic and eschatological, it relies on an aesthetics of catastrophe, what recent critics have termed a *via negativa*.[81] Through the ashes of the old theatre, the new would be reborn, phoenix-like. So it does not seem inappropriate for him to stage his essay with a highly evocative sacrificial image that quotes the great Italian actress Eleonora Duse, as stated above, where the image of the plague is also prevalent. An image that Antonin Artaud would also mobilise later to talk of the sacrificial nature of acting.

This gesture of catastrophe, further on in the quotation, is followed by Duse's equally demanding call for 'a return to the Greeks', again following the double turn towards the past and the future. And this return is echoed throughout Craig's essay in a number of ways: in the ways that, like Plato, it too utilises the discourses of drama to attack it. Craig, like Plato, uses highly theatrical tropes, the dramatic dialogue, the creation of personae and the structure of death/resurrection. Craig's writing too can be read as radically reworking both the discourses of the philosophical dialogue and of theatricality as a way to stage the oldest debate in the history of aesthetics – the ancient quarrel – the quarrel about mimesis itself, its philosophical, aesthetic and political efficacy. And as in Plato, this debate is located on the body of the actor:

> Acting is not an art. It is therefore incorrect to speak of the actor as an artist. For accident is an enemy of the artistic. Art is the exact antithesis of Pandimonium [sic], and Pandimonium is created by the tumbling together of many accidents; Art arrives only by design. Therefore, in order to make any work of art it is clear we may work in those materials with which we can calculate. Man is not one of these materials.[82]

The shift from acting to art in general and the denouncing of 'Man' as an inappropriate material for art is characteristic. It can be read as echoing Plato's concerns about the 'confusion of forms', a confusion that results in aesthetic but also political chaos (theatrocracy). It is not surprising in this context to find that Craig's seminal essay is itself punctuated by two equally important quotations from 'the Greeks' whom he so often summons throughout it. One is from Plato's *Republic*; it is the famous section about the rhapsode:

> And therefore when any one of these pantomimic gentlemen, who are so clever that they can imitate anything, comes to us, and makes a proposal to exhibit himself and his poetry, we will fall down and worship him as a sweet and holy and wonderful being; but we must also inform him that in our state such as he are not permitted to exist; the law will not allow them. And so, when we have anointed him with myrrh and a garland of wool upon his head, we shall lead him away to another city.[83]

How fitting that Craig uses this iconic passage – one that has generated so much philosophical reflection about mimesis – to frame and also to justify his own theories about the Übermarionette. Like Plato, he too is concerned about the power of the actor to distort reality and to *mesmerise*, to act as a kind of charismatic demagogue who threatens the political order itself ('the law will not allow them'). And, as in Plato, this power of the theatre and theatricality is seen to be at the core of the problem of mimesis itself. To do full justice to the debate itself, Craig also calls upon Aristotle in support of his manifesto for the actor – or more generally, we could claim, for a modern theatre. The quotation he uses from Aristotle is the equally famous passage from the *Poetics*, where the 'spectacle' is denounced as the work of 'the stage machinist' rather than the poet, and where tragedy 'is felt even apart from representation and actors' (note xxvi, 1–4).[84] This quotation appears at the end of the essay, while the one from Plato is in an earlier note. Along with Duse's epigraph at the start, they serve to frame his manifesto, to give it a historical lineage and to theatricalise it. So when Craig calls upon 'the Greeks' to help him construct and articulate his argument, he is not simply being nostalgic, calling upon a unifying and homogenising rhetoric that would give his argument the aura of the classical. In many ways he is calling upon 'the Greeks' as both a philologist and a theorist of performance. Indeed, his own essay may be said to rehearse the ancient quarrel itself. As in Plato, this quarrel is given shape and form through the workings of theatre and in particular is located on the performing body; a performing body, however, that has been conceptualised and embodied through the figures of the puppet and the dancer.

If we consider the role of puppets and automata (*thaumata*, wondrous, almost magical things, as Plato calls them) in Plato's philosophical writings, we can perhaps even claim a lineage for Craig's Übermarionette that places it within a genealogy of writing about the efficacy (both aesthetic and political) of mimesis through the figure of the automaton. And if in turn we read this Übermarionette in conjunction with Duncan's dancer, not in opposition, but as its double – as indeed both Plato and Artaud understand the double in theatre – then they can be seen to be locked in an embrace and possibly dancing in the same chorus, a chorus that at once looks back to Greek tragedy and forward to modern dance.

NOTES

1. Duncan, *My Life*, p. 58.
2. Ackerman, *The Myth and Ritual School*, pp. 29–30.
3. Quoted in Blair, *Isadora*, p. 35.
4. Duncan, *My Life*, p. 5.
5. Ibid. p. 35.
6. For an account of the impact of the theories of Anton Mesmer (1734–1815) – mesmerism – on acting, see Goodall, *Stage Presence*, pp. 84–121.
7. Ibid. p. 107.
8. Quoted in Goodall, *Stage Presence*, p. 106.
9. See Blair, *Isadora*, p. 30.
10. Ibid. p. 46.
11. See Peters, 'Jane Harrison and the Savage Dionysus'.
12. See Chapter 2, 'Scene Changes', in Innes, *Edward Gordon Craig*, pp. 11–37.
13. Wilde, *The Works of Oscar Wilde*, p. 36.
14. Oscar Wilde quoted from *The Dramatic Review*, 22 May 1886, p. 162, in Stokes, *Resistible Theatres*, p. 55.
15. Quoted in Peters, 'Jane Harrison and The Savage Dionysus', p. 11.
16. John Stokes writes of this production of *Helena in Troas*, 'Yet in every respect the standards of the production were amateurish, and to the professional critics it seemed that archaeology had, in the hands of Bedford Park, become merely an excuse for Aesthetic nostalgia. For the most part the performers were sadly

below par, and except for Florence Farr, who survived by virtue of her voice, none emerged unscathed,' – *Resistible Theatres*, p. 66.

17. In British Library, MS 58407, vol. 35 of the Darwin-Cornford Papers.

18. Apparently Cornford also sent Craig a copy of his wife's play, and Craig responds that he is 'Glad to get your wife's play' although he goes on to state that he is opposed to women writers in general. Craig's reply and three further letters to Cornford are in the British Library in MS 58428, vol. 56 of the Darwin-Cornford Papers. The first is from Munich, dated Dec. 19, 1911.

19. Cornford, *The Origin of Attic Comedy*, p. 204.

20. See Blair, *Isadora*, p. 60.

21. Ibid. p. 61.

22. See Duncan, *My Life*, p. 69.

23. See LaMothe, '"A God Dances through Me"'.

24. Duncan, *Art of the Dance*, p. 96.

25. Ibid. p. 108.

26. Ibid. p. 96.

27. Franko, *Dancing Modernism/Performing Politics*, p. 17.

28. Ibid. p. 20.

29. Badiou, *The Century*, p. 159.

30. Plato, *The Laws*, 700 a–b.

31. See LaMothe, '"A God Dances through Me"', p. 262.

32. Nietzsche, *Thus Spoke Zarathustra*, in *The Portable Nietzsche*, p. 153.

33. See Duncan, *Art of the Dance*, p. 260.

34. Jowitt, 'Images of Isadora', p. 2.

35. See LaMothe, '"A God Dances through Me"', p. 260.

36. Craig writes in *The Mask* of the impact of Duncan on the Ballets Russes: 'The two most perfect Russian Dancers are Pavlova and Nijinsky. These two have been the most successful in acquiring the grace taught them by the American, and every performance of theirs becomes less and less the old French thing and more and more American.' *The Mask*, vol. 4, no. 2 (1911), pp. 83–4.

37. See Potter, 'Designed for Dance', pp. 154–69.

38. Stein, *A Stein Reader*, pp. 123–4.

39. Terry, *Isadora Duncan*, p. 115.

40. Craig, 'A Note on Masks', p. 9.

41. Ibid. pp. 9–10.

42. Edward Gordon Craig, 'The First Dialogue', in *The Art of the Theatre*, reproduced in *On the Art of the Theatre*, pp. 140–1.

43. Walton, 'Craig and the Greeks', p. 7.

44. Count Harry Kessler, quoted in intro. to Newman (ed.), *Edward Gordon Craig, Black Figures*, p. 17.

45. Albright, 'Knowing the Dancer, Knowing the Dance'.

46. See Chapter 3 for a detailed analysis of this concept.

47. See 'Gentlemen, the Marionette', in Taxidou, *The Mask*, pp. 141–74.

48. See Albright, 'Knowing the Dancer, Knowing the Dance', p. 302.

49. Quoted in Aymes, 'Woodcuts and Some Words', p. 53.

50. Buckley, *Beyond Text*, p. 28.

51. Ibid. p. 31.

52. Aymes, 'Woodcuts and Some Words', pp. 54–5.

53. Craig, quoted in intro. to Newman (ed.), *Edward Gordon Craig, Black Figures*, p. 20 (emphasis original).

54. See Franko, 'The Invention of Modern Dance', in *Dancing Modernism/Performing Politics*, pp. 1–25, p. 6.

55. Craig in 'A Note on Masks', p. 22.
56. Ibid. p. 22.
57. Ibid. p. 23.
58. Kurke, 'Imagining Chorality', p. 124.
59. Ibid, p. 147.
60. Quoted in *The Mask*, vol. 1, no. 2, p. 64.
61. See Kurke, 'Imagining Chorality', p. 127.
62. Ibid. p. 72.
63. Ibid. p. 15.
64. Quoted in *The Mask*, vol. 1, no. 2, p. 2.
65. See Aymes, '*Woodcuts and Some Words*', p. 63.
66. Craig, 'The Actor and the Über-marionette', pp. 14–15.
67. See Buckley, *Beyond Text*, pp. 52–3, where she writes: 'Although Craig never built an Über-marionette, the Black Figures exhibit the characteristics he ascribed to his ideal actor. Their features and poses severely formalized, the figures are so de-individuated that even those familiar with them frequently had trouble determining which character they represented. Their facial expressions are indicated either very broadly or not at all, a graphic choice consistent with Craig's conviction that actors should always be masked to eliminate the temptation toward emotionally inspired facial mobility.'
68. I am grateful to Fiona Macintosh for pointing this out in discussion after a paper I delivered at the Archive of Performances of Greek and Roman Drama (APGRD), at the University of Oxford, February 2019.
69. Schopenhauer, *On the Suffering of the World*, p. 108 (emphasis original).
70. See Duncan, *My Life*, p. 58.
71. See Taxidou, 'The Director, the Playwright and the Actress,' *Modernism and Performance*, pp. 43–58.
72. Burt, *The Male Dancer*, p. 3.
73. On rhythm in Plato see Kowalzig, 'Broken Rhythms in Plato's *Laws*'.
74. See Kurke, 'Imagining Chorality', pp. 150–1.
75. Ibid. p. 158. Kurke writes: 'We could say that in Platonic theology, the gyration of the human as mechanical (a puppet) is in no way a demeaning or negative image, because for Plato the entire cosmos is itself a magnificent and perfectly ordered machine. Thus, the human as puppet is sutured into that larger machine via mimetic cords of reason and sympathy.'
76. Rood (ed.), *Gordon Craig on Movement and Dance*, p. xvii.
77. See Duncan, *Art of the Dance*, pp. 99–100.
78. Preston, *Modernism's Mythic Pose*, p. 146.
79. Rancière, 'The Archaeomodern Turn', pp. 28–9. For the significance of this concept for modernism in general see Vassiliki Kolocotroni, 'Still Life.' Also see Rancière's comments on Craig's Übermarionette in his analysis of the Craig/Stanislavsky collaboration on the 'Moscow *Hamlet*' of 1909–11, in Rancière, *Aisthesis*, pp. 171–90.
80. Craig, *The Theatre – Advancing*, p. 260.
81. See Patrick McGuinness, 'Mallarmé, Maeterlinck and the Symbolist Via Negativa', in Ackerman and Puchner (eds), *Against Theatre*, pp. 149–67.
82. Craig, 'The Actor and the Über-marionette', p. 3.
83. Plato, *Republic*, III, 395. Quoted in *The Mask*, vol. 1, no. 2, p. 5.
84. Aristotle, *Poetics*, VI. 19 and XXVI, 1–4. Quoted in *The Mask*, vol. 1, no. 2, p. 11.

3

POETIC DRAMA: THEATRICALITY, PERFORMABILITY AND TRANSLATION

The encounter between Greek tragedy and the modernist stage is certainly, as this book has endeavoured to trace, a series of exercises and experiments – sometimes successful, sometimes less so – in performance practice. Whether the modernist theatre-makers had studied the Greek play-texts or not, it is clear that a strong notion of Hellenism informed some of their most radical experiments in performance practice, be that acting, dance and movement or scenography. In addition, this chapter claims that this intricate relationship to Greek tragedy acquires a more immanent urgency when it comes to actually translating, rewriting, adapting, reworking (all terms that I would claim have their origins in these modernist experiments) classical Greek plays for the stage. This enterprise is all the more heightened when it is undertaken by leading modernist poets. Although by no means a singularly anglophone project, this chapter will look at some of the ways the experiments in mostly anglophone modernist poetic drama are informed and inflected by the ways that leading modernist poets – T. S. Eliot, Ezra Pound, W. B. Yeats and H.D. – both practised and theorised translating 'the Greeks'. These concerns about transposing ancient texts onto the present, especially for the purposes of performance, are at the heart of some of the main concerns of the modernist project itself. The relationships between tradition and innovation, between experimentation and classicism, between individual talent and collective creativity, between play-text and stage, between the poetic word and the performing body are all creative tensions that are central to modernist experimentation, both as a literary and as a performance practice.

The term 'poetic drama' itself may need some further clarification before we proceed to examine the ways it engages with Greek tragedy. Usually coined in opposition to the more daring theatricality of the avant-garde, the term has come to describe the dramatic works of writers we otherwise associate with literary experimentation. In its more canonical guise, poetic drama refers to the dramatic works of W. B. Yeats and T. S. Eliot, accompanied by the dramatic works of W. H. Auden and Christopher Isherwood. This categorisation tends to posit European symbolism (as in the works of Maurice Maeterlinck and Stéphane Mallarmé) as its predecessors and sees as its successors the theatres of Harold Pinter and Samuel Beckett. It is a tradition that focuses on the tension between the written word and the stage, predominantly highlighting the power of the written word. However, most of these modernist poet-playwrights also display a profound attachment towards the workings of the stage: an attachment that is at once informed and undermined by a characteristic modernist anti-theatricality. This becomes all the more heightened as most of these writers are primarily poets. So the tension between the written word and the stage is endemic to these experiments. I would claim that in most cases the formal and thematic concerns about the 'word as flesh' and the 'flesh as word' form a constitutive element of poetic drama itself. This becomes all the more significant and precious when the word itself, and the cultural capital it carries, is the WORD of the great classics.

This sometimes fraught relationship between the poetic word and the stage is also a prime concern of many Continental experiments of the period, prompting Jean Cocteau to differentiate between 'poetry in the theatre' and 'poetry of the theatre' in his famous preface to his own poetic drama, *Les mariés de la Tour Eiffel* (1922). This 'poetry of the theatre' was soon to be shaped by his own excursion into Greek drama with *La Machine Infernale* (1934), a version of *Oedipus Rex*. This poetry of the stage we might today term as theatricality. It is fascinating that these modernist attempts to formulate theatricality and retheatricalise the stage bear a distinctly Greek stamp; one that at the same time addresses the difficulty of transmitting poetry onto the stage, and reconfigures the Platonic tradition of anti-theatricality. The difficulty of transmitting poetry onto the stage creates its own language of theatricality, one that is also accompanied by its own body of theory in the form of essays, debates and manifestos. Rather than feed into a Platonic anti-theatrical tradition, one that opposes the workings of 'poetry/philosophy' to those of the stage, these experiments gesture towards a new modernist relationship between the 'word' (with all its philosophical efficacy), the body of the actor, and the theatrical event in general.

This use of poetry is further complicated by the fact that the *poetic* is usually underscored by an equally strong *philosophical* and *ethico-political* imperative. Whether it is Eliot's Christianity, Yeats's mysticism, Pound's pronouncements on *Kulchur* (*Guide to Kulchur*, 1938) or H.D.'s essays on psychoanalysis, most of these poetic dramas are philosophically framed. And these philosophies also entail theories about translation. In each case this philosophy and theory of translation is not simply a frame or backdrop, but also appears as a theme, enacted through dramatic character and action, and comes to define the conventions and modes of dramatic presentation itself. In this sense, poetic drama is very classically Platonic, as it rehearses all the debates about the fraught relationships between philosophy and the stage, between the written word and the body of the actor, between the acts of reading and seeing, between individual and collective responses.

It is fascinating to note in relation to this philosophical imperative that poetic drama very deliberately rewrites another moment of separation between theatre and philosophy. Indeed, these modernist reworkings of Greek tragedy also address the violent banishment of theatre from the public sphere by Christianity in the fourth century CE, an event that modernist theatre directly or indirectly re-visions. The absence of the divine or the 'death of God' has been hailed as one of the main reasons for the impossibility of tragedy within modernity, both as a motor for philosophical thinking *and* as a mode of performance. For the absence of the divine is read as depriving tragedy of both its metaphysical aspirations and its ritualistic discourses of performance. According to George Steiner's well-rehearsed and much repeated notion, this creates an insurmountable difficulty for modern playwrights, dooming all their attempts to failure. However, an aspect of the modernist encounter with Greek tragedy that this chapter addresses is precisely its attachment to the metaphysical and the divine (albeit in the shadow of the 'death of God'), sometimes in a heady fusion of Christianity and Greek tragedy, as in the work of T. S. Eliot or through equally interesting fusions of orientalism, primitivism, and Hellenism.

This intriguing interface between Hellenism and primitivism that we find in the theatrical works of T. S. Eliot, W.B. Yeats, and in Ezra Pound's and H.D.'s translations of Greek plays results both from the fascination with the theatres of South-East Asia, Japan and China, and – in the case of H.D. – Egypt, and from the more direct influence of the modernist classicists known as the Cambridge Ritualists. Although, as previously mentioned, the grouping itself has been challenged (Gilbert Murray was professor of classics at Glasgow and not Cambridge) and their theories are constantly reassessed within classical studies, their impact on modernist languages of performance and especially on the translations of classical plays was formative. For in as much as these poetic dramas/translations were experiments in modernist poetry, they were also experiments in modernist performance, where the notion of performance is heavily influenced by ideas of ritual and continuity as conceptualised by James Fraser, the Ritualists and by modernist anthropology more generally (as in Pound's *Kulturmorphologie* of anthropologist Leo Frobenius). For these charismatic modernist classicists offered the modernist playwrights and theatre-makers ways of reviving notions of ritual and the sacred. These translations and reworkings were also revivals, and indeed the whole idea of a 'revival' of the classics is radically reworked through these projects. These 'revivals' offered ways of addressing the sometimes tense relationships between tradition and newness, so central to the projects of modernism.

It is in this sense that the encounter with Greek tragedy for these poets goes to the heart of their modernism itself. And at its heart is a fraught, contradictory, but ultimately creative and reciprocal relationship to the notion of 'tradition'. For Eliot, writing in 'Tradition and the Individual Talent', this sense of tradition creates both a historical lineage and a sense of presentism. Not static, or even canon-making as we may perceive it today, this idea of tradition follows a reciprocal motion as Eliot claims that 'the past should be altered by the present as much as the present is directed by the past'.[1] Tragedy in performance, which is one way we could approach the notion of 'revival', offers an ideal platform/stage to experiment with ideas of historicism and contemporaneity. In this context it is crucial to stress that for Eliot and these poets of the theatre, the languages of performance were as significant as the languages of poetry and translation. Eliot's famous 'Mythical Method', which triggers a 'continuous parallel between contemporaneity and antiquity',[2] can be seen to be enacted through the discourses of performance itself and the ways it creates presence. In some ways, and almost despite Eliot's attempt to endow this Mythical Method with elements of 'traditionalism' and canon formation, the performative coming into being of the event of revival itself, we could perhaps claim, acts as a corrective to the more conservative and totalising conceptions of Eliot's formulations. With distinct echoes of James Frazer's *The Golden Bough* (final edition in twelve volumes, 1906–15), Eliot coins this term in a review of Joyce's *Ulysses*, which is seen as the epitome of this method at work. He views it as 'a way of controlling, of ordering, of giving a shape and a significance to the immense panorama of futility and anarchy which is contemporary history'.[3] This sentence with its all-encompassing conservativism has been read as the hallmark of Eliot's Mythical Method, one that somewhat neatly feeds into his later Christian period. Still, I would like to stress the genealogy of this term as seeped in the modernist anthropology and classicism that it ventriloquises (Jane Harrison, Jessie Weston's *Ritual to Romance*, 1920). Sometimes, the application of this Mythical Method in *Ulysses* and in *The Waste Land* has been read as satirical or mock-heroic, where the whole edifice of a grand classical tradition is fragmented and debased in a familiar modernist turn. And far from advocating a formal, harmonious 'classicism' in the German Romantic mould that acts as the corrective to the anarchy of the present, it perhaps creates a more reciprocal relationship to that past. In this sense, and almost despite himself, Eliot's Mythical Method partakes in modernist myth-making that re-energises a version of the past that is pre-classical and pagan. This becomes much more accentuated in Pound's, Yeats's and H.D.'s use of myth-making, whose chosen sites are no longer classical Athens, but the broader Mediterranean/Egypt, China and Japan, and for Yeats the Celtic Twilight as well. In Pound's *Cantos*, Yeats's later poems like 'Parnell's Funeral' (1934), in H.D.'s *Helen in Egypt*, myth and ritual, rather than signal an organic past 'lost and regained', trigger a pagan violence that is seen to be at the foundation of culture and is based on the idea of the sacrificial – a sacrifice, however, that entails the possibility of regeneration.

We see the attraction within this paradigm of modernist myth-making that Greek tragedy exerts, both as a performance practice and as a model for poetic drama. This version of Greek tragedy, re-read through Gilbert Murray's pre-classical Greece and through Nietzsche's Dionysus, offers a broader canvas than solely poetry on which to experiment with this quintessentially modernist mode of myth-making. Eliot's quite restrained and somewhat conservative formulation is expanded, inflected and revised by this network of poets who turn into playwrights/directors. Yeats augments this with his interest in the occult, the Celtic Twilight and nationalism; H.D. expands and corrects this with her particular perspective of Freudian-infused Sapphic myth-making that relies more on the geopolitical sphere of the Hellenistic Hellas than on classicism. For Pound, *mythopoeia* appears as early as 1915 and informs his three-part definition of poetry: *phanopoeia, melopoeia, logopoeia*. This definition could also work for performance in general, especially as it stresses the phenomenological experience in ways that are now commonplace in performance studies. Pound states that the modernist work of art expresses 'an impersonal or objective story woven out of [the artist's] own emotion, as the nearest equation that he was capable of putting into words'.[4] Pound is advocating here a type of performance-poetry that at once embodies the phenomenological experience of the possibilities but also the limitations of expression, as this is both created/expressed and also received. This interlocking of all the above categories creates a view of poetry that goes beyond the binaries of visual/aural, text/body, and indeed proposes the poetic word itself as an embodied experience. For Pound this process that he charts in the *ABC of Reading* (1915) generates modernist texts that are myth-making machines, which can be read as being simultaneously *performing machines*. The term here is used in the Greek sense of *mechane* (as in the adjective for Odysseus *polymechanos*), that connotes a type of critical but also embodied thinking. Also crucial in this modernist vision of myth-making is the principle of 'impersonality'. As Pound mentions above, this dynamic between individual talent and impersonality is a tension that informs much modernist theorising and experimentation, especially in poetry. It can be read, as indeed it has been by structuralism and poststructuralism, as an attempt at rejecting the authorial function altogether, and is one of the kernels of modernist theory and practice. When Eliot uses the famous analogy of the artist's personality as a 'catalyst' in his influential essay 'Tradition and the Individual Talent' he is making an attempt at a type of scientism, which dissolves later in his life after his turn to religion and metaphysics. It is interesting to note that many of the metaphors that Eliot employs at the time of writing this essay see human consciousness, and by analogy perhaps authorship itself, as a kind of *mechane* – as an assemblage of neurological functions ('Like a patient etherized upon a table', as in 'The Love Song of J. Alfred Prufrock'). This parallels much thinking about both puppets and actors of this period. Indeed, one area in which this idea of modernist impersonality is practised and tested is in the field of acting theories and actor training, and it fundamentally informs the 'man or marionette' debate. We have seen in previous chapters how this debate also has a Hellenic/classical inflection. And the ways Greek tragedy conceptualises both authorship and dramatic character/persona also prove attractive for this sometimes ambiguous quest for impersonality.

The chorus, too, proves a challenging arena where the ideas of impersonality are tested. Isadora Duncan's proclamation 'I never danced solo' comes to mind, where the idea of individual creation and authorship is contested, even as she actually dances solo. Within the experiments of modern dance, as we have seen, the figure of the dancer, embodying a type of mediation between 'individual talent' and collective creation and between the past and the present, is conspicuous and perhaps somewhat easier to conceptualise. The dancer's body as ekphrastic machine enacts many of these concerns. What these excursions in poetic drama add to the dancers of Hellenist modernism is the power of the poetic word itself and the long tradition of lyrical poetry in Greek tragedy. For in textual terms the tragedies already encompass and configure a convention whose primary role is to negotiate the complex relationships between individuality and impersonality, between movement and stasis, between lyric and prose, between the written word and music, between textuality and performance, and that is the chorus itself. All of the poets we are examining in this chapter engage with the potential offered by the Greek chorus, as both philosophical and performance vehicle. Sometimes, the relationships between tragedy and modernity, particularly in its purely and primarily German philosophical guises, express an awkwardness regarding the chorus. As Miriam Leonard states: 'To be a modern critic of tragedy is to have a problem with the chorus.'[5] Against this reading, and in a gesture that highlights the contribution of this performative perspective on Greek tragedy, all these modernist poets/playwrights grapple with the 'problem of the chorus' in a highly sophisticated manner and bring to it all their modernist formal and thematic concerns. In the choruses of Eliot's translations/reworkings (and already apparent in *Murder in the Cathedral*), in Pound's *Women of Trachis* and *Electra*, in Yeats's translations of the Oedipus plays and in H.D.'s of Euripides, the chorus offers a site where the formal relationships between poetry and prose, between language and music and between the performing body and the word are tested and contested.

Importantly, in all these endeavours the work of translation is highlighted. As the New Modernist Studies stress, anglophone modernism is inconceivable without the work of translation. Joyce's debt to Homer but also to Henrik Ibsen; Yeats's to Maurice Maeterlinck; Pound's, F. S. Flint's and H.D.'s debts to French symbolism in their formulation of imagism; Virginia Woolf's and Bloomsbury's debts to French post-impressionism; Craig's to Stanislavsky and Italian futurism; the Hogarth Press's both literary and primarily psycho-analytical translations. Within this rich tapestry of relationships, the concept of translation itself is broadened and expanded, given a modernist twist in order to capture the multivocal and polymorphous nature of these encounters, which exceed the simple and direct relationships between source and target text or between mother and foreign tongue. Through their own translations and through contributions to the Little Magazines of modernism, all the poets in this chapter helped to forge an understanding of their own work in which translation is formative. Eliot, a dedicated translator himself, as editor of *The Egoist* 1917–19, *The Criterion* 1922–39, and as literary editor at Faber and Faber 1925–65, personally commissioned and oversaw translations of Jean Cocteau, Paul Valéry, Proust, Hermann Hesse and Eugenio Montale, as well as critical studies of Gourmont. Pound's prolific translation output includes the work of Cavalcanti, Li Po, Propertius, Old English poetry, Italian, Provençal, French and classical Greek plays and fragments woven into his *Cantos*, and H.D.'s radical feminist revisions of Euripides in both her poetry and play trans-lations, all attest to the centrality of translation to their overall projects. This is a radically revised view of translation, one that departs from the domains of classical philology, which was up until that point probably the privileged discipline when it came to theorising and practising translation. Although its seeds can be traced in German Romanticism and mainly in the translations of Hölderlin, who in many ways acts as the predecessor of many a modernist take on Sophocles, these experiments open up the field of translation itself, at once making it central to modernist poetics and reconfiguring its own parameters. Here we have translation as reworking, as adaptation, as intertextuality and sustained allusion, as play-text but also as performance-text. These modernist translations of classical plays are both homages and acts of catastrophe; they perform both the neo-classical work of restoration and the modernist work of deconstruction and blasphemy.

Walter Benjamin's famous essay 'The Task of the Translator' (1923) is helpful in trying to analyse this modernist view of translation, especially in the ways it reconfigures classical texts. In many ways, translation can be seen to form part of modernism's linguistic turn, focusing on the power of linguistic experiment (especially in modernist poetry) to help us unhinge the seemingly 'natural' and 'organic' relationship between language and the world. After Wittgenstein, Saussure and mainly the Russian formalists, modernist poetics strives to create that sense of estrangement and 'alienation' (*ostranienie*) that may help us realign our sense of ourselves and the world. The 'unhomeliness' that Heidegger derives from Hölderlin's translation of the famous 'Ode to Man' in *Antigone* (*deinon*) is seen to potentially lie within linguistic experimentation itself. It is this idea that made modernist poetry so attractive for structuralism and poststructuralism alike. Benjamin's essay appears at this moment in modernism where linguistic experimentation is theorised and accorded a philological/literary but also an ethico-political (even metaphysical) dimension. This is an aspect of linguistic experiment that all the modernist translators grapple with. When Benjamin, in the quotation that follows, states that translation is a form, the term 'form' is here articulated in the wake of the Russian formalists (and his own visit to Moscow). Form is to be differentiated from content; it bears its own autonomy, and this is primarily linguistic:

> Translation is a form. To comprehend it as a form, one must go back to the original, for the laws governing the translation lie within the original, contained in the issue of its translatability. The question of whether a work is translatable has a dual meaning. Either: Will an adequate translator ever be found among the totality of its readers? Or, more pertinently: Does its nature lend itself to translation and, therefore, in view of the significance of this call for it?[6]

Translatability is an important term in this context, in terms of reception but also in terms of the linguistic make-up of the original itself. So according to this view, translation unearths something in the original itself, and that something is what makes it immanently translatable. This is the formulation, perhaps, that Roland Barthes would later rework as a writerly versus a readerly text, or texts that invite the reader (here possibly the translator) to act as co-creator. And of course, for Barthes and later Julia Kristeva, this is where the radical potential of the modernist text lies. This 'ability' that Samuel Weber analyses as central to all Benjaminian thinking about language points to the fact that beyond the axes of fidelity and licence, a translatable text helps us to revise both the target and the source language. In these translations Benjamin claims that 'the life of the originals attains its latest, continually renewed, and most complete unfolding'.[7] He calls this their 'afterlife', in a term that may also be read as one of the first modernist formulations of reception theory. The evocative term unfolding is helpful here, as it marks not only a linguistic relationship between the original and the translation but also a haptic, performative one.

And this is how Benjamin views translation, using imagery of birth/death/resurrection:

> Translation is so far removed from being the sterile equation of two dead languages that of all literary forms it is the one charged with the special mission of watching over the maturing process of the original language and the birth pangs of its own.[8]

In the process of this rebirth, Benjamin claims that what becomes transparent and what translation helps us to come to terms with is the apparent 'foreignness of [all] languages'.[9] So this process of making strange that Benjamin adopts from the Russian formalists, and that he will also mobilise later in his life in his *Understanding Brecht*,[10] is reciprocal. This quintessentially modernist reformulation of translation not only helps to birth a new work; it also radically re-visions the original. Both works are seen through the prism of 'strangeness'. He claims that part of 'the task' of the translator is to allow 'his [own] language to be powerfully affected by the foreign tongue'.[11] He also believes that this process is more effective when dealing with old and remote languages. We can view this theory of translation as emblematically modernist, but we can also discern a romantic and idealist lineage. Benjamin references Hölderlin, and we can claim that it is his translations that might be read as examples of what Benjamin claims here. And, of course, they are translations of classical Greek plays, mainly Sophocles. The term 'translatability' foreshadows another term that was to prove central for Benjamin's thinking about the relationships between tradition and modernist innovation, authenticity and reproduction, classical 'auratic' works of art and modernist radical ones. Inspired by the sometimes uncritical and somewhat romantic faith in the emancipatory potential of modern developments in technology, Benjamin's famous essay of 1939, 'The Work of Art in the Age of Mechanical Reproducibility', can be read as in some ways reiterating the arguments initially articulated in 'The Task of the Translator'. The terms 'translatability' and 'reproducibility' can be read as mirroring each other. For Benjamin it is not a simple case of 'technical' reproduction, as he claims this has always been possible regarding works of art. The particular modernist take on ideas of reproduction is to bring out, to help surface, an 'ability' inherent in great works themselves, and that is their 'ability' to be reproduced, rewritten and rethought. Far from expressing a simple and unmediated 'technical' trope, this suffix '-ability' (-*barkeit* in German) becomes the hallmark of the modernist, and for Benjamin the avant-garde work of art, a work that is open to reiteration, rewriting and reproduction. For Samuel Weber, in his analysis of Benjamin's -*abilities*,[12] this adds a sense of potentiality to the work of art, a potentiality that also entails a utopian strand. In this context we can perhaps also read another -*ability* that is ignited by these modernist translations of classical plays, and that is *performability*. To the notions of Benjamin's translatability and reproducibility, I would add performability and, as an adjunct, *adaptability*. All the translations by these modernist poets throughout the received critical tradition, whether in strictly literary contexts or in performance theory, have raised the spectre of performability. Like their poetic counterparts, these plays are *difficult*. This principle of difficulty, so desirable for modernist poetics more generally, complicates the act of performance as much as it complicates the act of reading (or one could also state that it rewrites the act of reading itself *as* performance). The specific difficulty of finding an English poetic idiom to carry/translate Greek prosody; the general difficulty of the poetic word on the stage; the difficult relationships between poetry, recitation and acting; the difficulty of reconciling the Greek concept of 'character'/persona with the modern idea of psychology; the tension between stylisation and expressiveness; and the list could go on. Rather than view this as a shortcoming, it might be more helpful to view this challenging relationship that all these translations pose for performance as part of their *-ability*, as expressing a possibility or a potentiality, a capacity rather than a defined existing reality. I would like to highlight this somewhat expanded and *strong* sense of performability, where the demands that these plays place on performance are read not as a failure or an inability to engage with the workings of the stage, but in a sense as inhabiting a classic modernist trope where the form – in this instance, the stage and theatricality itself – is radically reworked and experimented with. This experimentation does not necessarily throw up and offer closed and specific modes of theatricality that are to be emulated by each concrete performance; rather it invites the reader, actor, director, to also experiment with theatrical form. In ways that parallel the demands that modernist poetry places on the act of reading itself, this principle of *performability*, we might claim, asks us to engage with these plays as a reader, but also as an actor, director and theatre-maker in general.

Together with the discourse of failure that haunts many of these plays/translations, another common trope is that of belatedness, or being 'ahead of their time'. So in a sense we are only now beginning to grapple with Pound's translations; perhaps modern technology can help create Craig's designs and his Übermarionette; our contemporary knowledge of Noh is more detailed and 'authentic'; our knowledge of H.D.'s relationship to Freud may allow us to approach her translations with more insight. These are all, of course, true and are empirical and sometimes biographical facts. However, they do posit quite a linear, developmental and positivist model of the understanding of performability itself, and view it somewhat schematically as a puzzle that needs to be solved. Rather, perhaps viewing this trope in the sense that Samuel Weber conceptualises Benjamin's *-abilities* as a capability that is initiated, as a trope that may be even *mechanical* (in the Greek sense of practical, embodied thinking), asks us to renegotiate theatricality every time anew whenever we approach these texts. Rather than creating a determined performance text that needs to be repeated, in making the whole trope of performance *difficult* these texts, I would claim, might be interpreted along the lines of Brecht's *models*, or rather foreshadow and echo these, as we know how endemic Benjaminian thought was to Brecht's conceptualisation of epic theatre. And in doing so, we are drawing another somewhat incongruous parallel that this book is attempting to trace between these experiments in anglophone modernist poetic translations of Greek tragedy and Brecht's epic theatre. In this way, the notions of *translatability*, *adaptability*, *performability* and the notorious *reproducibility* might be read as forming a constellation of ideas that have a distinct modernist prominence, but also enact a modernist neo-classicism, or Hellenism. Tragedy, with its reliance on myth, we may claim is already premised on adaptability, and this central principle is constitutive of its very physiognomy (Benjamin). Eliot's Mythical Method, Pound's Mythopoeia, Phanopoeia and Logopoeia and H.D.'s 'clatter montage' are all modernist techniques that highlight a formal imperative but also mobilise what we may call modernism's obsession with the 'ideology of form', which occupies all these poets in terms of their ethico-political projects. So when Benjamin calls translation a 'form', far from being 'formalist' in the strict or negative sense, he is opening up the *mechanics*, the *process* of translation to all the vicissitudes of the relationships between form and meaning, past and present and, in this context, poetry and theatricality. And it is in this sense that translatability and performability may be viewed as sister terms, as doubles, in the way that theatre in particular from Plato to Antonin Artaud conceptualises and embodies the idea of the double. A 'doubleness' that at once allows these play-texts/translations to pay homage to the past, to embody their modernist present and gesture towards the possibility of all future performances.

T. S. ELIOT: 'HE DO THE POLICE IN DIFFERENT VOICES'

Throughout his writing life Eliot was preoccupied with the issues of translating, adapting and staging Greek tragedy and the possibilities this presented for poetic drama. Eliot's famous attack on Gilbert Murray's translations was primarily based on what Eliot considered an appropriate use of poetry in the English language. He wrote, 'Greek poetry will never have the slightest vitalizing effect upon English poetry if it can only appear masquerading as a vulgar debasement of the eminently personal idiom of Swinburne.'[13] For Eliot the path that Greek tragedy was to follow in order to have the required 'vitalizing' effect on English poetry was primarily through experimentation. Crucially, this experimentation was both linguistic and theatrical. Equally vital for Eliot were the demands that poetic drama places both on matters of verse and matters of voice:

The first thing of any importance that I discovered was that a writer who has worked for years, and achieved some success, in writing other kinds of verse, has to approach the writing of a verse play in a different frame of mind . . . In writing other verse, I think that one is writing, so to speak, in terms of one's own voice: the way it sounds when you read it to yourself is the test. For it is yourself speaking. The question of communication, of what the reader will get from it, is not paramount: if your poem is right to you, you can only hope that the readers will eventually come to accept it . . . But in the theatre, the problem of communication presents itself immediately. You are deliberately writing verse for other voices, not for your own, and you do not know whose voices they will be.[14]

So for Eliot the problem of translating Greek tragedy for the stage is also a problem of voice and authorship, in addition to addressing the issue of transposing poetry onto the stage when there is no living tradition of verse drama in English. Eliot's forays into Greek tragedy as a form of contemporary poetic drama are paralleled by his equal interest in matters of staging, and particularly the staging of the chorus. After his attack on Murray (1920), Pound dared Eliot to translate the *Agamemnon*, a venture he was to take up himself, with both men eventually abandoning the task.[15] Perhaps this initial unsuccessful attempt shaped their later engagements with Greek tragedy; Eliot would write mainly heavily disguised adaptations and Pound would translate Sophocles. Before Eliot wrote his drawing-room adaptations of Greek tragedy, *The Family Reunion* (1939), *The Cocktail Party* (1949), *The Confidential Clerk* (1952) and *The Elder Statesman* (1954), he wrote the two fragments of *Sweeney Agonistes* (1926) as an attempt to combine Aristophanic comedy with music-hall-style verse, and his early plays *The Rock* (1934) and *Murder in the Cathedral* (1935). Of these, *Murder in the Cathedral* presents a fascinating precursor to his attempts at 'Greek' plays. Indeed, we may claim that in form and theatrical conventions it is much closer to Greek tragedy than his actual adaptations of the Greek plays. In some ways it functions as a more successful attempt at a modernist Greek tragedy than his drawing-room dramas. The play at once engages the idea of tragedy, reworking it through Christian theology, and the formal demands of training actors and chorus, while also dealing with audience reception. It presents what some scholars (in the tradition of George Steiner) would consider an impossibility: tragedy that is *both* modernist and Christian. Eliot's conflation of a Christian martyr (Thomas Becket) with the tragic protagonist, and the tragic chorus with the women of Canterbury, can be read as the direct influence of the Cambridge Ritualists and their ritualistic, evolutionary model of drama. He writes in *The Criterion* in 1923, in an article entitled 'Dramatis Personae', in terms that echo the writings of the Ritualists:

> Instead of pretending that the stage gesture is a copy of reality, let us adopt a literal untruth, a thorough-going convention, a ritual. For the stage – not only in its remote origins, but always – is a ritual –, and failure of the contemporary stage to satisfy the craving for ritual is one of the reasons why it is not a living art.[16]

Eliot was also familiar with the work of Craig and his writing on acting. He had read Craig's *The Art of the Theatre* (1905) while an undergraduate and was well versed in the debates about puppets and actors (he had defended Craig in an article in *The Dial* in 1921). The invitation from the Friends of Canterbury Cathedral to write a play allowed Eliot to bring together his experiments in poetic drama with his interest in reviving Greek tragedy through the prisms of both Christianity and modernism. This attempt offered Eliot the opportunity to address the 'problem of the chorus'. Although it is viewed by most philosophical traditions as the quintessential anti-modern aspect of Greek tragedy, modernist experiments in performance find in the Greek chorus a space (both conceptual and physical) to rehearse new theories of acting and audience reception. And in this respect Eliot's views are quite pioneering:

> In making use of [the chorus] we do not aim to *copy* Greek drama. There is a good deal about the Greek theatre that we do not know, and never shall know. But we know that some of its conventions cannot be ours. The characters talk too long; the Chorus has too much to say and holds up the action; usually not enough happens; and the Greek notion of climax is not ours. But the chorus has always fundamentally the same uses. It mediates between the action and the audience; it intensifies the action by projecting its emotional consequences, so that we as the audience see it doubly, by seeing its effect on other people.[17]

This is quite a sophisticated reading of the chorus both in terms of what it can offer theatrically and for the ways that Eliot considers it strange ('we will never know'). It posits the chorus as a mode of mediation that enables a kind of 'double vision' in the audience, and foreshadows a contemporary phenomenological understanding of spectatorship. The chorus here for Eliot functions almost as a Brechtian technique to help create distance, the critical double-take and, crucially, to mediate emotional responses. This metatheatrical and quotational use of the chorus, as commenting both on the action and on the audience, is a trope that many modernist theatre-makers will employ. For Eliot it marks the beginning of his experiments with the chorus, always parallel to those in poetic drama, which continued throughout his life. In this instance these choruses helped to create the ritualistic aspects of this modernist tragedy that is at once a Christian liturgical drama. Sometimes, however, due to the cumbersome nature of these very choruses, they are neglected in discussions about both poetic drama and translations of Greek tragedy. For Eliot, they proved fundamental for both these ventures.

Murder in the Cathedral proved to be a success, unlike his later attempts at translating/adapting Greek tragedy. Eliot was very aware, however, that undertaking to translate and possibly stage Greek tragedies would prove to be a more demanding endeavour. He was very conscious that he could not repeat the success of *Murder in the Cathedral*, despite the fact that it was a very useful training ground for approaching Greek tragedy. This was partly due to the fact that he could not repeat those stylised, ritualistic, poetic choruses, and partly because in his later ventures he could not have access to that 'organic audience' that participated in the play as a religious experience, as the play was created specifically for the congregation of Canterbury Cathedral. The term 'organic' in this context also has undertones of continuity and ritualistic, anthropology-inspired thinking that Eliot himself designates as 'modern'. He writes in 1950, looking back at this event, in *Poetry and Drama*:

> The writer of poetic drama is not merely a man skilled in two arts and skillful to weave them together; he is not a writer who can decorate a play with poetic language and meter. His task is different from the 'dramatist' or that of the 'poet', for his pattern is more complex and dimensional . . . The genuine poetic drama must, at its best, observe all the regulations of the plain drama, but will weave them *organically* (to mix a metaphor and to borrow for the occasion a modern word) into a much richer design.[18]

Fascinating that Eliot considers 'organic' to be a modern term, a term that helps to create a genealogical link with the quintessentially anti-modern term 'tradition'. However, in this context, as in the German idealist legacy of *Gemeinschaft* (versus *Gesellschaft*) it is the very modernity of the enterprise that helps create this organic co-existence facilitated by poetry itself. Eliot claims that he was fortunate that for (in the instance of *Murder in the Cathedral*), 'a beginner . . . the path was made easy' and attributes this to three main factors: the subject matter was 'generally admitted to be suitable for verse'; the play was produced 'for a rather special kind of audience'; and 'finally it was a religious play'.[19] These three factors – heightened language, an 'organic' audience and the play as religious experience – also characterise Greek tragedy, and all three place their own particular demands on translation and performance. As Eliot could not necessarily count on repeating this experience with his other Greek plays, he followed a slightly different path. Still, the significance of this apprenticeship with *Murder in the Cathedral* should not be underestimated.

Henceforth, Eliot deliberately chooses contemporary themes, drastically reworks the chorus and makes every attempt to mask any direct references to the Greek plays he approaches. This makes for an approach to Greek tragedy that was different both from Gilbert Murray's translations, whose use of blank verse Eliot attacked viciously,[20] and Reinhardt's daring arena-style productions. *The Family Reunion*, the play that Eliot himself deemed to be a failure, is the one that has the most direct links to Greek drama, as it is a reworking of the *Oresteia* trilogy:

> You will understand, after my making criticisms of *The Family Reunion*, some of the errors that I endeavored to avoid in designing *The Cocktail Party*. To begin with, no chorus, no ghosts. I was still inclined to go to a Greek dramatist for my theme, but I was determined to do so merely as a point of departure, and to conceal the origins so well that nobody would identify them until I pointed them out myself. In this at least I have been successful; for no one of my acquaintance (and no dramatic critics) recognized the source of my story in the *Alcestis* of Euripides.[21]

The errors that Eliot refers to above relate primarily to the function of the chorus. For although *The Family Reunion* is notionally based on the *Oresteia*, the parallels are deliberately oblique and far from straightforward. It is written partly in blank verse and partly in prose. The roles are contracted and syncopated and do not neatly map onto the ancient characters. The figures of Orestes and Agamemnon are fused into one central character, Harry. The very name is emblematic of Eliot's and modernism's bathos. Crucial scenes in the original – the scene at Delphi and the trial scene – are missing. Amy, the lady of the house of Wishwood, is the Clytemnestra character, but so is Harry's dead wife, who drowned at sea (a death that haunts Harry, and this is never quite resolved – whether he murdered her or not). So this medley of detective narrative and redemption narrative, with fraught gender and parental relations, is loosely traced onto the *Oresteia* with a freedom and interpretive flair that we sometimes find in the ways that contemporary novels rewrite this foundational family drama. Still, it is the choruses that provide the strongest link to the original: one of the old uncles and aunts structurally linked to Amy/Clytemnestra; and the other Erinyes/Eumenides, initially horror-inducing, but ultimately leading Harry to some sort of redemptive truth. Eliot claimed: 'What we have written is not a story of detection, of crime and punishment, but of sin and expiation.'[22] It is difficult not to read Hamlet into this version of Orestes, as indeed it is impossible not to interpret the whole play as an attempt to fuse Hellenic, Christian and psychoanalytic notions of catharsis and redemption. For Eliot, it is the chorus that proves to be the strongest vehicle for such fusions. He states in a letter to E. Martin Browne, who was about to produce the play, that '[Orestes] follows the Furies as immediately and as unintelligibly as the Disciples dropping their nets'[23] – a creative fusion of Greek and Christian imagery. We could also claim almost counterintuitively (and possibly against the grain of Eliot's own intentions) that *The Family Reunion* helps unearth the gender politics of the *Oresteia* in ways that would be intelligible to a contemporary audience. Martha C. Carpentier writes about *The Family Reunion*, tracing a link between Harry and Eliot's earlier 'Sweeney' poems:

> Most analyses of the Sweeney poems and their culmination in *The Family Reunion* have focused on Eliot's ultimately Christian vision, while the powerful female archetypes in those works and their Hellenic parallels have been largely misunderstood or dismissed.[24]

In an insightful reading, Carpentier interprets Eliot's fascination with the feminine, albeit negatively, as inspired at least partly by Harrison. Hugh Kenner, too, in more traditional Eliot criticism, mentions his propensity for killing women in his work: 'Throughout *The Waste Land*, in *Sweeney Agonistes*, and in *The Family Reunion*, Prufrock disguised as Sweeney and as Harry, drowned this woman over and over.'[25] Still, in addition to Harry's drowned wife, Eliot's insistence on the double chorus as Erinyes *and* Eumenides, as sites of horror and redemption, does have echoes of Harrison's matriarchal daimones. Carpentier elaborates:

> This predilection is unique to her among the Cambridge Anthropologists, and because Eliot was also influenced by French sociology, his dramatic theory is closer in spirit to Harrison than to Cornford or Murray. He shared her desire to evoke a collective spiritual experience through resurrecting the ancient ritual 'mould' in Greek drama, not only in theory but on the modern stage.[26]

Interpreting the *Oresteia* as an *agon* between matriarchy and patriarchy, as the elemental site for the 'Battle of the Sexes', has become commonplace in post-war and late twentieth-century productions. Rather than view Eliot's attempts as failures or make them the target of a politics of blame, it might be more intriguing to see them as precursors of the now canonical reading of the *Oresteia* as a trilogy that deals with the politics of gender and how these are refracted through the workings of the patriarchal family. For Harry does not strike a heroic pose; he appears as much a victim of the patriarchal order as a perpetrator of it. As generous a reading as this may sound, it may help to underline the complexities of adaptations like Eliot's, where the interaction/ rewriting of forms and conventions (like the chorus) triggers its own formal and thematic potentialities (Benjamin's *-abilities*) almost despite and some-times in direct contradiction to the stated intentions of the author themselves. Eliot himself was ambivalent about *The Family Reunion*, but was still able to see an experimental aspect to it that gestured towards the future: 'For my own part, I am far from pronouncing it an irretrievable failure theatrically. It may prove to be an important extension of the drama not yet fully understood.'[27] Again the 'not yet' factor is stressed; this idea of being 'too soon', while at the same time being 'too late' for antiquity itself, creates a notion of time that is syncopated, compressed, where both the past and the future are filtered through the present. And the idea of presentness in all these reworkings is made visible and experienced through performance itself. Eliot was not only interested in performance, but in performance that would be accessible and successful. He writes:

> Audiences are prepared to accept poetry recited by a chorus, for that is a kind of poetry, which it does them credit to enjoy. And audiences (those who go to a verse play because it is in verse) expect poetry to be in rhythms which have lost touch with colloquial speech. What we have to do is to bring poetry into the world in which the audience lives and to which it returns when it leaves the theatre ... Then we should not be transported into the artificial world; on the contrary, our own sordid, dreary daily life would be suddenly illuminated and transfigured.[28]

It is for this primal function of theatre that Eliot goes to Greek drama. His remaining Greek plays were to keep their classicism well disguised, primarily by disposing of the elaborate choruses. *The Cocktail Party* (1949) was a reworking of Euripides' *Alcestis*; *The Confidential Clerk* (1953) was based on Euripides' *Ion*; *The Elder Statesman* (1958) was based on *Oedipus at Colonus*. All three premiered at the Edinburgh International Festival and went on to have runs in the West End, and some in the USA as well. All three had elements of farce and all were billed as drawing-room comedies, with their classical Greek references only there to be decoded possibly by the classicists in the audience. They fulfilled Eliot's desire to write successful, approachable middle-class – and, I would claim, middlebrow – dramas.

A brief synopsis of *The Cocktail Party* will provide an indication of the route that Eliot's forays into poetic, Greek-inspired drama followed: Two society couples – Edward and Lavinia (which may be a reference to O'Neill's Lavinia/Electra in *Mourning Becomes Electra*), and Peter and Celia – are entangled in love affairs. Lavinia, who has mysteriously disappeared at the opening of the play, is, unbeknown to her husband, having an affair with Peter. Edward is having an affair with Celia, but refuses to continue seeing her when his wife leaves. This leaves Celia desolate but makes her attractive again to Peter. This neat, over-schematic exchange is plunged into crisis by the news that Celia – whose despair has led her to join an 'austere order' in a tropical country – has been crucified beside an anthill. This female death, like the 'murder' Harry commits in *The Family Reunion*, forces everyone else to reassess their life and yet again explores the possibility of transcendence. In place of a chorus this play has a psychiatrist, Sir Henry Harcourt-Reilly, functioning as the slightly comic mediator and the voice of authority in this secular drama. The characters indulge in quasi-existential anxieties ('What is hell? Hell is oneself/Hell is alone, the other figures in it/Merely projections'),[29] always 'Contre Sarte', as Eliot whispered to Martin Browne when these lines were spoken on the opening night. It is the opinion of this reader that Eliot's attempts to abandon any visible references/citations to the original Greek plays make the plays following *The Family Reunion* certainly more successful but also certainly less modernist. Their farcical elements pander to their designated audience, the upper middle classes of England, and Eliot's desire to 'illuminate' and 'transfigure' our 'sordid and dreary' lives not only smacks of condescension but enacts all the critical clichés voiced against so-called 'high modernism'; but rather than making these works 'difficult', it makes them middlebrow and bourgeois. In this sense, the more successful Eliot's plays became, the less interesting they were in terms of modernist experimentation. Here is how one satirist of the time in *The New Statesman* responded to the success of *The Cocktail Party*:

Nightingale among the Sweenies
This is the vulgarest success, blasting
A hitherto immaculate reputation,
The voice
Par excellence of the waste land and the wilderness
Can the exalted oracle rejoice
Who, casting
Pearls before swine, wins swinish approbation?
Tereu, twit, twit, this metaphysical mime
That should have been
The most distinguished failure of all time
Proves quite the opposite.
Between the conception and the reception, between
The curtain calls the Shadow falls –
The deep damnation of a Broadway hit,
Groomed for some critic *coterie's* diploma,
Dear God, like *Oklahoma*!
(Oh what a terrible morning)
Seeing (let's face it) not alone the arty
But the dim rabble crash *The Cocktail Party*.
Has the hautboy of attenuated tone
Become the uncultured herd's unconscious saxophone?[30]

Unlike *The Family Reunion*, these later plays were eminently performable. However, what they gained through their momentary success they may have lost through all the concessions that Eliot made to make them more 'accessible'. And these concessions pandered to their middle-class audiences, mainly by burying and obliterating any references that might be considered obscure or difficult in terms of themes, but also crucially by relying on the quintessential bourgeois aesthetic of naturalism. In his early attempts at drama in *Sweeney Agonistes*, Eliot borrows from Greek drama mainly conventions and ideas about theatricality, combined with influences from the theatres of South-East Asia and Japan, in a modernist fusion of classicism, orientalism and primitivism. This fusion proves very enabling for performance. In a letter to the radical director of the Federal Theatre Project, Hallie Flanagan, who was considering staging *Sweeney Agonistes*, here is what Eliot has to say:

> In 'Sweeney Agonistes'; the action should be stylized as in the Noh drama – see Ezra Pound's book and Yeats' preface and notes to 'The Hawk's Well'. Characters *ought* to wear masks; . . . I had intended the whole play to be accompanied by light drum taps to accentuate the beats (esp. the chorus, which ought to have a noise like a street drill). The characters should be in a shabby flat, seated at a refectory table, facing the audience; Sweeney in the middle with a chafing dish, scrambling eggs. (See 'you see this egg.') (See also F. M. Cornford: 'Origins of Attic Comedy', which is important to read before you do the play.)[31]

In effect the Federal Theatre Project ended up producing *Murder in the Cathedral* instead, giving it a huge audience way beyond the reach of Canterbury Cathedral. And for that production, too, the above notes served as guidelines. Perhaps it is this play and the early *The Family Reunion* that we should consider as Eliot's modernist Greek plays. The later plays, in purging themselves of the Greek elements of theatricality (the mask, the chorus, music) also, and somewhat counterintuitively are as a result less modernist.

'THE CLASSICS, "ANCIENT AND MODERN", ARE PRECISELY THE ACIDS'

Pound's extraordinary translations of Sophocles' plays could not be further removed from the success stories of Eliot's drawing-room dramas. Written during his bleakest years at St Elizabeth's hospital in the 1950s, where he was incarcerated after having escaped charges of treason, they have been interpreted both as comments on his own state of mind and possibly as a critique of the cathartic power of the classics themselves, their ability or inability to contribute to the redeeming and emancipatory project of modernity.

For Pound this tackling of the two quite different Sophoclean dramas, *The Women of Trachis* (1954) and *Electra* (1949), was a return to some of his fundamental concerns:

> My pawing over the ancients and semi-ancients has been one struggle to find out what has been done, once and for all, better than it can ever be done again, and to find out what remains for us to do, and plenty does remain, for if we still feel the same emotions as those which launched the thousand ships, it is quite certain that we come on these differently,

through different nuances, by different intellectual gradation ... yet a man feeling the divorce of life and his art may naturally try to resurrect a forgotten mode if he finds in that mode some leaven, or if he thinks he sees in it some element lacking in contemporary art which might unite art again to its sustenance, life.[32]

In many ways this is the most 'classical' of neo-classicisms. It claims that we share the same human substance *and* that we can regain that organic unity of art and life lost to the moderns. However, as Pound's translations clearly exhibit, there are some significant variations to this model. On the one hand, what this modernist classicism claims to reunite us with is the ritualistic, primitive, disruptive side of that ideal Hellenism that 'launched a thousand ships', through a relationship that will prove distant, inorganic, savage and strange; and on the other, the styles, modes and conventions employed to create such a disjointed connection will be ones of catastrophe, estrangement and violence, where, as Pound claims, the 'classics' are the 'acids' to 'gnaw through the thongs and bull-hides with which we were tied by our schoolmasters'.[33]

This is a very compelling if violent image, in some ways not unlike the character of Hercules himself attempting to fulfil one of his tasks, or to break loose from the stronghold of some monstrous female that may be pursuing him. And the analogy is not as arbitrary as it may appear, for it is the role of Hercules that attracts Pound to *The Women of Trachis*. To this day *The Women of Trachis* is rarely performed and is considered to be an uneven play, one that has not attracted perhaps its due attention within the Sophoclean canon. This was not what Pound thought about the play. He writes:

> The *Trachiniae* presents the highest peak of Greek sensibility registered in any of the plays that have come down to us, and is, at the same time, nearest the original form of the God-Dance.
>
> A version for KITANO KATUE, hoping he will use it on my dear old friend Michio Ito, or take it to the Minoru if they can be persuaded to add it to their repertoire.[34]

As his translation was first performed on radio, on the BBC's Third Programme, Pound did not get the opportunity to put his ideas into practice. Although this translation appears quite late (1954) it still echoes the terminology of the Cambridge Ritualists. The God-dance is pure Harrison, and in the same gesture Pound remembers his old friend Michio Ito, the Japanese dancer who first inspired him and Yeats and with whom he had spent a summer at Stone Cottage in Sussex almost forty years earlier. In the Noh, Pound, like Yeats, finds a form of stylised drama that relies more on the epiphanic transformation of the central hero than on dialogue and development of action and/ or character.

Pound's attraction to the play has been read as primarily focused on the fate of Hercules, whose transformation and apotheosis the play charts – an apotheosis that results from the misplaced, misinterpreted and in some ways mistranslated actions of his wife Deianeira. However, the play itself is presented in two distinct halves: Deianeira's section and Hercules' section.[35] It might be worth outlining the plot and the main themes of the play in our attempt to see what drew Pound to this somewhat obscure Sophoclean tragedy. The first, feminine half refers to the life of the *oikos*, the domestic realm, and Deianeira accounts the woes of married life: a life of neglect, as Hercules is always on some adventure, ignoring her and her children. She sends their son Hyllus to find Hercules, as she is concerned about him due to bad prophecies. After Hyllus' departure the messenger arrives, announcing a recent victory of Hercules at the nearby Euboean town of Oechalia. This marks the distinct break in the plot and the possible reversal of fortune (the *peripeteia*), as Deianeira is fed a false story – literally a cock and bull story – by Lichas, a herald of Hercules, to cover up the fact that amongst the captive procession of women he brings is Iole, who is Hercules' most recent lover and for whom the siege of Oechalia was undertaken in the first place. Upon realising this, Deianeira decides to send a love potion that will win back Hercules. When she was a young girl, as she was being taken across a river by the centaur Nessus, he tried to rape her, and in that instance she was rescued by Hercules, who shot Nessus with an arrow. As Nessus lay dying he told her that his blood, now mixed with the blood of the Lernaean Hydra in which Hercules' arrow had been dipped, would have the power of keeping Hercules away from any other women. Deianeira dyes a robe with the blood potion and sends it to Hercules with Lichas. She makes a point of stressing that no one else is to wear it, and that it is to be kept in the dark until he puts it on. However, she has a bad feeling about it all, and decides to try it out for herself. She throws some of the leftover material into the sunlight and it reacts like scorching acid. Like Lichas, Nessus too was lying. Hyllus, their son, soon returns. Hercules was in such maddening pain that he killed Lichas. As a result of her shame, Deianeira kills herself. Only later does her son Hyllas reveal that it was not her intention to kill his father. Hercules arrives home in pain and feeling betrayed by his wife, but after Hyllas explains the truth, Hercules realises that the prophecy has been fulfilled: he was to be killed by someone who was already dead, that is, the centaur Nessus. His pain is so unbearable at the end that he asks for someone to kill him. At this stage he says that he is like a woman. He manages to make a final wish, or to give a final order to Hyllas, and Hyllas promises to obey and marry Iole – restoring some kind of order. As an end to his suffering and to the play, Hercules is carried away to be burned alive.

This strange story has been read as a play about the apotheosis of Hercules, or as a play about the suffering of Hercules, or as a play about the power of eros. There are a number of ways in which we can transcribe the narrative. Crucial in any interpretation we may have of the plot is, I believe, the function of translation, transcription, interpretation and transliteration. When Pound calls the 'classics' the 'acid' in the above quotation, it is impossible not to also think about Deianeira's 'acid'. For as much as *The Trachiniae* is a tale about Hercules as an *epiphanic* hero, it is also about the destructive power of Deianeira's 'acid'. And I would claim that Pound's attraction and overall approach towards this play, and translation more generally, can be said to follow this double motion of apotheosis *and* catastrophe.

This double flow can be viewed in the way that *eros* itself is reconfigured as desire that is driven by both vitalism and death, making it *thanatoerotic*. The term used by Sophocles to describe this force is *deinon*, a notorious term that features in the famous first stasimon of *Antigone* (*polla ta deina* . . .).[36] And this is how Pound, in a modernist twist of bathos, translates Hercules' destructive desire, when he has the Messenger declare that: 'All started when he had a letch for the girl.' The girl is Iole, and rather than feel animosity towards her, we see Daysair (Pound's version of Deianeira, 'The Day's Air', as he explains in PERSONAE), expressing pity in the Aristotelean sense of sympathy and identification. This is how she greets her:

> DAY: You look as if you were taking it worse than any of the others.
> Girl, wife, young; no, you can't have been married yet. And good family.
> Who is she, Likhas? I'm sorrier for her than for the rest of them.
> She seems to feel it.
> LIKH: How do I know? She might be top drawer, why ask me?
> DAY: Royal? Had Eurytus a daughter?
> LIKH: I dunno. I haven't asked her.
> DAY: Didn't anyone tell you?
> LIKH: I had plenty else to do, without asking that kind of questions.
> DAY (to IOLE): Well then, you tell me.
> What's happened? Who are you?[37]

Fascinating that this play, so premised on the imagery of darkness and light, should have the female protagonist's name syncopated to 'DAY'. Later on, when Hercules is suffering, literally burning due to the potion that his wife sent him, his name too is abbreviated to 'HER'. In the original he is compared to a woman in the midst of his deepest pain – and Pound quite beautifully reworks this in a typical imagistic manner that brings together the typescript, the word and the picture. Occasionally, this use of the typescript keeps it in its original, transcribed in Latin. This is something that Pound will employ more systematically in his *Electra*, and especially in the chorus. The Trachiniae chorus, or Khoros, makes it clear that this use of the Greek, transcribed, transliterated, is about beauty but also about violence:

> KHOROS : APOLLO and Artemis, analolu
> Artemis,
> Analolu, Sun-bright Apollo, Saviour Apollo,
> analolu, Swift-arrowed Artemis, analolu
> Artemis, Sylvan Artemis,
> By the hearth-stone Shout in male company:
> brides to be APOLLO EUPHARETRON.
> Sylvan Artemis, torch-lit Artemis.[38]

So, in this story of DAY and HER as the two protagonists are presented, Apollo, the sun-bright god, is also the god who carries the deadly arrows, albeit in a fine-encrusted case (Eupharetron). A fine case will also carry the deadly gift that DAY will send to HERcules, only to change her mind after the deed and declare that 'Something's gone wrong, my dears, terribly wrong, and I'm scared,'[39] as she enters wearing a tragic mask. The tragic mask is used twice by Pound in his version, once by DAY and once by HER as he is in the midst of his suffering, and in each case the protagonists wear it when they have come to a realisation, or rather a self-realisation. Together with the heightened quasi-classical references of using a mask, Pound's shift in register also helps create an unease, a modernist bathos, where the sublime and the everyday co-exist. DAY says, 'Something too creepy's just happened . . . [the jacket] . . . Seemed to corrode of itself [. . .] I found it flaming all there in the sunlight.'

Sunlight, shining, electrifying, are all images that abound throughout the translation, leading to HERcules's epiphanic moment, when he utters the famous lines:

> I thought it meant life in comfort.
> It doesn't. It means that I die.
> For amid the dead there is no work in service.
> Come at it that way, my boy, what
> SPLENDOUR, IT ALL COHERES
> [*He turns his face from the audience, then sits erect, facing them without the mask of agony; the revealed make-up is that of solar serenity. The hair golden and as electrified as possible.*][40]

This startling image of HERcules might even be read as an imitation of the Lernaean Hydra, whose blood poisoned him in the first place, as if at once embodying and expressing the deadly blood of the Hydra through his golden and electrified hair. For the figure of the Hydra haunts this play, as much as the figure of Kupris Aphrodite, whom Pound presents as the *dea ex machina*. A *dea ex machina*, however, who does not intervene to provide a solution or to release HERcules from his suffering. Rather, she acts as a silent witness, almost as a member of the audience:

Attest
That Kupris stood by and never said a word,
Who now flares here the contriver manifest . . . and indifferent.
*[The dea ex machina, hidden behind a grey gauze in her niche, is lit up
strongly so that the gauze is transparent. The apparition is fairly sudden,
the fade-out slightly slower: the audience is almost in doubt that she has
appeared.]*[41]

What are these acts that proceed, or appear, or happen (*taut' oun . . .
lampra sumbainei*) together in such splendour, so as to provide the desirable
coherence? We may claim the two distinct sections of the play, the female and
the male section, are both embodied in this final image of the *deinon* quality
of eros turned to violent desire, turned to death. In a note Pound claims that:
'This is the key phrase, for which the play exists, as in the *Elektra*.' And as
in the *Elektra* all 'things' that come together to create this violent epiphany
include man and woman, the text and the stage, and the original Greek and
its translation.

'The classics, "ancient and modern", are precisely the acids to gnaw through
the thongs and bull-hides with which we are tied by our schoolmasters,'[42] states
Pound in one of his early letters. The idea of acid gnawing is repeated through
his version of *The Women of Trachis*. The acid of the Hydra, 'gnawing into
his bones';[43] the net of the furies, 'gnawed through to my furtherest in'nards';
a death 'rattle', 'gnawing again, budding, blossoming',[44] are all images used by
both the chorus and Hercules himself. The idea of 'blossoming' also perhaps
allows for a kind of regeneration through the violent act of gnawing. And
Pound's translation itself can be read as a kind of acid that gnaws away at the
both the original Greek and the English language. In doing so it also reworks
the classical idea of apotheosis through a modernist understanding of epiphany
where the gender politics and the politics of linguistic representation mirror
each other. So in this instance, if we are looking for Pound in this translation
(not necessarily a desirable or effective critical strategy), we can find him both
in Hercules (HER) and in Deianeira (DAY).

This androgynous quality is also present in the persona of *Elektra*, the play
that Pound translated prior to *The Women of Trachis*. A few years earlier
(1949) and in the same confinement, Pound approaches another play by
Sophocles and produces a translation/reworking which is even more extraordinary in its linguistic variation and in the demands it places on performance.
As several scholars have noted,[45] this variation, which includes transliterated
classical Greek, African American, Scots, Irish, archaic English lyrics and
Cockney, could be indicative of Pound's attempt to create a sense of poetic
metre that bears some kind of analogy with the metre in Greek tragedy. To this
day, the discrepancy between classical Greek metrical systems which rely on

length (qualitative) and those of English which rely on syllable stress (quantitative) create problems for poetic translations of Greek tragedy.[46] At the same time, Pound is adamant that rhythm is central to any poetry that claims to be modernist, and in particular imagist. He writes:

> I believe in an ultimate and absolute rhythm as I believe in an absolute symbol or metaphor. The perception of the intellect is given in the word, that of the emotions in the cadence ... The rhythm of any poetic line corresponds to emotion. It is the poet's business that this correspondence be exact, i.e. that it be the emotion which surrounds the thought expressed.[47]

So, this technique of fusing, jamming, different types of English unsettles the relationships between language and dialect, between the word and the performing body and between the past and the present. Much more than in *The Women of Trachis* Pound maintains a lot of the original Greek, especially in Elektra's *keening* sections, as he calls them. This transliterated Greek might serve well in keeping the 'aura' of the original *melos*, but it also poses problems of readability and especially performability. In an insightful article on Pound's use of language in this translation, Christine Syros writes:

> Pound was not timid about maintaining in several passages of his *Elektra* the Greek melos intact instead of sacrificing it for the intelligibility of English prose-poetry. At the same time, maintaining the Greek meter untranslated kept him from causing it aesthetic damage, as well as from committing a translative fallacy by not discerning that the meters of the Greek text often had a different function from that possible in English verse.[48]

This transliterated Greek might also be seen as at once expressing a kind of literal faithfulness to the original Greek, but at the same time it seems to be pouring 'acid' on the English language. For what are we to make of these long sequences of transliterated Greek that appear mostly in Elektra's mourning sections, or *keening*, as Pound calls them? Here is how Elektra's famous opening lines are presented:

OO PHAOS HAGNON
Holy light
Earth, air about us,
THRENOON OODAS
POLLAS D'ANTEREIS AESTOU
Tearing my heart out.[49]

The demands placed on readability and performability are multiple. Is the reader/performer meant to recite these sequences; are they meant to be understanding what they are articulating, or is it preferable that they remain unintelligible? And surely when these utterances are pronounced in English, they are no longer either classical Greek or English, as they form a kind of hybrid language. In some ways we could read these translations as an imagist poem, or even as a concrete poem, where the act of translation itself is part of the theme of the endeavour while the formal linguistic requirements, in ways that parallel Pound's adopting of the Chinese ideogram appear on the page as if it were a stage. So this transliterated Greek underlines the materiality of the language as an aesthetic object *and* as a medium of communication. And Pound's stage directions throughout perhaps indicate that he was writing both as a poet and as a director: *sinks into step*; *quasi sotto voce*; *emphatic and explicit with meaning to ram it in*; *chorus moving/clear cut position: pause/ move*; *pause: very clearly enunciated*; *different tempo*; *pausing between each word*. It is characteristic that all the stage directions refer to movement, tempo and voice. There are none that propose any interpretive or psychological reading of the roles.

Here is how this amazing translation ends:

CHORUS (*sings*)
O SPERM' ATREOOS
Atreides, Atreides
come thru the dark.
(*speaks*)
my god, it's come with a rush
(*sings*)
Delivered, Delivered.
TEI NUN HORMEI TELEOOTHEN
swift end
so soon.[50]

Pound's translations have been compared to Hölderlin's before him. And the parallel is valid in the Benjaminian sense of making the target language just as strange (*deinon*) as the original Greek to its audience. At the same time, they also rewrite in complex and intriguing ways another key trope of theatricality: the trope of *epiphany* or *apotheosis*. This is clear in *Women of Trachis* but is also present in his version of *Elektra*. The final *lambra sumbainei* in *Women of Trachis* is foreshadowed in this ending of *Elektra*. The ambivalent coherence of *Trachiniae*, which blends Eros and Thanatos, can also be read in these closing lines of *Elektra*, where the violence of the house of Atreus, reeked through the SPERM, might be seen to return to the House of the Father from where it originated. This final chorus sequence, read as a performance event and as an imagist poem that combines ideograms, movement, song and speech, perhaps allows us to interpret Electra's deed, literally mediated and enacted 'thru'

Orestes, as both originating from and returning to the house of 'ATREOOS', as combining the life-giving 'SPERM' with the 'rush' (HORMEI) of death.

In reworking this trope of epiphany through his translations and in ventriloquising the roles of Deianeira, Hercules and Electra, we may claim that Pound is also creating a mode of epiphany that is mediated through an androgynous persona rather than through a sacrificial female figure. Or rather, in mirroring the ways modernist experimentation plays with epiphany (as in James Joyce's *Portrait of the Artist as a Young Man* and *Dubliners*) the reliance on the mediating presence of the female body as sacrifice/love-object/muse in the trope of epiphany is problematised and given an androgynous or hybrid dimension. This is pertinent in the context of classical Greek tragedy, as in addition to the linguistic experiments of translation, when it comes to the notion of embodiment, acting more generally, Pound's translations might also be read as being sensitive to and aware of the classical convention of men playing women. If we add this aspect into the heady mixture of all the formal conventions that Pound is reworking, then perhaps more interesting possibilities may open up in terms of performance.

The *difficulty* that Pound's translations pose for contemporary performance has sometimes been approached through recourse to dance. Dance seems to offer an appropriate form that can perhaps address the demands of rhythm, movement and expression that they place. In this respect Stephe Harrop's work is very enabling:

> Stephe Harrop's project is to uncover, in the light of an historical understanding of the nature of the theatre familiar to those translators, a sense of what the dancing or moving actor is invited by the language to do. Printed texts suggest appropriate systems of movement in many different ways, ranging from obvious authorial stage directions through to the performative implications of textual structure, rhythm, tempo, rhyme, sound patterning, and imagery.[51]

This is a very exciting approach, one that probably yields very interesting choreographical versions of these translations. Still, I believe that the experiments undertaken by these translations might be read as being even more far-reaching. It is not so much a case of the dancing body going places where the acting body cannot, or even of the body itself offering interpretive solutions somehow 'beyond' the poetic word. It is not simply a case of the body offering the material dimension of the poetic word. Surely the acting/dancing/moving body of the performer is invited to 'do' things by language. However, this modernist take on translation and performance goes beyond the divide between language and the body. Embodiment is not simply and empirically the transposition of the poetic word onto the body. Rather the binary between the poetic word and the body is elided and the body and the word are seen as being both textual and material. In this sense the poetic word is already embodied and the human body is already textual. The word as flesh and the flesh as word is a trope that many modernist experiments in performance engage. And these translations can also be seen in partaking in this modernist legacy. In some respects, this can also be read as a phenomenological understanding of the performing body; indeed, this trope has inspired much recent thinking in performance theory. This thinking about the performing body also finds precedents in these difficult modernist translations of classical Greek plays.

Dance is surely one route that contemporary performance follows in addressing the demands of Pound's translations. Another route might be offered by puppets. In drawing on the parallels between the dancer and the puppet examined in previous chapters, where the physical and the mechanical are not viewed in opposition and where the mechanical itself is read as a type of critical embodied thinking, then perhaps in addition to dance, puppetry might also offer exciting solutions to the demands placed by Pound's difficult, modernist translations.

Another possible way of approaching these complex translations might be by recourse to Pound's notion of *paideuma*, which he borrows from the German anthropologist Leo Frobenius. More layered and performative a term than the Romantic *zeitgeist*, *paideuma* denotes, we could claim in Raymond Williams's terms, a kind of 'structure of feeling' that is rooted in time and space, and combines 'ideas that are in action'.[52] For Pound, the etymological link with paideutics (the science and art of learning and teaching) is not lost, as these translations are called upon to train the English language but also the performer who approaches them. In Brechtian terms we could even claim that they are a type of *gestus*, a performance/performative trope where the political, the historical and the linguistic come together to create a mood, an attitude or a pose. Again, in this instance we can further understand Pound's attraction to Noh theatre.

'TO BE SUNG AND SPOKEN':
W. B. YEATS'S VERSIONS OF THE OEDIPUS PLAYS

It is in Yeats's plays that we find the more direct impact of the Noh drama. Together with Pound he spent a summer in Sussex in 1913, in many ways urging the Japanese dancer Michio Ito to remain 'traditional' for the sake of their aesthetic contemplation, while also engaging with the Fenollosa Noh manuscript. Translation, dance, movement and embodiment more generally were always linked in their endeavours. Yeats started working on what he labelled 'versions' of the Sophocles plays as early as 1900. He continued to work on them until the late 1930s. In contrast to Pound, Yeats's lack of classical Greek and his reliance on the translations of Sir Richard C. Jebb, which were published together with the Greek text between 1883 and 1896, create yet another notion of translation. For Yeats clearly did not work from the original, but reworked the Jebb translations for the purposes of performance. He writes:

> I put readers and scholars out of my mind and wrote to be sung and spoken. The one thing that I kept in mind was that a word unfitted for living speech, out of its natural order, or unnecessary to our modern technique, would check emotion and tire attention.[53]

The language that Yeats chose in his translations was a combination of prose and verse (prose for the protagonist and verse for the chorus). The quest for a language that could speak to big national themes and attract large audiences fitted in quite neatly with Yeats's fascination with the oral and popular tradition. Unlike Pound, for whom there is no 'organic' myth at work in his relentless attack on all forms of language, Yeats finds inspiration and a redemption of sorts in the critical legacies of the Celtic Twilight. The difficulty of reviving the poetry of the Greek plays is viewed by Yeats as a general symptom of a modern 'malaise'; a world where language has been debased and lost its 'organic' unity with a living, breathing community. Yeats finds this alternative, ideal audience on the Aran Islands, and in line with the linguistic experiments of the Celtic Twilight (also undertaken by J. M. Synge and later Louis MacNeice in his translation of *Agamemnon* in 1937), uses rhythms and patterns that he considers to be part of an organic community that somehow has not been marred by modernity. For Yeats the revival of Sophocles was also a return to this organic community. He writes to Lady Gregory: 'You and I and Synge, not understanding the clock, set out to bring again the Theatre of Shakespeare or rather perhaps of Sophocles . . .'[54]

Yeats brought to his versions of the Oedipus all his concerns: 'I had three interests: interest in a form of literature, in a form of philosophy, and belief in nationality,'[55] and despite the initial problems with the censor, his *Oedipus Rex* was produced at the Abbey on 6 December 1926. Before it reached production, however, it had accompanied all his other theatrical ventures and influenced his playwriting more generally. Of all the anglophone modernists (apart from Gertrude Stein, who wrote seventy-five plays and operas), Yeats is probably the most prolific writer for the stage. And it is in his theatre work as a whole, not solely in his Jebb-inspired versions, where we can trace the impact of Greek tragedy. Like Eliot, Yeats's quest for poetic drama also bears a Christian inflection, where the figures of Oedipus and Christ are conflated. He writes in *A Vision*: 'What if Christ and Oedipus, or to shift the names, Saint Catherine of Genoa and Michael Angelo, are the two scales of a balance, the two butt-ends of a seesaw?'[56]

This conflation of Christian ritual, Greek tragedy and Noh is more pronounced and clearly articulated in Yeats's own plays. His 1927 play

Resurrection acts as a fine example of this creative polyphony. It presents, in the form of questions and answers (antiphones, perhaps), a discussion about the nature of Christ among three emblematic figures: a Greek, a Hebrew and a Syrian (or Egyptian in the *Adelphi* version). This debate is threatened by an offstage ecstatic chorus of Dionysus performing horrific rituals. This brief play, which combines prose and verse, exhibits many of the traits that were to characterise Yeatsian drama: it features a chorus of musicians, it uses the mask, the folding and unfolding of the curtain, and it was specifically written for a small studio audience such as that of the Peacock Theatre (the smaller stage of the Abbey). Here is the opening song that, as Yeats states in his directions, is for 'the folding and the unfolding of the curtain':

> I saw a staring virgin stand
> Where holy Dionysus died,
> And tear the heart out of his side,
> And lay the heart upon her hand
> And bear that beating heart away;
> And then did all the Muses sing
> Of Magnus Anus at the spring,
> As though God's death were but a play.[57]

All these formal aspects are borrowed from the Noh, and have parallels in Yeats's earlier *Four Plays for Dancers* (*At the Hawk's Well*, 1919; *The Only Jealousy of Emmer*, 1919; *The Dreaming of the Bones*, 1919; *Calvary*, 1920). *Resurrection* is dedicated to a Japanese admirer called Junzo Sato. While he is writing *Resurrection* he also returns to the Oedipus plays. In general, we could claim that these translations/versions shadowed all the stage work that Yeats was involved with. Probably more than his contemporary anglophone modernist poets, Yeats was engaging with the practice of performance as much as he was with the writing of poetic drama. This practice brought together his version of Hellenism, primitivism and Christian ritual. It was also informed by Craig's ideas about scenic space. Craig's designs and his theories of acting were formative for Yeats. One of Craig's early designs and the first use of his notorious screens was for Yeats's *The Hour Glass* (1910). Earlier, as part of his plan to stage his version of *Oedipus Rex* for the Abbey (1907), Yeats considered using Craig's scenery but was discouraged from doing so and had second thoughts, as he was worried that the design might be overwhelming and distract from the poetic language on the stage. This is a pity, as at this stage of his career Craig had already attempted and failed to collaborate with Reinhardt, and a Yeats/Craig Oedipus cycle could have been a major theatrical event. Still, it remains one of theatrical modernism's great unfinished projects.

In 1950, when Eliot is writing one of his final 'manifestos' for poetic drama, it is Yeats's late *Purgatory* (1939),[58] that he hails as the perfect paradigm for poetic drama. This is a brief play which could be read as a variation or version of both the *Oresteia* and *Oedipus Rex*. It is written in four-stress verse and has no songs and no masks. The set comprises a ruined doorway (perhaps a nod to Craig) and bare trees: 'wicked, crooked, hawthorn tree'. It is minimal and haunting. The narrative revolves around guilt, repetition, parricide and the possibility or not of redemption. An old man and his son visit the ruins of the great house where the father was born. This house of the father is also the site where he hopes to redeem the rape of his mother, a rape, however, that resulted in his birth. The primal Oedipal story is enacted as the son – the old man in the story – narrates how he grew up to kill his father. In the fight that occurs between the onstage father and his son, the father (and not the son this time) kills his son, thinking he is ending the cycle of repetition, only to discover that he is 'but twice a murderer and all for nothing'. These final words he addresses to God. This play, with its *Oresteia* and *Oedipus* echoes, its Craigian setting and its Noh influences, is the one Eliot chooses to hail as the finest example of poetic drama. It certainly presents a modernist version of tragedy – in the way that Yeats's translations are also 'versions' of Sophocles, as he calls them – and in looking back towards Greek tragedy, also looks forward and anticipates ('watch that tree') the ways that Samuel Beckett was to rewrite tragedy.

This poignant and evocative play can be read as a version of the Oedipus plays, but also as a Yeats Noh play and as a modernist Christian drama, and it is in this energising concoction where both its homage to the past and its originality lie. In this sense Eliot, too, was prophetic in hailing *Purgatory* as the highest achievement in poetic drama. It allows us to also see the work of Samuel Beckett in this genealogy of poetic drama that fuses Christian ritual and Greek tragedy.

Berlin Dada: (Not) Simply Classical

While Greek tragedy was approached within a spirit of reverence that despite the modernist formal experiments still carries the cultural capital of both classicism and tradition, there is an instance of a radical reimagining of the form within the workings of Berlin Dada, which relies more on the equally modernist tropes of blasphemy and deconstruction. *Simply Classical! An Oresteia with a Happy Ending* opened on 8 December 1919 at the Schall und Rauch (Sound and Smoke) cabaret beneath the Großes Schauspielhaus at the same time as Reinhardt's famous *Oresteia*. It is astonishing that one of the most successful Reinhardt renditions of Greek tragedy was shadowed by this irreverent production that embodied all the contours of Dada performance. Written by Walter Mehring with music by Friedrich Holländer, it was performed by puppets designed by George Grosz and constructed by John Heartfield. Fascinating to note that all these artists who were to become prominent within Berlin Dada, and whose work was to have a sharp political dimension, saw in

Greek tragedy an opportunity to experiment with their artform. And indeed, this short piece came to embody all the traits that were to become 'stock' – one could say 'classical' – of avant-garde performance: the use of satire and caricature; the use of music; the use of puppets; the irreverent attitude towards authority; the use of 'modern' technology like the telephone, the phonograph and the use of film on stage; the episodic use of narrative; cabaret techniques like direct address to the audience; the 'epic' labelling of scenes. Not only does this performance event act as a precursor to the political theatres of Piscator and Brecht, but it also acts as an early example of the ways that Greek tragedy was to be used in overtly political and sometimes even agitprop renditions later in the twentieth and twenty-first centuries. That it appears, quite literally, in the basement of Reinhardt's Schauspielhaus makes a strong statement about the interconnectedness and the dialogical/dialectical relationships between the 'high' uses of Greek tragedy, practised by Reinhardt, and the more 'low' and popular ones evidenced in *Simply Classical!* It is included in this analysis as an example of avant-garde and non-anglophone poetic drama that engages directly with the classical tradition; that is at once cognisant of both the cultural capital of the original, and of its prestigious position within the critical legacies of the German philological tradition.

The play is divided into three sections: (1) Agamemnon in the Bath; (2) The Dawn of Democracy; (3) The Classical Flight from Taxation. Agamemnon appears as a representative of the old guard, a 'commanding General in his best years'. Clytemnestra and Aegisthus are presented as heralding the Dawn of a New Democracy, and interestingly *not* Orestes, who appears as an officer of the Attic Free Corps. Electra has joined the Salvation Army. Apollo is Woodrow Wilson, with an 'unmistakable similarity to President W.' All the roles of the original are presented through puppetised caricatures of the leading political figures of both the German and Allied forces. The chorus that hounds Agamemnon and Clytemnestra is made up of the Press and also doubles as the 'Tax Eumenides', who make sure that millionaires leave behind their money before they abandon the country. The state court that indicts Orestes is established by 'Woodrow Apollo', who, however, withdraws his leadership, and in this way allows for Orestes' military takeover as the play concludes – prophetically and alarmingly – with him advancing on the Baltic states.

This kind of direct reference to contemporary events went beyond the tropes of allusion, citationality and general 'modernising' of the Greek plays. Its blatant critique of German politics and especially the military is more reminiscent of late twentieth- and twenty-first-century restagings/adaptations of Greek tragedy. All the instances we have examined encapsulate not only formal/aesthetic, but also political/ethical concerns as part of their attempts at making the Greeks modern. However, nowhere do we find this direct reference to contemporary political figures and events. And here is how the Dadaists unapologetically write themselves into the workings of German politics of the time, and into the workings of Greek tragedy. Here is Aegisthus, commenting on trying to run a democratic government with direct references to the Weimar Republic in an almost Aristophanic vein:

AEGISTHUS: *(In a morning gown, practising in sweat at the punching ball).*
Ladies and gentlemen! It's easy to laugh!
But do better! Do better than that!
     After all, have you ever ruled a country?
(Begins throwing some hard punches.)
Sometimes they stab you on the Left, and sometimes on the Right.
Sometimes they bloody you in the morning papers.
Or caricatured by Zillie –
You are searched, ridiculed, spied upon.
There is no romanticism to it anymore,
No heroic posture, no gigantic iambics.
There are no more crowns, no more kingly ways.
The Dada-rebels will begin their riots.[59]

This reading of Aegisthus as a 'writer and professional moralist' who tries to establish a democratic government after Agamemnon's demise presents quite a sympathetic view of the role and of his relationship with Clytemnestra, again acting as a precursor to more contemporary political and feminist readings of these roles. At the same time, it displays a deep knowledge of the original trilogy and of its modes of theatrical representation. The light from Troy that the night watchman sees in the original, announcing the victory of the Greeks, is here turned into a telephone, which like that original light is metaphorised throughout the *Oresteia* and comes to stand in for progress and civilisation, where technology becomes the emblem of modernity. It is no coincidence that many an avant-garde production from the period features telephones as characters. The Pythia section appears as a 'Filmic Interlude', again foreshadowing the use of film on stage that would later be used in the political theatre of Piscator. The production is fully aware of its irreverent style and does not hesitate to cite both Aeschylus and Reinhardt, always in Dadaist manner:

If only Aeschylus were to know
With happiness he would overflow
A bit of classicism in a modern way
Redoubles the humor, he would say.
In school we already learn Greek
And students think it is quite chic

To see such an old Greek gent
Exposing himself indecent.
If only Aeschylus . . .
Go to Reinhardt when he curses
It is classic how he rehearses
Smoothly runs the Oresteia
All with his machinery.[60]

This is an astonishing sequence that at once references the centrality of the classics for the German middle classes and pokes fun at Reinhardt's famous directing 'machinery'. Erika Fischer-Lichte has convincingly written about the ways in which philhellenism and especially Greek tragedy was foundational for the ethico-political identity of the educated German middle classes (the *Bildungsbürgertum*).[61] So it seems appropriate that this Dadaist critique of the German middle classes will also attack the centrality of a classical education that helped to create their cultural and hegemonical identity. It also appears, as several scholars have noted, to be influenced by Nietzsche and his irreverent attacks on the German classical tradition in scholarship. Indeed, in line with much of the modernist re-visioning of Greek tragedy, this version seems to be critiquing the dominance of the German tradition classical reception. And it does so at its heart. At the same time, its satirical take on Reinhardt repeats a criticism of the period: that his production and directing methods were organised like a well-oiled machine. This echoes Craig's criticism of Reinhardt, as he too felt that he ran his company like a huge production machine. This is an interesting perspective coming from the Dadaists, as they were hardly technophobic. Still, to them the concept of the 'mechanical' possibly carried nineteenth-century connotations, as a process that seamlessly covers up the creative process. The Dadaist use of technology (as opposed to machinery), however, was to help fragment and deconstruct this process, so Agamemnon could be a telephone and the telephone itself could be a dramatic character. This is a very innovative use of stage technology to reinvent the notion of dramatic character, one that doubtless was facilitated by the use of puppets, an aspect too of stage technology.

The central position that classicism and particularly Greek tragedy occupies within Berlin Dada cabaret is not surprising, given the educational and cultural background of its members. This is German classicism, reinvented through a combination of Nietzschean philosophy and Dadaist irreverence. The programme notes for *Simply Classical!* featured cover artwork by Grosz and Heartfield, a photomontage of a puppet from the production, a monologue from the play itself by Mehring, and a short text by Huelsenbeck titled *Talking about the Hat*.[62] It is fascinating that throughout their collaborations with the Schall und Rauch cabaret these prominent, and very radical politically, Dada artists also see fit to rework notions of classicism and give them the Dadaist treatment. Raoul Hausmann also contributed an article/Dadaist poem titled *Percival and Klytemnestra*, where he references Nietzsche's ideas on tragedy combined with medieval legend, no doubt with a nod to Wagner. *Simply Classical!* also goes to the heart of classical humanism and to its economies of representation. The use of puppets at once nods to all the modernist discourses about technology, mechanical reproduction (that Benjamin will soon articulate, partly inspired by the Dadaists) and their critical potential, but also helps to once again rehearse the ancient quarrel, as for these Dadaists their classical education and cultural inheritance was anything but *Simple!*

This irreverent production was also in some way commenting on the function of translation. Not in the least concerned with the linguistic intricacies of translating the classics, it is bold and brash in the ways it quotes them. Its creators were obviously aware of the triumph of the Reinhardt performances, and located as they were in the basement of his theatre (its subconscious, perhaps), through their cabaret version present a blasphemous version of this most classical of tragedies. Ironically, of course, as theatre conventions themselves come with a genealogy, the use of puppets can be read in both its Dadaist flair and in its classical Platonic context. *Simply Classical!* showed how a classical text can be used and abused in order to voice political dissent by creating incongruous connections between classical drama, agitprop, puppetry and overall Dadaist aesthetics. At the same time, it can be viewed as expanding the whole field of translation to include the linguistic text, but also the body of the performer, the stage and theatricality in general. This is indeed translation as total theatre.

NOTES

1. Eliot, 'Tradition and the Individual Talent', in *Selected Essays*, p. 22.
2. Eliot, '*Ulysses*, Order and Myth' (1923), in *Selected Prose of T. S. Eliot*, p. 176.
3. Ibid. p. 177.
4. Pound, *Literary Essays*, p. 431.
5. See Leonard, *Tragic Modernities*, p. 132.
6. Benjamin, *Selected Writings, Vol. 1*, p. 254.
7. Ibid. p. 255.
8. Ibid. p. 256.
9. Ibid. p. 257.
10. Benjamin, *Understanding Brecht*.
11. See Benjamin, 'The Task of the Translator', in *Selected Writings*, p. 262.
12. See Weber, *Benjamin's –abilities*.
13. Eliot, 'Euripides and Professor Murray', in *The Complete Prose of T. S. Eliot, Vol. 2*, pp. 195–201, p. 201.
14. Eliot, *Poetry and Drama*, p. 20.
15. Pound, *Guide to Kulcher*, p. 93.
16. Eliot, 'Dramatis Personae', p. 434.

17. Eliot, quoted in Jones, *The Plays of T. S. Eliot*, p. 52. From essay, 'The Need for Poetic Drama', *The Listener*, 25 November 1936, p. 95.
18. See Eliot, *Poetry and Drama*, p. 72.
19. Eliot, 'Poetry and Drama', in *Selected Prose of T. S. Eliot*, pp. 132–47, p. 139.
20. See Eliot, 'Euripides and Professor Murray', n. 14.
21. See Eliot, *Poetry and Drama*, p. 31.
22. See Eliot, *Selected Essays*, p. 104.
23. Eliot, quoted in Browne, *The Making of T. S. Eliot's Plays*, p. 108.
24. Carpentier, *Ritual, Myth and the Modernist Text*, p. 102.
25. Kenner, *The Invisible Poet*, p. 339.
26. See Carpentier, *Ritual, Myth and the Modernist Text*, p. 106.
27. Quoted in Jones, *The Plays of T. S. Eliot*, p. 122.
28. See Eliot, *Poetry and Drama*, p. 27.
29. Eliot, *The Complete Poems and Plays of T. S. Eliot*, p. 39.
30. Quoted in Browne, *The Making of T. S. Eliot's Plays*, p. 247.
31. Letter (1933) to Hallie Flanagan, quoted in Crawford, *The Savage and the City*, p. 162.
32. Pound, 'A Retrospect' (1918), in Kolocotroni, Goldman and Taxidou (eds), *Modernism*, p. 387.
33. Pound, *The Letters of Ezra Pound*, p. 113.
34. Pound, 'Sophokles' *Women of Trachis*'.
35. For an elaboration of this reading see Liebregts, '"No Man Knows his Luck 'Till He's Dead"'; for the most informed and comprehensive philological study of Pound's translations, see Liebregts, *Translations of Greek Tragedy in the Work of Ezra Pound*.
36. A notoriously ambivalent term, it has been translated as wondrous, horrific, monstrous, strange, alienated, extremely capable, always carrying at least a double connotation. Famously, Heidegger translated it as the *unheimlich* (the unhomely) and Freud as the *uncanny*.
37. Pound, 'Sophokles' *Women of Trachis*', p. 495.
38. Ibid. p. 492.
39. Ibid. p. 505.
40. Ibid. pp. 519–20.
41. Ibid. p. 510–11.
42. Pound, *The Letters of Ezra Pound*, p. 113.
43. Pound, 'Sophokles' *Women of Trachis*', p. 505.
44. Ibid. p. 519.
45. See Syros, 'Beyond Language', and Stergiopoulou, '"And a Good Job"?'.
46. See Wiles, 'Sophoclean Diptychs'.
47. Pound, quoted in Ayers, 'H.D., Ezra Pound and Imagism', p. 6.
48. See Syros, 'Beyond Language', p. 122.
49. Pound and Flemming, *Elektra*, p. 33.
50. Ibid. p. 115.
51. Harrop and Wiles, 'Poetic Language and Corporeality in Translations of Greek Tragedy', p. 55.
52. Pound, *Guide to Kulchur*, p. 58.
53. Yeats, 'Preface to Sophocles', p. v.
54. Yeats, 'A People's Theatre: A Letter to Lady Gregory', *The Irish Statesman*, 29 November and 6 December 1919, rtp. in *Plays and Controversies*, pp. 209–10.
55. Yeats, *Explorations*, p. 263.
56. Yeats, *A Vision: The Revised 1937 Edition*, p. 21.
57. W. B. Yeats, *Collected Works of W. B. Yeats, Vol II: The Plays*, pp. 481–2.

58. Ibid. *Purgatory*, pp. 537–44.
59. 'Simply Classical!: An Oresteia With a Happy Ending', in Gordon (ed.), *Dada Performance*, pp. 66–79 (p. 73).
60. Ibid. p. 71.
61. See Erika Fischer-Lichte, *Tragedy's Endurance*.
62. See Jelavich, *Berlin Dada*; and Taxidou, *Modernism and Performance*, pp. 168–72.

4

H.D.:
FEET, HANDS AND HIEROGLYPHS

The act of translation as a composite activity, involving the word, the image and the body, is perhaps nowhere more evident than in H.D.'s translations. H.D.'s excursions into translation shadowed all other artistic, general creative and possibly personal activities that she undertook throughout her life. Unlike her male contemporaries, H.D. was drawn not to Aeschylus or Sophocles but to Euripides, unearthing a proto-feminist aspect of his work that proved very alluring for later twentieth- and twenty-first-century productions of his plays. At the same time H.D. locates in Euripides a formal experimentation that proves attractive both for the purposes of translation and for the purposes of acting. Although H.D. did not act in her own translations, she did act in the avant-garde films made by the experimental group of filmmakers in the 1930s, the POOL Group, associated with the short-lived but highly influential little magazine *Close Up* (1927–33).[1] So far in this study we have drawn analogies, intertextual relationships and modernist network clusters between the tasks of translation, imaging and general modernist linguistic experimentation with poetry on the stage. Of course, the concept of embodiment is formative in all those instances, but in H.D.'s case this is not simply a metaphor or an instance of imagistic *phanopoeia*. Her forays into cinematic acting and her general interest in the theory of cinema – a theory which she developed in a series of articles entitled 'The Cinema and the Classics'[2] – invites us to attempt to trace a number of threads that perhaps connect her overall approach of and practice in translation with her theorising of and acting for the cinema. And the trope that possibly best describes this interconnection might be that of the *hieroglyph*. When Ernest Fenollosa claims in aphoristic tone that 'Thinking is *thinging*',[3] he surely has the Chinese ideogram in mind that Pound later developed into the visibly concrete, direct 'word-thing'. However, he also had the dancer Michio Ito in mind. H.D.'s experiments in thinking/thinging/dancing/acting take this analogy further, establishing the hieroglyph as its trope and emblem, adding an embodied kinetic sensibility to this central imagistic kernel.

H.D.'s long association with Euripides spanned her whole career. Between 1912 and 1919, during the First World War, she translated choruses from *Iphigenia at Aulis* (1915) and *Hippolytus* (1919). During the late 1920s she wrote a long lyric poem, *Hippolytus Temporizes* (1927). She continued writing essays and translating plays (*Helen, Ion, Bacchae, Hecuba*) throughout the 1920s and early 1930s. Between 1933 and 1934 – a period some scholars mark as a turning point in her life and work – she engaged in psychoanalysis with Freud.[4] Throughout this period H.D. continued her involvement with Euripides, which culminated in the composition of *Helen in Egypt* in the early 1950s. This is a long lyric poem that brings together and rewrites five Trojan plays of Euripides.

The kinds of Hellenism that H.D. engaged with bear striking parallels to the work of the Cambridge Ritualists, and Jane Ellen Harrison in particular. As Eileen Gregory states, there are no direct contacts here, as there are with Virginia Woolf, but it would have been almost impossible for H.D. not to have been aware of Harrison's work, or not to have read her books. H.D. would have found the anthropological take on the origins of religion quite appropriate – as she also discusses this with Freud. It would also suit H.D.'s interest in an Alexandrian-based hybrid Hellenism that framed much of her work, and that also finds an interpretive parallel in the hieroglyph. At the same time, she too is interested in developing a matrilineal model of genealogy (again something that Freud would pathologise). Gregory writes that, 'like Harrison, H.D. attempts to reassemble from its refractive facets in Greek cults the occluded image of the divine mother'.[5] And this attempt always bears with it the marks of nostalgia, a characteristic texture of H.D.'s Hellenism that Pound and Eliot had found sentimental, unreliable, feminising and verging on the pathological. For H.D., however, this nostalgia towards the Greeks presented a way of reviving the past for the purposes of the present. During the First World War in particular this nostalgia proved restorative, offering a possible cure (a *pharmakon*) for the trauma of war and the ills of modernity. 'My work is creative and reconstructive, war or no war, if we can get across the Greek spirit at its highest I am helping the world, and the future.'[6] In some ways this is the most classical of classicisms. It is, at the same time, double-edged, looking both towards the past and the future, combining her interest in Greek tragedy with her own modernist poetic experiments. Like her reworking of Helen in *Helen in Egypt*, it is both *'phantom and reality'*.[7]

She writes in Book 2: 'Lethe, as we all know, is the river of forgetfulness for the shadows, passing from life to death. But Helen, mysteriously transposed to Egypt, does not want to forget. She is both phantom and reality.'[8]

It is, perhaps, the act of translation/adaptation/rewriting that provides at least one of the main frames (or poses, or *gestus*) or threads that weaves together all of H.D.'s endeavours as both a classicist and a modernist; in a sense it provides the rhythm and the beat for her writing (biographical, poetic and theoretical) and for her acting. H.D. as performer and H.D. as translator might offer an enabling interface that may allow us to read theatricality into her act of translation.[9] So it may be illuminating to read her translation projects in conjunction with her involvement with the POOL Group of avant-garde film-makers, and with her attempts to develop an acting *style*. In the cinema H.D. found a medium that could bring together her interest in classicism, imagism and psychoanalysis. Her faith in the function of 'vision', 'projection' that is evidenced in her poetry finds in the cinema the ultimate modern trope that provides access to the psyche. This access, for her, is also mediated through the encounter with the classics. She writes eleven articles for *Close Up*, the first three of which appear under the general tile of 'The Cinema and the Classics'. Here she develops her theories of cinema, montage and acting in relation to her particular revision/rewriting of the classics. As Laura Marcus states, quoting Robert Herring, H.D. viewed the screen as a site of magic:

> There is the screen, and as you know the projector is at the back of you. Overhead is the beam of light which links the two. Look up. See it spread out. It is wider and thinner. Its fingers twitch, they spread in blessing or they convulse in terror. They tap you lightly or they drag you in. Magic fingers writing on the wall, and able to become at will . . . a sword or an acetylene drill, a plume or waterfall, black glass and crystal flowers . . .

> You need not be a chamber to be haunted, nor need you own the Roxy to let loose the spirit of cinema on yourself. You can hire or buy or get on the easy system, a projector. You then have, on the occasions on which it works, people walking on your own opposite wall. By moving your fingers before the beam, you interrupt them; by walking before it, your body absorbs them. You hold them, you can let them go.[10]

Marcus insightfully claims that Herring's images in this article (rod, snake, flower) anticipate the 'hieroglyphs' of H.D.'s epic poem *Trilogy*. This image of the screen and projector could also be read as rewriting Plato's Allegory of the Cave, where the light of the sun that is located behind the audience (who are chained in Plato's vision) projects a fantasy of reality onto the walls of the cave. In this instance, however, and in creating a model of cinema that, as Marcus claims, destructs the 'aura' 'and of a blurring of a body/world division as the spectator inserts him or herself into the spectacle', Herring's vision 'imagines a future for cinema, an "avant-garde", in which images would be rendered visible without the mediation of the screen, bodies and beings becoming solid projections of themselves'.[11] What Marcus describes here can also be read as an anti-Platonic utopia, as the dream of pure mediation; one that, perhaps, would not have been lost on H.D. So in this sense it is no coincidence that she goes back to the classics in order to help her construct a theory of cinema. The Greece she goes 'back' to, however, is not the Greece of the golden, classical era; it is the primitivist Greece, the one that inspired Murray and Harrison, and perhaps this is a more appropriate route to follow in revisiting and lighting up the darkness of Plato's cave. She writes: 'We would be, like pre-Periclean Athenians, without fear, really ready for an Art Age'.[12] This modernist medium, which she calls experimental, at the same time harks back to mysteries that were pre-classical, like the Eleusinian mysteries, themselves cryptic and coded in obscure references by the time we get to the Periclean era:

> Elaborate experiment – *that* was well enough – and waste and waste and waste must inevitably precede perfection of any medium. But don't let's put up with too much of it. Here is our medium, as I say here is the thing that the Eleusinians would have been glad of; a subtle device for portraying of the miraculous. Miracles and godhead are *not* out of place, are not awkward on the screen. A wand may (and does) waft us to fabulous lands, and beauty can and must redeem us.[13]

The above quotation, differently lined across the page, could easily be read as one of H.D.'s poems. The aligning of the miraculous with the Godhead is also matched in other sections of these three articles, where the miraculous is read in parallel with the mechanical. In her pamphlet accompanying the film *Borderline* in 1930 she describes the director Kenneth Macpherson working in the film as 'giant mechanical Perseus'. And together with the orgiastic pleasures of the Eleusinian mysteries, H.D. also accords to film a Sophoclean lyricism. And this tension between a eudaimonic 'Beauty' and 'Restraint', the subtitles of two of her three essays on 'Cinema and the Classics', comes to form a structuring narrative device throughout these essays:

> The 'classic' as realism could be better portrayed by the simplest of expedients. A pointed trireme prow nosing sideways into empty space, the edge of a quay, blocks of solid masonry, squares and geometric design would simplify and at the same time emphasize the pure *classic* note . . . Beauty restrained and chaste, with the over-weaving of semi-phosphorescent light, in a few tense moments showed that the screen can rise to the ecstatic level of the poetic and religious ideals of pure Sophoclean formula.[14]

These are extraordinary images that manage to fuse the ultra-classical with the ultra-modern. Could this trireme also be a reference to *The Battleship Potemkin*, as H.D. in her criticism praised the work of Sergei Eisenstein and his theories of montage? And perhaps her image of the 'blocks of solid masonry' might also be traced onto the famous scene with the Odessa steps. So when it came to actually acting in the films of the POOL Group, H.D. approached her acting style as a film theorist, as a poet, as a classical scholar and as translator. And it is this particular combination, one that we may possibly even read as an expression of her hyper-theory of montage – clatter montage – that we might be able to read back into her practice of translation and forward into her theory of acting.

An Act/Acting of Translation

H.D. seized the opportunity to act in three films created by the POOL Group, funded by Bryher and directed by Macpherson. These were *Wing Beat* (1927), *Foothills* (1928) and *Borderline* (1930). All were silent films, and the one that received the most attention both at the time (Macpherson writes about it and H.D. writes a pamphlet-libretto to accompany it) and in the critical canon of both modernist cinema and H.D. studies is *Borderline*. It has been read as a study of the intricate relationships between cinema and psychoanalysis, on the ways that cinema helps to create personal and collective phantasy, and on the ways it is both mechanical and miraculous. In the words of Anne Friedberg, '*Borderline* contained everything that seemed important to the POOL group, combining, as it did, the psychoanalytic insights of Hanns Sachs and the montage theories of Eisenstein.'[15] We could also add H.D.'s interest in the classics, as it may be read as parallel to the structure of a Greek tragedy in the ways the workings of a fraught *oikos* are emblematic of both the interior psychic lives of the protagonists and their *public/political* lives that are located on a number of borderlines, between races, genders, countries (just as Greek tragedies always take place on the threshold between the *oikos* and the *polis*, between the private and the public). Harry A. Potamkin, who had just published an article in *Close Up*'s special issue devoted to black cinema in 1929 (where he argues for a 'pure' 'Afroamerican' cinema ('Not black films passing for white, and not, please, white passing for black')[16] introduced Macpherson to Paul and Eslanda Robeson, who agreed to take part in the film. The film enacts a melodramatic narrative of sexual jealousy through the entanglements of an African American couple, Adah (Eslanda Robeson) and Pete (Paul Robeson), with a white couple, Astrid (H.D.) and Thorne (Gavin Arthur), exploring anxieties about race and sexuality, using a highly experimental, montage-based cinematic language. Here is how H.D. presents the plot in the 'libretto' handed out at the early screenings of the film:

> In a small 'borderline' town, anywhere in Europe, Pete, a negro, is working in a cheap hotel café. His wife, Adah, who left him some time previously, has arrived also in the same town, although neither is aware of the presence of the other.

> Adah is staying in rooms with the white couple Thorne and Astrid. Thorne is a young man whose life with Astrid has become a torment to them both. Both are highly strung, and their nerves are tense with continuous hostility evoked by Thorne's vague and destructive cravings. He has been involved in an affair with Adah, and the film opens with the quarrel that ends their relationship.[17]

The drama reaches its climax when, after a quarrel between the white couple, Thorne stabs Astrid (H.D.) in 'self-defense'. The progamme notes offer a narrative and an explanation for this act: 'The negro woman is blamed ... Thorne is acquitted ... the mayor, acting for the populace ... ordered Pete ... to leave town. Pete goes ... a scapegoat for the unresolved problems, evasions and neuroses for which the racial "borderline" has served justification.'[18] Although the story has been read as melodrama, it can also quite neatly map onto the structure of a Greek tragedy. The references to Pete as a 'scapegoat' (elsewhere he will be referred to as the 'Godhead' or 'daemon') and the chorus-style understanding of the 'populace' may also allow for a reading of tragedy mapped onto the workings of cinematic form. Fascinating in this context is how H.D. (Helga Doorne – stage name) is cast so negatively, and although she is stabbed, she refuses to call herself 'the scapegoat'. Rather she is cast as a racist 'neurasthenic', where the 'neurasthenia' and being 'highly strung', as she notes, reference both Marinetti's misogynist and proto-fascist praise-indictment of the female performer, *and* Plato's puppets. We could also perhaps read into this the above interpretation of the cinema as a reworking of Plato's cave, the original site of representation through the actors as puppets/*neurospasta*. And indeed, H.D.'s acting style, with its jerky, fragmented gestures, might be seen as a neurospastic externalisation of the character's neurasthenia. In turn this is parallel to the experiments in montage that the film also undertakes. 'Clatter montage' itself, her evocative term, may be read as a 'neurospastic/neurasthenic' reconfiguration of montage, as put together by a puppet.

At the same time, H.D.'s formulation of the idea of clatter montage, a rapid cutting of shots, that the film and acting style have come to present, also need to be read in the context of the notion of 'Restraint' that she develops in her essays on 'The Cinema and the Classics'. On the one hand, there is definitely a jagged quality to her acting and to the film in general, but at the same time I would claim that this needs to be read not simply as a jumbling together of inchoate images and movement. There is a level of stylisation at work that, as in Plato's puppets, presents the body of the performer as a well-wound-up machine. This in turn has an impact on affect and audience spectatorship. It is indicative that H.D. herself was not unreservedly embracing of montage, for despite its critical and political potential she also saw the ways it could be manipulative for the audience. In quite a nuanced reading of Carl Dreyer's *The Passion of Joan of Arc*, which goes against the grain of its mostly enthusiastic reception at the time, she writes:

> Do I *have* to be cut into slices by this inevitable pan-movement of the camera, these suave lines to left, up, to the right, back, all rhythmical with the remorseless rhythm of a scimitar? . . . Do we have to have the last twenty-four hours' agony of Jeanne stressed and stressed and stressed, in just this way, not only by the camera but by every conceivable method of dramatic and scenic technique? . . . I am shut in here, I want to get out.[19]

One wonders where she is shut? Perhaps she is returned to Plato's cave and to the relentless, manipulative force of the shadows on the wall. The 'pan-movement' refers to the totalising trompe l'oeil effect of the camera, but it is also impossible not to see the other pre-classical Pan here, whose wild primitivism is read in conjunction with the 'suave' lines, an adjective usually reserved for a particular kind of slick, even manipulative masculinity. As ever with H.D.'s writing, her criticism and her poetry inhabit similar registers. And the register/trope of being cut up features throughout her work, especially when dealing with the power of representation and, even more specifically, the possibility of feminine representation. A characteristic example appears in an early poem (1914–17):

> Envy
> IV
> So the goddess has slain me
> for your chance smile
> and my scarf unfolding
> as you stooped to it,
> so she trapped me,
> for the upward sweep of your arm,
> as you lifted the veil,
> was the gesture of a tall girl
> and your smile was as selfless
> Could I have known
> Nay, spare pity,
> though I break,
> crushed under the goddess' hate,

though I fall beaten at last,
so high have I thrust my glance
up into her presence.
Do not pity me, spare that,
but how I envy you
your chance of death.[20]

This evocative early poem, which could also be read as foreshadowing the fate of Isadora Duncan, highlights the image of being cut and slain while also alluding to Greek tragedy (perhaps Helen or Iphigenia), so it may not be too strained to connect H.D.'s later technique of clatter montage with these early images. This is also the time she starts translating choruses from Euripides. In Yopie Prins's evocative study of H.D.'s translations in *Ladies' Greek*, she proposes the notion of the 'rhythmic body', a way of integrating the body within the act of translation itself, where the body and the word form a kinaesthetic whole. Prins insightfully elaborates on this embodied trope of inhabiting the classical verse of Euripides:

> More than an exercise in versification, this imaginative transformation of Greek meter marks another way of being in, and out of, time not only for Hipparchia and Hippolytus, but also for H.D. herself. As we have seen, her 'free' versions of Euripidean tragedy superimpose an idea of classical quantitative meter on English accentual verse, so that her feet also 'quickened out of proportion to its measured beating'. In H.D.'s Euripides, past and present are formed and re-formed to make the ancient Greek look like modern free verse and vice versa.[21]

This is indeed a truly inspired way of solving the problem of transposing quantitative Greek metre onto qualitative English verse. This modernist (and I would say not Victorian) syncopation of time, which H.D. practises through this rendition of 'free verse' in her translations of *Hippolytus* and in her dramatic poem *Hippolytus Temporizes*, is enacted through the rhythm of the verse itself, where, as Prins states in reference to *Hippolytus Temporizes*, 'Instead of stomping "feet, feet, feet, feet" to the "beat" of a tune, Hippolytus tries to reimagine accentual verse in metrical feet that can measure time on a larger scale. What he has in mind is a temporization of meter . . . Hippolytus seeks to transform song from "a thing" into a more expansive spiritual experience within and beyond time.'[22] This takes the modernist trope of the word/thing and *thinking/thinging*, and intersperses it with the presence of the body itself; the body not simply as the medium of the poetic verse but as its performative, synaesthetic and kinaesthetic interlocutor. And this may also possibly offer one way of reading H.D.'s cinematic technique of clatter montage and her stylised acting in conjunction with her approach to translating.

The theme of being 'slain', 'cut', by eros is, of course, what probably attracted H.D. to *Hippolytus* in the first place and it is also the theme that is quite literally enacted in *Borderline* on her character Astrid. The way that this is enacted, we can claim, brings together the 'feet, feet, feet' of Prins's evocative proposition of 'dancing Greek letters' with the 'hands, hands, hands' of H.D.'s acting style. This way of addressing the difficulty faced in approaching Euripides' prosody, in the choral odes in particular, creates a view of character that is also choral, very much parallel to the modernist ideal of the actor as the laboratory of the collective soul or the body politic.[23] This approach to collective character is something that H.D. surely also gets from her study of Eisenstein and cinematic montage, but it is also fascinating to see it inflected by her understanding of prosody and her overall approach to translation. So in this sense the body of the performer itself becomes a kind of translating machine, mediating between the individual and the collective, between the poetic word and the body and between the past and the present. We may once again evoke ekphrasis as a bodily activity. It is in this sense that H.D.'s acting style may itself be read as an elaboration of her studies in 'The Cinema and the Classics'.

It may be somewhat incongruous to try to impose this primarily aural interpretation of H.D.'s translation tropes onto an acting style that is silent. Still, I would maintain that there is rhythm and rhyme to that silence. The soundscape is also created in conjunction with the music, and it is a soundscape that creates its own world. Here, too, we might be able to draw parallels with H.D.'s translations and the aural landscape they create. Catherine Theis calls this a 'processional poetics':

> Processional poetics involves multiple entrances and exits, where language, landscape and meaning are interconnected. Processional poetics enacts a revolution, a flight from inside the cross-hatched lines of language.
>
> [. . .]

And she elaborates:

> H.D. willingly writes a kind of minor literature: a tradition that works against the more visible and accessible kinds of literature. A minor literature is no less interested in telling major stories, but its agency comes from participating outside recognized social, political, or linguistic systems of order. Desire is procedure, then, the molten lava flown from a form. H.D.'s project involves writing and reading out of form.[24]

The above quotation could function as a comment on both H.D.'s translating and on her acting style. Interesting also that Theis here evokes Deleuze's notion of minor literature, which as she too acknowledges is not about minor works but about works that create a new formal and thematic landscape. Deleuze is possibly also appropriate when discussing H.D. due to his re-visioning of the Oedipal understanding of literary production, and his contributions to film theory.[25]

THE POETICS OF LANDSCAPE

The idea that H.D.'s translations create a landscape that she herself inhabits as a performer brings to mind another modernist experimental writer who also wrote plays: Gertrude Stein. The concept of the landscape play is elaborated by Stein in her own rich theatrical output. There are quite a few parallels that we could draw between H.D. and Gertrude Stein: both inhabit a type of aristocratic Sapphic modernism; both write in a register that challenges formal poetics; the body, and specifically the female body is central to their poetics; the relationship between the word and the image is central to this poetics for both; both propose an anti-Oedipal relation to the past; and both rewrite notions of classicism.

Elaborating on Theis's understanding of H.D.'s Euripides translations (especially the choruses of *The Bacchae*) as creating their own landscape, Eileen Gregory writes:

> The speaking voice, in H.D. the collective voice of the chorus, enacts a kind of cosmopoesis, a landscape which the voice brings bodily into being through sound. Thus the choral poems are performative, evoking the context of the theatre, yet standing outside of territorial containment.[26]

I would like to further reflect on this concept of cosmopoesis and connect H.D.'s translations with Gertrude Stein's plays, in this way creating a place for H.D. as a dramatist/playwright as well as a translator within the broader experiments in modernist performance.

Between 1913 and 1946, Stein wrote almost eighty plays. All her plays, from the early *It Happened, a Play* (1913) to the last, *Yes Is for a Very Young Man* (1946), consistently defy referentiality, exhibit an awareness of and play with dramatic genre (comedy, tragedy, satire) and, in ways similar to H.D.'s translations, create landscapes of their own. For Stein, the notion of the landscape, which she develops in her essay 'Plays' (1934),[27] was to provide the possibility of fusing the pictorial and the textual arts. The materiality of the poetry, the actor and the stage would all fuse into the idea of the landscape. This was not meant metaphorically, but presented a material being-in-the-theatre. Of course, as is the case with H.D.'s translations, this theatre was the page. Again, like H.D.'s translations, which are also rarely performed, they are themselves a performance. And in both the question of performability is central. Bonnie Marranca writes about Stein's dramaturgy:

This spatial conception of dramaturgy elaborates the new, modern sense of a dramatic field as performance space with its multiple and simultaneous centers of focus and activity, replacing the conventional nineteenth-century, time-bound and fixed setting of the drama. The effect is a kind of conceptual mapping in which the activity of thought itself creates an experience.[28]

Stein's plays set out to reconstitute the very essence of the theatre itself. This is not simply an exercise in reconciling the ancients with the moderns. This view of the stage rewrites the mould itself and offers a phenomenological take on spectatorship in the process. Here is a characteristic example of the ways Stein uses genre, classical dramatic structure, character and plot in her *Doctor Faustus Lights the Lights* (1938). The story starts after Faustus has sold his soul and without one he is unable to go to Hell. The power of the divine is replaced by technology and the familiar story is given a feminist twist with the introduction of the female character Marguerite Ida – Helena Annabel (with a dual identity, like Helen in H.D.'s *Helen in Egypt*, both phantom and reality). This play also features a chorus, in one of the few explicit modernist renditions of the form in a play:

> *Woman at the window*
> A viper has bitten her and if Doctor Faustus does not cure her it will be all Through her.
> *Chorus in the distance*
> Who is she
> She has not gone to hell
> Very well
> Very well
> She has not gone to hell
> Who is she
> Marguerite Ida and Helena Annabel
> And what has happened to her
> A viper has bitten her
> And if Doctor Faustus does not cure her
> It will all go through her
> And he what does he say
> He says he cannot see her
> Why cannot he see her
> Because he cannot look at her
> He cannot look at Marguerite Ida and Helena Annabel
> But he cannot cure her without seeing her
> They say yes yes.[29]

The way this sequence appears on the page, the use of repetition, the question/answer format, the use of image and symbol, could all also feature in an H.D. poem or translation. In H.D.'s 'Choros Translations', this is how Dionysus, from *The Bacchae*, is introduced by a collective chorus speaker:

Who is there,
who is there in the road?
who is there
who is there in the street?
back,
back,
each to his house,
let no one,
no one speak.

Or this, a few pages later:

This,
this
this
this;
escape
from
the
power
of
the
hunting
pack.[30]

This could not be a more Steinian translation of *The Bacchae* chorus. Stein, of course, never translated classical Greek plays. Still I feel the concept of the landscape play can be expanded to also apply to H.D.'s translations, if we think of them as works of dramaturgy. In her essay 'Plays', Stein presents one of the first modernist attempts at a phenomenology of theatricality and spectatorship. The crucial elements are the notion of experience-through-the-senses (which draws on the classical understanding of the aesthetic as *aesthesis*) and the different experiences of time that a theatrical event involves (time past and time present; the actors' time and the audience's time). She writes:

Is the thing seen or the thing heard the thing that makes most impression upon you at the theatre. How much has the hearing to do with it and how little. Does the thing heard replace the thing seen. Does it help or does it interfere with it.

[. . .]

So then for me there was the reading of plays which was one thing and then there was the seeing of plays and of operas a great many of them which was another thing.[31]

In Stein's plays, the actions of seeing and hearing, the eye and the ear are in some ways 'torn apart', unlocked and put back together again in cubist manner on the surface of the page as stage. When she writes that 'the play really is a landscape', we are reminded of the ways that H.D.'s poetry too is a landscape, from her first collection, *Sea Garden* (1916) to her startling translations. This is how H.D. conceptualises Stein's double time of plays. She writes in her translation of *Ion*: 'What time is it?/Greek unity gives us freedom,/it expands and contracts at will,/it is time-in-time,/and time-out-of-time together,/it predicts modern time estimates'.[32]

Indeed, this notion of time does mirror or 'predict', at least in poetological terms, the modernist preoccupation with narrative time. For Stein, the disparity of time experienced between the goings-on of the stage and the emotions of the audience was precisely what led her to formulate the concept of the landscape play. She states: 'I felt that if a play was exactly like a landscape then there would be no difficulty about the emotion of the person looking on at the play.'[33] This notion of landscape extends the theatrical space to include the whole event with the audience as well. It has traditionally been read as a way of creating an enlarged *mise-en-scène*, a type of performance space rather than a traditional theatrical space, where the poetics, the emotion and the physicality of theatricality all merge. In this respect and in a predominant modernist vein, Gertrude Stein's experimentation has predictably been read as anti-Aristotelean. This may be true regarding Aristotelean notions of narrative plot and character, but regarding the Greek plays themselves, H.D. constructs a very different genealogy for the landscape play. This is a view of translation that in truly Benjaminian terms rewrites and makes foreign both the original Greek and its modernist rendition.

Adam Frank has experimented intuitively and insightfully with Gertrude Stein's plays through the medium of recorded sound and has opened up very enabling ways of understanding her notions of the setting through 'landscape theatre'. He claims that this process might be relevant to our critical appreciation of modernism more broadly:

> . . . the treatment of setting in Stein's landscape theatre shares something with the modernist practices across the arts: with flatness in Cezanne and the Cubists; with serialism in European music, and with the lucid yet oblique compositions of Erik Satie and (early) John Cage; with an emphasis on parataxis in modernist poetry; with an evenly distributed attention in phenomenology and psychoanalysis.[34]

This paragraph concludes a reading of Stein's notion of the landscape play that re-visions it in tandem with her lecture/essay 'Plays' through theories of affect and emotion influenced by William James, Silvan Tomkins and Wilfred Bion, who was a member of the Melanie Klein group of object relations analysts. To inflect this reading, I would propose that H.D.'s translations occupy a similar trajectory to Stein's plays in the ways they reconfigure notions of theatrical setting, acting through a radical reworking of character/plot and audience affect and reception.

Frank locates much of his analysis in the interface between phenomenology and psychoanalysis. For the psychoanalytical strand of his reading he relies on Bion's reworking of some fundamental Kleinian notions regarding projective identification, reintrojection, regressive phantasy and group experience. Klein's emphasis on the constitutive and formative relation to the body of the mother finds parallels with H.D.'s fascination with the mother, as with her emphasis on projection as both a primal psychoanalytic function and as a function of both poetry and cinema. However, the most evocative idea, which I believe could also be read into H.D.'s translations as landscape plays, is Frank's reading of Bion's relationship between the terms of container and contained, initially experienced of course within/without the mother's body:

> The container-contained relation is fundamentally reciprocal or reversible. A group may contain an individual, but so may an individual contain a group; similarly, a word (or other aesthetic form) may contain a meaning, but so may a meaning (such as a dream, a feeling, a perception) contain words (and other forms). In my reading of her landscape poetics, Stein seeks to compose plays that are reversible containers in Bion's sense in which experiences of reverie permit thinking to become possible both for audience members and for players on the stage. The problem of narrative theater lies in its failure to accommodate the to-and-fro of emotional coordination that leads to thinking; it leads, instead, to the 'nervousness' of emotional syncopation.[35]

Perhaps this is one way of comprehending and expanding Gregory's idea above that H.D.'s translations enact a kind of 'cosmopoeisis', yet still stand 'outside territorial containment'. For in a sense all theatre creates a vision/version of the world, one that always threatens with its own totality (Plato's theatrocracy, the renaissance and baroque notions of the *theatrum mundi*). However, the radical potential of the landscape play, both in the Stein and H.D. iterations, may lie in its ability (to reference Benjamin again) to render the container–contained relationship reciprocal and reversible, as Frank claims. This clearly undoes the binaries between form and content, word and image, and makes plays 'reversible containers'.

This impacts the ways in which an audience experiences the theatrical event through time, avoiding the confusion or collision of time systems between the time of the play and the time of the audience; it creates a flow of time, which in H.D.'s terms can be read as 'time-in-time' and 'time-out-of-time together'. That H.D. calls this the freedom of 'Greek time' is astonishing indeed, as it is parallel to Stein's modernist time. The function of the voice is crucial in this context, as the way the voice 'projects' time in both H.D. and Stein is premised not solely on meaning, but also on formal qualities like rhyme and rhythm. Here Frank's experiments with Stein's plays and recorded sound are very evocative. In similar ways, we could perhaps claim that the way time is employed by H.D. in her translations through the uses and 'abuses' of prosody, and through her attempts at what Prins calls 'the temporization of meter', also turn the container/contained dyad of the relationships between metre and voice inside out.

This landscape poetics, what Theis also calls processional poetics, has a huge emotional impact both on the players/performers and on the audience. Reading this poetics in terms of affect once again leads us to considering theories of spectatorship, but crucially also of acting. The 'nervousness' that Stein mentions in her essay relates to the emotional syncopation experienced by an audience due to the dissonant notions of time at work. However, we can also read this 'nervousness' as echoing Plato's *neurospasta*, where the physicalisation and embodiment of this temporised language creates an unease, a confusion, of body/voice, container/contained (what Plato calls 'a confusion of forms'). Viewed from another angle, however, this confusion and 'nervousness' may make physical an emotional awareness that reconstructs the body of both performer and spectator as a *machine*, a thinking, feeling machine. And this may be another way of drawing parallels between H.D.'s practice of translation and her practice of acting. The jagged, stylised, cutting movements of the character Astrid might already be contained in the temporising metres of the character of the translator H.D. This is how Theis further elaborates on Prin's work on H.D.'s poetological practice:

> Prins' understanding of how H.D.'s poetic feet integrate poetry, music and dance into phenomenological appreciation of 'dancing Greek letters' illuminates how H.D. performs a free-verse approach when negotiating the difficult prosody of classical choral odes. H.D. translates against a backdrop of tragedy, a form ideally suited for pursuing how the speaking voice's rhythm performs its drama upon the listening, landscaped world, visualizing these broken sentences and unfinished rhythms as rocks.[36]

This landscaped world is as much created and 'projected' as performed upon. So when we claim that H.D.'s translations enact a version of the original Euripidean plays, they also recreate these as landscape plays, where the relationship between the original and the translation is itself reversible and reciprocal. The conventions of theatricality are crucial in this context. This is not simply a case of performance acting as a metaphor for the whole enterprise. Rather, this kind of translation/landscape play is located at the interface between theatricality as a set of formal conventions, which comes with a history and a genealogy, and performativity as a linguistic/philosophical category.

Of course, *pace* Judith Butler and queer theory, but also the references to Melanie Klein mentioned by Frank, it is impossible not to read gender into this landscape. For Klein the primal container is the mother's body, and according to Kleinian psychoanalysis it is that initial relationship with that body that could be seen to be reworked, enacted in this schema of the landscape play. Interesting, too, that Benjamin's theorising of translation as that process that makes strange both the original language and the target language is given shape and metaphorised through images of motherhood and birth. Translation has the ability to create something new but also to rebirth the original, as he states in his essay.

The Translator as Dramaturg

More often than not this process of 'landscaping' theatre has been read as anti-Aristotelian. The emphasis on speech, song, movement and theatricality, what Aristotle calls *opsis*, at the expense of his supposedly more privileged concepts of plot, character and dramatic action, has been viewed to be at the heart of this quintessentially modernist practice. This is a reading of Aristotelian poetics that is dominant throughout many a modernist theatrical project (Brecht and the avant-garde are emblematic examples) and in many ways also pre-empts their scholarly and critical reception. This reading of Aristotle and Greek tragedy posits both the plays and their Aristotelian poetics as representative of an aesthetics (and politics) that is read as fundamentally anti-modernist in its discourses of representation, reception and spectatorship. It creates a somewhat schematic binary trope that may be useful for modernist manifesto-making, but may also miss some of the more nuanced and complex aspects of Aristotelian poetics. If we attempt, as we have been doing throughout this book, to read Aristotle in tandem with his teacher Plato, then a more critically enabling discourse may transpire, in the ways the 'ancient quarrel' is reinscribed within modernist experimentation in performance.

In turn, reading H.D.'s engagement with the plays of Euripides as works of translation but also as works of dramaturgy allows us to perhaps also reassess the dominant position of Aristotelianism (and not necessarily Aristotle) in the modernist encounter with Greek tragedy. H.D.'s translations/plays exhibit a very intimate knowledge of Euripides while also being experimental and radical, both in their formal/aesthetic and political/gendered aspirations.

More than her anglophone contemporary modernists, her work on the classics did not preclude her from working on the most modernist of media, the cinema. And when she brings her classicism to help her conceptualise the radical potential of cinematic form, she characteristically uses the paratactic 'and' in titles of her essays ('The Cinema and the Classics'). There is none of the Oedipal anxiety of influence and succession that we find in some of her contemporaries, with whom it has to be acknowledged she also worked with very closely. It is as if she bypasses the complex and sometimes inhibiting legacies of cultural capital inherited from the classics and Aristotelianism, and approaches the plays themselves directly. It is as if she unhinges the plays from their Aristotelian mould and their sometimes Oedipal critical reception, and rediscovers them. And in doing so, H.D. creates a relationship between the original Euripidean works and her modernist versions that is reversible and reciprocal, rendering both versions equally classical and modernist.

Notes

1. See Donald, Freidberg and Marcus (eds), *Close Up, 1927–1933*.
2. H.D., 'The Cinema and the Classics'.
3. Ernest Fenollosa, quoted in Chisolm, *Fenollosa*, p. 168.
4. See Friedman, *Penelope's Web*; Friedman, *Psyche Reborn*.
5. Gregory, *H.D. and Hellenism*, p. 118.
6. Ibid. p. 207.
7. H.D., *Helen in Egypt*.
8. Ibid. p. 3.
9. See Carrie Preston, 'Ritualized Reception: H.D.'s Anti-modern Poetics and Cinematics', in *Modernism's Mythic Pose*, pp. 191–238.
10. Quoted in Donald, Freidberg and Marcus (eds), *Close Up, 1927–1933*, p. 99.
11. Ibid.
12. H.D., 'The Mask and the Movietone' in Donald, Freidberg and Marcus (eds), *Close Up, 1927–1933*, p. 117.
13. H.D. 'Restraint', in Donald, Freidberg and Marcus (eds), *Close Up, 1927–1933*, p. 112.
14. Ibid. p. 110.
15. Anne Friedberg, 'Introduction to *Borderline* and the POOL Group', in Donald, Freidberg and Marcus (eds), *Close Up, 1927–1933*, pp. 212–20, p. 218.
16. See Harry A. Potamkin, 'The Aframerican Cinema', in Donald, Freidberg and Marcus (eds), *Close Up, 1927–1933*, pp. 65–72.
17. H.D., '*Borderline*: a POOL Film with Paul Robeson', in Donald, Freidberg and Marcus (eds), *Close Up, 1927–1933*, pp. 221–35, pp. 234–5.
18. Ibid. p. 234.
19. H.D., 'Joan of Arc' in Donald, Freidberg and Marcus (eds), *Close Up, 1927–1933*, pp. 130–3, p. 132.
20. H.D., *Selected Poems*, p. 35.
21. Prins, *Ladies' Greek*, pp. 200–1.
22. Ibid. p. 197.
23. See Chapter 4 for ways in which this notion of dramatic character also ties in with epic acting techniques and with what classical philosopher Christopher Gill calls the 'objective-participant' notion of tragic personhood.

24. Theis, 'Braving the Elements', pp. 100–1.
25. See Guattari and Deleuze, *Anti-Oedipus*; Guattari and Deleuze, *A Thousand Plateaus*.
26. Gregory, 'Respondent Essay', p. 121.
27. Stein, 'Plays'.
28. Stein, *Last Plays and Operas*, 'Introduction', p. x.
29. See Stein, *Doctor Faustus Lights the Lights*, pp. 415–16.
30. H.D., 'Red Roses for Bronze', in *Collected Poems, 1912–1944*, p. 223, p. 227.
31. See Stein, 'Plays', p. 429, p. 433.
32. H.D., *Hippolytus Temporises & Ion*, p. 185.
33. Stein, 'Plays', p. 438.
34. Frank, 'The Expansion of Setting in Gertrude Stein's Landscape Theatre'.
35. Ibid. p. 2.
36. Theis, 'Braving the Elements', p. 103.

5

EPIC, TRAGIC, DRAMATIC THEATRE AND THE BRECHTIAN PROJECT

This project has attempted to approach the modernist encounter with Greek tragedy as a performance practice. It has tried to tease out some of the ways modernist theatre-makers, translators and performance theorists thought through and experimented with some of their basic premises *through* Greek tragedy. Almost counterintuitively, the modernist quest for the ideal of performance as an autonomous aesthetic event takes shape and form through these sometimes tense, sometimes creative encounters. As phantom, ghost, nostalgic longing, spectre, scholarly/pseudo-scholarly/philosophical reflection, the relationship with ancient drama informs most experimental modernist theatrical endeavours. Calling upon 'the Greeks' acts as a type of shorthand that adds the aura of a classical lineage with its attendant cultural currency, while also facilitating risk-taking and experimentation. From Duncan's dances to Craig's designs to Pound's and H.D.'s translations, 'the Greeks' are present in order both to legitimise and to be reworked in a radical modernist manner. With Bertolt Brecht, however, the presence of 'the Greeks' and tragic drama in particular performs a slightly different function. Brecht too defines his edifice of epic theatre in relation to Greek drama, but this relationship is markedly different from all other cases within modernism, as epic theatre defines itself in direct opposition to the Greek model, or at least to a construction of it. At the same time, modernist performance would be unthinkable without Brecht.

The term 'Brechtian', we could claim, has acquired the same schematic and iconic status as 'Greek drama' and 'the Greeks' when discussing modernist performance, but also in literary and cultural theory. On the one hand, Brechtian aesthetics has been read primarily within the ideological constraints of the cold war as a form of cultural critique that lacks affect and is no more than crudely applied dialectic materialism. On the other hand, and in particular from poststructuralism onwards and in the ways that Brecht was championed by thinkers like Roland Barthes, Susan Sontag, Darko Suvin, Frederic Jameson and more recently in the writing of Hans-Thies Lehmann, his project had been adapted/adopted as part of the attempt to theorise the aesthetic encounter as embodied, reciprocal and political, where notions of pleasure and pedagogy are not read in binary opposition. Within this concept of the remobilisation of Brecht and Brechtian aesthetics,[1] it might be worthwhile revisiting, and perhaps complicating, Brecht's somewhat contentious relationship with Greek tragedy.

What does it mean to define a project against Greek tragedy and Aristotle? As we know, Brecht had no knowledge of classical Greek, nor was he versed in classical scholarship, which in his case would most certainly have been in the German vein. However, as the recent work of Martin Revermann has shown, he did own a copy of *Poetics*, which he marked up with his own typewritten pages of commentary inserted.[2] So when Brecht creates his famous binary list of traits, juxtaposing epic with dramatic theatre, he is performing a number of functions. This is a list that has helped to articulate and schematise many modernist experiments in performance. The way it appears on the page is equally important. Its stark use of binary columns attests to Brecht's debt to the aesthetics and politics of the avant-garde manifesto, while also acting as an imagistic example of his own idea of 'crude thinking'. This much-quoted *agon* of ideas and practices is worth quoting again, stressing both its uniqueness and its iterability, as Brecht's friend Walter Benjamin may have claimed:

DRAMATIC THEATRE	EPIC THEATRE
plot	narrative
implicates the spectator in the stage situation	terms the spectator into an observer, but
wears down his capacity for action	arouses his capacity for action
provides him with sensations	forces him to take action
experience	picture of the world
the spectator is involved in something	he is made to face something
suggestion	argument
instinctive feelings are preserved	brought to the point of recognition
the spectator is in the thick of it, shares the experience	the spectator stands outside, studies
the human being is taken for granted	the human being is the object of inquiry

he is unalterable	he is alterable and able to alter
eyes on the finish	eyes on the course
one scene makes another	each scene for itself
growth	montage
linear development	in curves
evolutionary determinism	jumps
man as a fixed point	man as a process
thought determines being	social being determines thought
feeling	reason

This much-reproduced table is once more presented here in an attempt to read it within a number of contexts: within the context of its own narrative; within the context of the avant-garde manifesto, as mentioned above; within the context of modernist aesthetics more generally; and, somewhat counterintuitively, within the context of 'the Greeks'.

What is initially striking about these two columns is that they appear to be rather more binary than dialectical. Read, however, as a prop or a modernist ready-made, which literally pops up out of the page and is itself part of a broader argument, might lend it more nuance and more poetry. The immediate precedent that may come to mind here is Sergei Eisenstein's 'Montage of Attractions', which was first published in the Soviet journal *Lef* in 1923. Like Brecht's piece, it appears as an accompaniment/commentary to a production: Brecht's to *The Rise and Fall of the City of Mahagony*, and Eisenstein's to the production of A. N. Ostrovsky's *Enough Stupidity in Every Wise man*. Brecht would have been aware of this, if not directly, then almost certainly through his friend Walter Benjamin, who had visited Moscow[3] before he scripted his own take on epic theatre, *Understanding Brecht*, originally written between 1930 and 1939.[4] The links between Brecht, the Russian formalists and the radical theatre-makers of the early Soviet era are well established, and much of his terminology echoes theirs. Meyerhold spoke of the 'dialectical actor'; Victor Schklovsky's notion of estrangement maps onto Brecht's *Verfremdunseffekte*, as does the fundamental formalist opening up of the relationship between *fabula* (plot) and *syuzhet* (narrative), and Brecht's ideas about a theatre of amazement and naivety also appear in Eisenstein's notion of the 'Attraction'.[5]

When Brecht sketches out these two columns almost in the tradition of the agitprop performances of the Soviet Blue Blouses, he does so within the broader context of his polemic about opera, and he states in a note, framing his lists, that 'the table does not show absolute antitheses but mere shifts of accent. In a communication of fact, for instance, we may choose whether to stress the element of emotional suggestion or that of plain rational argument.'[6] So much for the criticism that sees this list as prescriptive. Again, viewing it as a stage within a stage, or as an imagist poem, or as a manifesto, or as a ready-made strategically placed/animated within his broader argument, will stress its performative character rather than its programmatic one. It might be worth stressing that Brecht formulates these thoughts about epic in conjunction to opera, highlighting the significance of music. He states that '*a radical separation of the elements*' is crucial for the development of epic theatre. '*Words, music and setting must become more independent of one another.*'[7] The main target here is Wagner's *Gesamtkunstwerk* and Brecht is very explicit about this. The terms he uses to describe the totalising power of these 'fused' arts are equally damning – 'muddle, degraded, feed' – and the impact they have on the 'passive/suffering' spectator are equally troubling – 'hypnotic, witchcraft, sordid intoxication'. These are, of course, terms that we have also come to associate with Brecht's critique of what he understood to be Aristotelian theatre. At the same time, however, they tap into the long tradition of anti-theatricality and indeed remobilise or refunctionalise its basic premises for the purposes of his own thinking. One could even claim that they remobilise the ancient quarrel, reworking quintessentially Platonic terms that also underline the function of music as a crucial motor for affect in terms of the overall impact on spectatorship.

During the same period that Brecht is formulating his ideas, Walter Benjamin (following on from his trip to Moscow, where he observed Meyerhold at work) also begins to write his seminal essays on epic theatre. His writings on epic theatre, in many ways more philosophically grounded than Brecht's own and less aphoristic, are also less shy about proclaiming their sources, and in true Benjaminian style are more quotational. Here is how Benjamin conceptualises similar ideas about spectatorship:

> Simply by the fact of appealing to an 'audience' – which continues to exist in its old, opaque form only for the theatre, but characteristically, no longer for film – the critic becomes, whether he means it or not, the advocate of what the ancients used to call 'theatrocratia': the use of theatre to dominate the masses by manipulating their reflexes and sensations – the exact opposite of responsible collectives freely choosing their positions.[8]

Here Benjamin appears as an insightful reader not only of Plato, but of Brecht as well. He situates epic within its contemporary developments in film (with a nod to Eisenstein), and connects it with the longue durée of the anti-theatrical tradition, referencing Plato's famous quotation in the *Laws*. At the same time, further on in the same paragraph, he reworks Brecht's notions of ' innovations' and 'renovations', quoting his friend from the above text ('The Modern Theatre is the Epic Theatre')[9] while also anticipating the criticism against this project that it is fundamentally against 'free choice'. And here again is the quotation from Plato that I believe both writers remobilise:

Afterward, in the course of time an unmusical license set in with the appearance of poets who were men of genius, but ignorant of what is right and legitimate in the realm of the muses. Possessed by a frantic and uncontrolled lust for pleasure, they contaminated laments with hymns and paeans with dithyrambs, they actually imitated the strains of the flute on the harp, and created a universal confusion of forms . . . By composition of such a kind and discourse to the same effect, they naturally inspired the multitude with a contempt of musical law, and a conceit of their own competence as judges. Thus our once silent audiences have found a voice, in the persuasion that they have understood what is good and bad in art; the old sovereignty of the best, aristocracy, has given way to an evil sovereignty of the audience, a theatrocracy. (*Laws*, 700a–b).[10]

Again Plato re-emerges as a performance theorist, and a Brechtian one at that. In this way we could even claim that in its attack against Aristotelian theatre, epic theatre refunctionalises Platonic thinking. In many ways, Benjamin's own 'aestheticisation thesis' could also be read as yet a further development of his thinking about epic and theatrocracy. Plato's fear of a theatre that allows the 'silent audiences' to have a voice and indeed to be judges is, however, exactly the function of theatre that Brecht wants to reignite through his view of epic. In many ways, to call Brecht a Platonist might be counterintuitive. On the other hand, the ways that Brecht describes the 'culinary' experience of theatre spectatorship chimes well with Plato's view. In a sense, Brecht confirms that many of the tenets of anti-theatricality might indeed carry the kind of politico-ethical tarnish of which Plato accuses them. Which is exactly why Brecht sets out to redefine, rework, rewrite the whole edifice of theatrical practice itself. Rather than simply dismissing the anti-theatrical legacies of Plato, Brechtian thinking – and Benjaminian thinking – reiterate them in such a way that at once fully acknowledges the power of the spectacle to deceive and mesmerise[11] (to turn aristocracy into theatrocracy). In this instance, however, that very idea of theatrocracy is now rewritten as a fundamental and constitutive element of *democracy*. So, like Plato, Brecht believes that theatre creates the ability of an audience to act as judges, but this is no longer a conceit; it becomes a political imperative.

We can trace similar Platonic echoes in Benjamin's aestheticisation thesis, which also scrutinises the complex and fraught relationships between aesthetics and politics. For him and for the radical critical thinkers that followed in the wake of the historical avant-garde, whose chief proponent can be seen in the Situationist Guy Debord's *Society of the Spectacle*,[12] theatricalisation, the spectacle, becomes the locus of both salvation and damnation. When Benjamin claims in *The Work of Art in the Age of Mechanical Reproducibility* (1939) that 'Fascism tends towards an aestheticization of politics,' he is in a sense reiterating Plato's theatrocracy:

> Humankind, which once, in Homer, was an object of contemplation for the Olympian gods, has now become one for itself. Its self-alienation has reached the point where it can experience its own annihilation as a supreme aesthetic pleasure. *Such is the aestheticizing of politics, as practiced by fascism. Communism replies* by politicizing art.[13]

We can see how Plato's idea of the 'conceit' is worked into Benjamin's idea of the false consciousness of an audience that thinks it is 'expressing itself' (which has become the mantra of identity politics). But the very same artwork can become refunctionalised to bring about redemption and critique. And for Benjamin that politicising of art finds its prime example and paradigm in epic theatre. It is also noteworthy that his Greek reference here is not tragedy (as it is for Brecht), but Homer. Homer wrote epic, and when Plato refers to ideas about performance and spectatorship, he too is referring to the performance of epic.

Modernist Epics

In order to perhaps better scrutinise how Brechtian aesthetics relates to tragedy and the tragic, it might be worthwhile also examining the ways his project adapts the ideas of epic. In many ways part of the modernist effort to 'rehabilitate' various traditions of epic from the literary/poetic, oral and theatrical traditions and to align them with the critical/radical experiments in both arts and politics, Brecht's reworking of the term 'epic' is in line with more recent research in the field that both presents a renewed understanding of the form and 'reignites' its critical potential. In a recent study, *Epic Performances: From the Middle Ages into the Twenty-First Century*, Fiona Macintosh stresses and insightfully discusses Brecht's evolution of the term 'epic':

> Moreover, whilst Brecht in the late 1920s and early 1930s followed Schiller and Goethe in his apparent misapprehension that, according to Aristotle, epic and drama were opposites, by 1935 both his position and his understanding of any Aristotelian polarity had evolved ... Now, it seems, 'epic drama' and 'dramatic epic' are both possibilities according to his schema.[14]

The ways that Brecht 'misunderstands' tragedy through German Romanticism have been well charted. Equally fascinating, however, are the ways that he remobilises epic in a model where epic and dramatic are no longer seen to be in opposition. Again, the parallel we might perhaps draw here is with Sergei Eisenstein, who in his theorising of montage and its political efficacy turns to the epic of John Milton, *Paradise Lost*, and to epics of his fellow modernist

James Joyce, *Ulysses* and *Finnegan's Wake*. This view of epic expresses a distinct modernist attempt to disassociate it from its perceived structural links with notions of empire, from its problematic gender politics and from the perception that it is formally conservative, while aligning it with the radical formal and political experiments of modernism and the avant-garde; particularly with the possibilities offered by that quintessentially modernist medium, film. In this context Brecht's redefinition of epic can be read as parallel to the ways the genre has been reworked by James Joyce and by Sergei Eisenstein. The latter, writing in his foundational text on montage, 'Word and Image', that Milton offers 'a first rate school in which to study montage', draws an iconic comparison between his own directing of the 'Battle on Ice' scene in his film *Alexander Nevsky* and Milton's 'The Battle in Heaven' in Book VI of *Paradise Lost*, stating that 'there is much in it that is very instructive for the film-maker'.[15] In this context we can perhaps claim that Brecht, like Eisenstein, draws upon a constellation of writers usually not grouped together (Milton, Keats, Shelley, Mayakovsky)[16] in his attempt to revitalise the epic tradition for the purposes of a politically engaged, modernist aesthetic practice; for Eisenstein this is film, for Brecht it is theatre.

Another attraction of epic for Brecht may also be seen in the ways it valorises the popular and oral traditions, drawing on a genealogy of literary creation that is more or less authorless or relies on a model of authorship that is multivocal and collective, delineating a sometimes imagined, sometimes perhaps real understanding of 'the voice of the people'. In terms of theatre historiography, this locates epic not solely negatively against 'dramatic theatre', but positively within a tradition that itself has a long and distinguished history and comes with its own formal conventions and modes of representation. Again, where Brecht – somewhat counterintuitively for a Marxist – obfuscates his sources and predecessors, Benjamin makes these more explicit. He writes in *What is Epic Theatre?*:

> For the fact is that ever since the Greeks, the search for the untragic hero on the European stage has never ceased . . . This is not the place to trace the path which winds through the Middle Ages, in Hroswitha and the mystery plays . . . If, that is, one can speak of a path at all, rather than an overgrown stalking-track along which the legacy of medieval and baroque drama has crept to us over the sublime but barren massif of classicism. This track reappears today, rough and untended as it may be, in the plays of Brecht.[17]

Here Benjamin almost creates a counter-genealogy for epic theatre, locating it within the workings of the medieval mystery plays and in the works of the legendary canoness of Gandersheim Abbey, Hroswitha (*c.* 935–973), who is also the first female historian and poet of Germany. It is extraordinary to place epic within this tradition, at once taking it away from its modernist 'newness' but at the same time placing it within a legacy that is counter-hegemonical in other ways. Like many theatre-makers and theorists of the avant-garde, and particularly the Russian constructivists like Tretyakov and Meyerhold (whose work Benjamin had experienced in Moscow), the oral and popular tradition becomes a site for an emancipatory and revolutionary aesthetic. Despite what may be considered a 'theocratic' and Christian legacy, this medieval aesthetic is viewed as anti-Renaissance, anti-anthropocentric, anti-humanist and anti-individualistic, carrying with it a world-view that is at once collective and ritualistic. And it is these conventions and forms that Brecht finds attractive for the uses of epic (allegory, non-psychological characters, etc.). We see this in the ways that Brecht himself rewrites biblical tropes (in *The Caucasian Chalk Circle*, for example). We also see it in the ways that the figure of the 'sage' and the storyteller become central for Benjamin's thinking. This historiography of epic places it within a popular and irreverent tradition that is anti-tragic and anti-dramatic. As such, it proves useful – as it did for many radical modernist theatre-makers – in the quest for an engaged form of theatre that is both popular *and* formally experimental. It is no coincidence that in the same breath, and continuing the vivid imagery of the 'overgrown stalking track', Benjamin aligns Plato with Georg Lukács, as both recognising 'the undramatic nature of the highest form . . . the sage'. This sage, however, despite being 'undramatic' (i.e. untragic in this configuration), helps to create a notion of epic theatre that is 'any the less philosophical'.[18]

The Sage, the Rhapsode and the Epic Performer

The figure of the sage, Plato's rhapsode, also inflects the ways epic understands the role of the actor. Both Benjamin and Brecht insightfully pinpoint a fascinating aspect of Platonic thinking regarding the art of the actor and its ethico-political efficacy. David Wiles highlights that contemporary scholars are somewhat frustrated by the fact that Plato's theorising about the art of the performer chooses to focus on Ion, the rhapsode, rather than on the more obvious figure of the tragic actor. Wiles – rightly, I believe – states that 'Ion served Plato's turn better because he recited words of the *Iliad* that had been performed many times before, with the consequence that his craft was more obviously a second order of mimesis.'[19] This notion of 'a second order of mimesis' that Wiles insightfully stresses can be read as parallel to what Benjamin believes to be the epic actor's 'most important achievement': 'To make gestures quotable'.[20] This idea of the quotable gesture, which is further developed by Brecht through the concept of *gestus*, is arguably one of the most fascinating but obscure contributions of epic to theories of acting. Positioning it within this Platonic lineage, which starts with the figure of the sage, helps to create a genealogy for epic acting that views it as rewriting both oral and classical theories of acting. These theories may start with Plato's rhapsode, but also have affiliations with modes of recitation and rhetoric – and, as Wiles states, also inform Shakespearean styles of acting. In this sense, this view of classical acting, which originates in the figure of Plato's sage rather than on the Athenian tragic stage, could also perhaps help us to better understand Brecht's somewhat illusive term *gestus*.

A central kernel of epic acting, *gestus*, has inspired considerable reflection within performance theory, partly because Brecht remained quite vague about it and partly because it is an evocative term that itself invites rewriting, quoting and reinterpretation. In effect, it is a term that could very well be mapped onto the more contemporary term 'performative'. The ways that the performative originates from speech act theory, phenomenology and queer theory might also find analogies in the concept of *gestus*. As that quotable gesture that comes into being through embodiment, theatrical phenomenology and audience reception, *gestus* may also be located at that very enabling interface between performance, as a set of theatrical conventions with a history and a genealogy, and performativity, as a distinct philosophical term that has a lineage in both linguistic theory and phenomenology and – crucially – has a distinct political efficacy. Indeed, we may claim that *gestus* may be one of the epic conventions that facilitates a theatrical experience which is at once naïve, and, crucially, *philosophical*. For Benjamin this proves to be one of the ways that the epic actor is linked both to the popular tradition and also to the philosophical tradition of modernity, with self-reflection, quotability and critique acting as its prime emblem:

> If, then, the actor on the old stage sometimes found himself, as 'comedian', rubbing shoulders with the priest, in epic theatre he finds himself beside the philosopher.
>
> [. . .]
>
> 'Making gestures quotable' is the actor's most important achievement; he must be able to space his gestures as the compositor produces type.
>
> [. . .]
>
> The actor must show an event, and he must show himself. He naturally shows the event by showing himself, and he shows himself by showing the event. Although these two tasks coincide, they must not coincide to such a point that the contrast (difference) between them disappears.[21]

In other words, performance and the performative are not identical, and in a fascinating way, again theatrical conventions do the work of elucidating both that difference and that parallel relationship. Sometimes in contemporary theory the two terms are conflated (everything is performance). What epic theatre teaches us through the constellation of ideas that fall under the term 'gestus' is that conflating these two terms is bad philosophy, in the way that perhaps a psychological actor may conflate role and character and create bad theatre, both in Brechtian and Platonic terms. And it is a similar warning that is voiced by Plato through his presentation of the figure of the rhapsode, or the 'sage', as Benjamin re-terms the classical epic actor.

FROM HÖLDERLIN TO THE POSTDRAMATIC (VIA BRECHT'S EPIC)

Another crucial concept that may be seen to have at once a modern and a classical cast is the term 'caesura', which Benjamin borrows from Hölderlin. Brecht's notions of both an acting and a narrative style that is based on 'interruption' rather than on linear continuity also has an epic lineage. It is the same principle that Eisenstein found attractive in his reworking of classical epic as montage. The *in medias res* trope of epic narration folds over into the opening up of the relationship between 'plot' and 'narrative', and also into the notion of the actor, who at once plays and comments on the role. This caesura that Hölderlin conceptualises in his essays on Oedipus creates the jolt, the cut and that fundamental 'doubleness' of theatre – a 'doubleness' that Plato labelled as a mind-numbing 'double phantasy', but that epic theatre rewrites as the possibility of a critically engaged and politically aware theatre for the purposes of modernity.

Interestingly enough, this is another term that has had more of an impact on musicology than on acting theory, in a similar trajectory to the term *gestus*. Hölderlin's definition of this term also combines classical resonances, poetic theory and, primarily through his crucial concept of the 'counter-rhythmic', music theory.[22] We may see another Platonic parallel here in the ways that Plato also conceptualises the art of the rhapsode and the 'confusion' – interruption – of forms by drawing on music. We can see such a similar conflation of ideas from poetics, acting and music in Hölderlin's definition of the caesura:

> The tragic transport is actually empty and the least restrained. So, in the rhythmic sequence of the representations wherein transport presents itself, there becomes necessary what in poetic meter is called caesura, the pure word, the counter-rhythmic rupture, namely in order to meet the onrushing change of representation at its highest point in such a way that very soon it is not change of representation which appears but representation itself.[23]

Hölderlin's complex reworking of the term 'caesura' adds to it a physical, almost violent dimension that allows it to enact his notion of the 'counter-rhythmic rupture'. In effect a classical philological term is materialised, given a performative inflection and turned into its theatrical equivalent. We might even say it is turned into a Brechtian *gestus*, providing Brecht's equally dense term with a philological lineage. For Philippe Lacoue-Labarthe, this poetic form as read by Hölderlin becomes the basic premise of theatricality itself:

> The *caesura* is the condition of possibility for manifestation, for the (re)presentation (*Darstellung*) of the tragic.
>
> Such is the law or, if you prefer, the principle of its theatricality.[24]

In some ways Hölderlin's own translations can be read as manifesting such a caesura, one that at once creates a 'rupture' from the Greeks but also points towards their modernity. These wonderful translations entail their own theatricality, where the texts themselves enact and embody a fundamentally new relationship to the Greek model of theatre. Rather than posing an example that needs to be imitated, as in previous forms of classicism and revivalism, Hölderlin's translations of Greek tragedy use them as a springboard and open up a more ambivalent and fraught relationship with the prototype, one that is free to radically rewrite it but also to 'correct' its failures and shortcomings, no doubt creating the possibility of more failures and shortcomings in the process (as contemporary scholars have noted about the use of systematic errors in his own translations). Françoise Dastur claims that this makes us 'distinguish between the model and the example, between what has to be imitated in a static sense of reproduction, and what can be followed in a dynamic and inventive way'.[25] We can see this dynamic echoed in Benjamin's aestheticisation thesis as the difference between mechanical reproduction and the work of art that is constructed according to the principle of reproducibility itself.[26] In this sense Greek tragedy itself emerges as such a work that is structured along the principle of reproducibility itself; one that allows it through its theatricality to act as a springboard for modernist experiments in the relationships between form and content, textuality and embodiment, and in the relationships between the ancients and the moderns themselves. Importantly, we could also claim that this reconfiguration of the relationship between the example and the model resurfaces in Brecht's own creations of 'models' for his epic theatre – the first of which, significantly, was based on his production of Hölderlin's *Antigone*, the *Antigone-Model 1948*.

As Hans-Thies Lehmann rightly claims, Hölderlin's remarks on Oedipus and Antigone not only had the function of critically elucidating ancient tragedy, but importantly, also aimed at creating a *model* for modern tragedy. He provides a necessary gloss on Hölderlin's term that also pre-echoes its Brechtian reworking:

> Hölderlin sketches the concept of a *caesura* of seeing that bears on theatre as a whole: it affects the positions of spectator and knowledge, as well as the precarious relation between rational insight, affect and mimetic identification. His model, which posits necessary interruption

in tragedy, also holds in an age that no longer has seers and understands mythology only in aesthetic terms. According to Hölderlin, the involved spectator must, at certain points, become an *exvolved* spectator for tragic experience to take place.[27]

And it is precisely this *exvolved* spectator that Brecht evokes as well. However, as Lehmann clearly analyses for Hölderlin, the caesura 'does not break with the tragic; it elucidates it. For Brecht, the caesura invalidates the tragic'. Lehmann adds a revealing parenthesis: '(at least according to his stated intention)'.[28] If we read Brecht against the grain of his own intentionality and in conjunction with Hölderlin and Benjamin, then perhaps a more involved relationship with tragedy emerges. And in this context the constellation of terms aligned around the term 'caesura' – innovation, renovation, interruption, self-reflection, *gestus* – prove very enabling in creating a kind of genealogy that at once links Brecht with Hölderlin, and less obviously through him to Greek tragedy, or at least a particular reading of Greek tragedy. This genealogy of Greek tragedy also goes back to German Romanticism, not so much through the idealist interpretations of Schelling, but through the more radical lens of Hölderlin and Nietzsche. And this 'tradition' is one that approaches tragedy not solely in terms of its great ideas, themes and humanist anxieties, but also, and crucially, as a performance practice. In this sense the notion of the caesura – reworked as *gestus* by Brecht – becomes a 'toolkit' of sorts; a method, as Fredric Jameson would claim in his work on Brecht.[29]

It might be useful in this context to tease out some of the ways that the term 'caesura' folds over into performance practice. When Hölderlin states in the above 'definition' of the term that it interrupts 'tragic transport', we could perhaps read this on the level of narrative and action, the plot/narrative binary from Brecht's list. It is here where the ideas of interruption and innovation work to create epic notions of an episodic narrative, one that this study has linked to traditional epic narratology. In addition, 'tragic transport' might also be the way Hölderlin understands classical ideas about metaphor, in an attempt to read the classical etymology of the term – the transference of meaning from one term, idea or image to another on a syntagmatic level. So, when Hölderlin claims that this 'transport' is interrupted, we could in turn perhaps read this notion of 'tragic transport' as going 'against metaphor', as Giles Deleuze would claim.[30] What is interrupted in this sense is the spectator's desire to impose, interpret a direct and 'simple' metaphorical meaning onto the narrative/plot. This in turn creates what Hölderlin calls the 'counter-rhythmic rupture' which in a sense 'pushes' the spectator to consider representation itself, what Lacoue-Labarthe calls 'the principle of its theatricality' and Lehmann terms 'the exvolved spectator'. To this double function Lehmann also adds a third, indicatively relating to the way this jolt of the caesura once again doubles up, fractures upon the spectator as subject, proposing a new and, I would claim, modernist concept of subjectivity itself:

> Tragic experience deals a blow to the half (or entirely unconscious idea) that the subject possesses self-identical status (whether familial, national, religious etc.) In other words the subject experiences caesura. What is more, everyone physically present in the theatre – both performers and spectators – is denied affirmation of this presence. No position, thesis or claim is offered; instead, ex-position, de-position, occurs. 'Exposing' to be translated as a caesura inscribed into consciousness, the split between the subject and meaning.[31]

This is Lehmann's evocative rereading of the caesura through Hölderlin via Benjamin, on three levels: narrative, self-reflection and subjectivity. For Lehmann this also folds over into his reading of the relationship between tragedy and postdramatic theatre. Indicatively, he proceeds to cite as examples 'Certain productions by Jan Fabre',[32] who features as one of Lehmann's chosen directors whose work embodies his notion of the postdramatic. However, and even prior to the advent of the postdramatic and Lehmann's coining of the term, we may already see the seeds of this evocative term in the modernist encounter between classical tragedy and Brecht's epic theatre. For despite the misconceptions, misreadings, binary and manifesto-like formulations, Brecht's encounter with Greek tragedy in a sense sets the stage for the emergence of what Lehmann, himself working within a Brechtian tradition, would later term 'postdramatic'. This is more so the case if we read Brecht in conjunction with Benjamin as both expanding on and revising the radical legacies of German Romanticism through Hölderlin and Nietzsche. For whether consciously, intentionally or not, directors like Jan Fabre or Theodoros Terzopoulos (who actually trained with the Berliner Ensemble) and their radical takes on Greek tragedy are epigones of Brecht and all the modernist encounters with Greek tragedy. In this sense their work is both postdramatic *and* post-epic, where just like the term 'postmodern', the prefix signals both an opposition and a strong attachment, debt to the main noun.

The third level that Lehmann draws above in his formulation of the postdramatic falls under the label of 'subjectivity', which he reads both in the ways the subject/performer is presented on the stage and in the ways the subject of the spectator is reconfigured. This aspect is particularly pertinent in the ways theories of acting are reworked in the epic and Brechtian legacies. We have already teased out the ways some of these tropes could be read as revisiting traditions of the epic actor through the figure of Plato's rhapsode. It might be equally interesting to probe some of the ways that Brechtian acting might relate to, or even rework, tragic understandings of notions of subjectivity and the acting tropes that they entail. In some ways this approach would be going against one of the fundamental binaries created by Brecht, that between the 'tragic character' and the 'epic character'. For Benjamin the 'untragic hero' is a fundamental premise of epic theatre, and one of the ways it is linked to what he calls 'the path which winds through the Middle Ages' and locates epic within a genealogy of both popular, oral performance and ritualistic medieval drama. He writes:

> For the fact is that ever since the Greeks, the search for the untragic hero on the European stage has never ceased. Despite all the classical revivals, the great dramatists have always kept as far away as possible from the authentic Greek figure of tragedy.[33]

Here as elsewhere in the work of both Brecht and Benjamin we see a conflation of the 'Greek figure of tragedy' primarily with the ways that figure was interpreted by German Romanticism. The glaring exception is, of course, Hölderlin and his views on Oedipus and Antigone. As analysed above, this reading, one indeed that both Brecht and Benjamin can be read as following in relation to the concept of *gestus*, offers other avenues for understanding notions of the tragic hero. There may also be parallels and similarities in the ways character/role/subjectivity appear in the Greek tragedies themselves, to the ways that these notions are worked under the umbrella of Brechtian/Benjaminian epic. In turn this notional interface may also offer ways of reading Greek ideas of character and acting and epic ideas of character and acting, not necessarily as identical, but perhaps as part of a continuum of acting traditions that deal with anti-psychological, gestural, stylised and communal notions of character which in turn translate into equivalent acting styles. For the ways that the figures/roles of Greek tragedy are written, the textual ways they appear to us on the page, presuppose notions of acting that are primarily anti-psychological. In turn these figures might have more in common with epic anti-heroes than may be initially apparent, or at least as they are interpreted in Brecht's own writing.

Tragic and Epic Characters (or Once More with Feeling)

In order to propose this counterintuitive reading I will draw on recent studies of Greek tragedy, especially the recent 'emotional' turn in classical studies,[34] where ideas of affect and reception become central on the one hand to the understanding of the workings of the 'tragic character' and on the other to the ways notions of sympathy, empathy, identification and/or distance are negotiated through the role of the spectator. Rarely is the Brechtian project read as inhabiting the same phenomenological trajectory as recent performance studies. However, read as a precursor to Lehmann's postdramatic, and in respect to the attention paid to the centrality of the spectator, we may claim that it is located on the same trajectory and may itself be read as ushering in

the contemporary phenomenological turn in performance studies. This is especially relevant in the ways the phenomenology of emotions has been studied
in recent classical scholarship. I would claim that this turn to 'feelings', which
might initially appear as somewhat incongruous within traditional classical
scholarship, may partly at least be the result of the the past twenty years or
so of reception studies. Within this context it also results from the particular
demands that the tragic protagonists especially place on the art of the actor.
The extremity of most of the tragic roles (Oedipus, Medea, Klytemnestra,
Antigone, Hippolytus, Orestes, Agave et al.) requires a radical rethinking
of acting, especially when it comes to the representation of emotions. And,
somewhat counterintuitively, Brechtian, epic ideas about acting have proven to
be some of the most enabling for late twentieth- and early twenty-first-century
renditions of tragic character, especially in the ways they negotiate the complex
relationships between empathy, sympathy, identification and estrangement.

Following the broad framework that we have been sketching out in this
chapter regarding the relationships between tragic character/role/subjectivity
and the epic renditions of the same trajectory (character/role/subjectivity), I
would like to revisit the seeming clash or binary that Benjamin sets up, following Brecht, between the so-called 'tragic hero' and 'untragic hero'. Rather than
viewing this in opposition, I would like to examine the interface between the
great tragic roles of Greek tragedy and the great epic roles of Brechtian theatre.
The binding link is the work of Hölderlin, to whom both Benjamin and Brecht
owe a huge debt, whether acknowledged or not. Possibly the most epic roles
are Brecht's epic mothers, whom feminist criticism and performance have both
critiqued *and* embraced. We can discern a similar double movement in the
ways the great tragic female protagonists have been received by contemporary
criticism and performance. Indeed, one of the most critically outstanding and
noteworthy repercussions of reception theory and the democratisation of the
classics has been the emphasis on the female roles and the shift from viewing
them either as direct reflections of the ancient Greek state of women or as
straight-out misogynistic renditions of women (either celebratory or critical),
to more complex, nuanced and enabling vehicles for performance and critique.
This is especially pertinent if we take on board the men-playing-women
convention, which opens up and examines the links between biological sex and
represented gender, or between the phenomenal body and the semiotic body
on the stage.[35] It is this aspect amongst many, I would argue, that makes tragic
characters attractive and open to an epic reading. Like Brecht's epic mothers,
Greek tragedy too is obsessed with various mothers: murderous, desiring,
caring, castrating mothers; and it is especially concerned with their reproductive function, their ability to create life and reproduce the world. I would
claim that Brecht's epic mothers share similar concerns. The anxieties about
parenthood, and fatherhood in particular, that many Greek tragedies express

are also parallel to the ways Brecht's mothers appear as emblems of the 'means of production' and, of course, reproduction. Both Brecht and Greek tragedy are concerned with the politics, ethics and representational aesthetics of reproduction, in a sense taking the most 'natural' of functions and making it strange (*deinon*). This way we could even claim that both modes are obsessed with mothers as reproduction machines, where the term *mechane* is again borrowed from Hölderlin, meaning not simple 'mechanistic' reproduction, but embodied critical thinking, as in the Greek terms *polymechanos* and *polytropos*.

Mothers prove useful for epic as a way of denaturalising and defamiliarising the most 'natural' of functions, motherhood. In similar ways they prove useful for Greek tragedies in the ways they embody, always through the male body, anxieties about fatherhood, autochthony, lineage, kinship and kingship. In exploring this theme and the formal demands it poses, this argument will follow a double trajectory. On the one hand, it will propose a fantastic dialogue or interface between the most monstrous or consummate of Greek tragic mothers – Medea – and Brecht's epic mothers (from *The Mother*, *Mother Courage* and *The Caucasian Chalk Circle*); and on the other, it will examine Brecht's own reworking of the anti-mother of Greek tragedy, Antigone. One focuses on the theoretical encounter between tragic and epic notions of character, and the other on the ways that Brecht's actual staging of *The Antigone of Sophocles* (partly based on Hölderlin's text) enacts his own more complex and nuanced relationship with Greek tragedy.

Writing about Brecht's early production of *The Mother*, Benjamin locates the central role solidly within the context of Marxist criticism that views the family itself as the laboratory of capitalism. He writes in his review, utilising a vocabulary that was also to prove enabling to the traditions of socialist feminism:

> It asks itself: can the family be dismantled so that its components may be socially refunctioned? These components are not so much the members of the family themselves as their relationships with one another. Of these, it is clear that none is more important than the relationship between mother and child. Furthermore, the mother, among all family members, is the most unequivocally determined as to her social function: she produces the next generation. The question raised by Brecht's play is: can this social function become a revolutionary one, and how? In a capitalist economic system, the more directly a person is engaged in production relations, the more he or she is subject to exploitation. Under the conditions of today, the family is an organization for the exploitation of the woman as mother.[36]

In the face of Pelagea Vlassova in *The Mother* ('widow of a worker and mother of a worker'),[37] we find an instance of a 'positive' mother figure. This is not always the case in Brecht's other plays, however, where we find sometimes good, sometimes 'good enough' and sometimes straight-out 'bad mothers'. In all instances these mothers appear as what Benjamin calls 'praxis incarnate'. He repeats the phrase 'the mother is praxis incarnate'[38] twice within the short review. Here the term *praxis* evokes Marxist terminology, but also, I would claim, could be read as an aspect of the *performative*, especially in the ways that it always entails embodiment ('incarnate'). This reading of the performative that I have been mobilising throughout this study sees it as located both within its origins in linguistic theory and philosophy of language,[39] and within its more recent rewritings in queer theory, which add to it a very definite political and activist dimension.[40] In this sense I propose to reimagine Benjamin's idea of epic mothers as 'praxis incarnate' as somehow located at the interface between performance – as a formal set of theatrical conventions – and performativity as a philosophico-political discourse.

In turn I would also like to examine how this notion of the performative may have a bearing on the contemporary understanding of tragic character, as evidenced in the role of Medea. The concept of the performative may also offer ways of approaching the function of the emotions of Medea, in terms both of the make-up of her character and its reception by the spectator. The *phrike*,[41] horror, that is experienced both on the stage and in the auditorium, and the emotional extremity it garners, places demands on both the actor and the spectator. How are we to understand this monstrosity, and why is it that within the context of all the horrific and abject events of Greek tragedy, Medea's killing of her children occupies a particularly distinguished position on the scale of horrors? As we know, Euripides also allows her to get away with it. Again, this to me seems like a very Brechtian move, in taking the most 'natural' of emotions and turning it into something utterly strange and incomprehensible. Still, the concept of the performative in this context may allow us to view the function of the emotions – in both role and spectator – as going beyond and somehow bridging the binaries between constructivism/essentialism, innate/external, universal/particular, embodiment/textuality. In a similar vein I suggest that we could also read the role of Medea as 'praxis incarnate'; a 'praxis' also in the Aristotelian sense which, through the function of motherhood, examines and enacts ideas about the relationships between men and women, mothers and fathers, Greeks and barbarians, autochthony and otherness, reproduction and patriarchy.

This reading, which locates Medea within a theatrical genealogy of dramatic character that leads right up to Brecht's Mother Courage, may not be as incompatible as it initially appears. Indeed, drawing on the work of classical philosophers, and particularly the work of Christopher Gill,[42] the notion of tragic character may be read as bearing possibly the initial traits, at least in the Western canon of theatre, of what we may today term epic character. Gill sets up a very helpful opposition between what he terms the 'subjective-individualist' and the 'objective-participant' understanding of personhood. The former chimes well with modern psychological views of character as conscious of itself as a unified 'I' – as an autonomous entity, able to make decisions and express emotions as a disinterested moral unit, abstracted from interpersonal or communal attachments; it presupposes a kind of 'transcendental freedom' that understands itself as possessing a unique personal identity. The latter views its existence in relationships with both other humans and other forms of life more generally. It derives its sense of self as contingent and its 'psycho-ethical life is seen as a dialogue'.[43] Gill insightfully calls this view of tragic character 'The Divided Self" and states that it is particularly clear when tragic roles like Medea actually conduct dialogues with themselves on stage. The instance he underlines is when Medea literally divides into two personas and debates with herself whether she should perform the horrific deed or not. This aspect can also be seen in the two different mothers of *The Caucasian Chalk Circle*.

It can also be read into that most iconic moment of *gestus*, Mother Courage's, and Helene Weigel's 'silent scream'. This much quoted and analysed performance event has sometimes been read as Weigel herself somehow going against Brecht's 'cold' and disinterested V-effect and channelling her own identity as a mother, hence bringing the much-desired and quintessentially feminine 'emotion' to her response. This reading on the one hand goes against the fundamental premise of the play, to read the mother-machine as part of the war-machine, and on the other it reintroduces the concept of psychological character as structurally bound with somewhat essentialist notions of the feminine and especially with motherhood. This approach, admittedly expressed by well-intentioned scholars, sets out to free the performer from Brecht himself and the emotionally restricting elements of his aesthetic.[44] Elin Diamond proposes a different reading of this scene:

> It's tempting by comparison, but it opens the rather tedious question of whether Weigel was caving into Dusean psychological expressivity ... It is more interesting, I think, to see that famous image not as a transcendence of thought, but as an anamorphic realization of 'dialectics at a standstill', in which what cannot be thought – death – becomes the felt other.[45]

Mother Courage's double refusal to recognise her dead son, Swiss Cheese, turns into a *gestus* not so much by drawing on the actor's own experience as a mother (although we may never know) but by quoting other similar moments and stylising them through her artform. We know that Weigel was already being quotational in the Benjaminian sense, as she was herself influenced by a newspaper photograph of an Indian mother crying over the dead body of her murdered son. We could also perhaps claim that the moment of recognition of Swiss Cheese's dead body through the silent scream might also be quoting another horrific recognition from Greek tragedy: that of Agave from *The Bacchae* recognising the dead head of her son Pentheus. In both cases this recognition also assumes some kind of responsibility. In this context Weigel's silent scream may be read as quoting the mask of tragedy itself. This intertexual connection through the art of the performer was apparent in Sophia Michopoulou's role as Agave in Theodoros Terzopoulos's production of *The Baccahae* (1985), where at the end she very directly quotes the silent scream after the recognition of her son. Terzopoulos himself trained with the Berliner Ensemble in the mid-1970s. The scream itself was never scripted, not because it somehow bothered Brecht, but because it belongs to the long history of *gestus* and the unscripted art of the performer. More appropriately, it has been photographed. This allows us to read it, as Diamond suggests, as both 'dialectics at a standstill' and 'praxis incarnate'. Reading Mother Courage within a trajectory of characters, which as Gill suggests interpret personhood (and interestingly not 'character') as 'objective-participant', with a sense of self that is constantly 'divided', also helps to bridge the binary between tragic and epic 'heroes'. This reading of dramatic roles, which opens up the dynamics between role-character-actor, sees the stage creation as a type of tableau that quotes (intentionally or not) other roles, the actor's performance history, the specific play-text and, we could also possibly claim, that invites the spectator to take part as an 'objective-participant', where responses of emotion and reason are intertwined and not in opposition.

Also, interestingly, Gill claims that both schemata – the objective and the individualist – entail reason; possibly different kinds of reason, but both approaches carry within them a rational attitude towards the world. One, the individualist, may be seen as expressing conscious acts of will and personal emotion; the other, the participant – and I would also agree to term it Divided Self – also performs acts of reason. Gill calls these 'reason-ruled' and 'action-guided'; in other words, they could also be interpreted as performative.

In terms of their aesthetico-political efficacy, these two modes might smoothly fold over into the two main categories of what Benjamin terms the 'tragic hero' and the 'epic hero'. However, we have already problematised this opposition in stating that perhaps this tragic sense of personhood might itself inhabit the same trajectory as the epic hero. To clarify further, and to perhaps also revise the various interpretations at work within this binary, I believe that Benjamin identifies the 'tragic hero' (or the ways it was interpreted by German Idealism) with the hero of bourgeois individualism, against whom the epic character revolts. In this sense Gill's notion of the 'subjective-individualist' understanding of personhood very neatly fits into the the bourgeois subject of naturalism, for example, with its emphasis on personal psychology and motivation, and *not* the tragic notion of personhood. In terms of the discourses of representation and theories of acting, the 'subjective-individualist' approach relies on psychological approaches to acting, whereas the 'objective-participant' approach presupposes an approach that is very similar to epic theories of acting. Indeed, Gill articulates this action-based discourse of the 'objective-participant' character as a series of 'exemplary gestures'. In this sense Medea's killing of the children is not read as an expression of her madness or unruly desire, but as a gesture that has rhythm and reason to it, that brings to the fore the main themes of the play: the politics of parenthood and childhood; the crisis through Jason's action in systems of *philia*, *philoxenia* and oath-taking; anxieties about autochthony, amongst others. In the same way, we may claim that Mother Courage's actions result in the death of her children, drawing links between the war-machine and the mother-machine. Gill reads these 'exemplary gestures' as themselves expressing a world-view. He writes:

> My claim is that, although these figures have sometimes been treated as social outsiders, or (in a different intellectual idiom) as marginal figures, their ethical stance is that of people who are deeply committed to (what they see as being) the norms of governing interpersonal relationships in their communities. What are sometimes taken as acts or statements of radical self-assertion or individualism are better understood as exemplary gestures, designed to dramatize what they see as fundamental breaches in these norms. These exemplary gestures imply, at least, a special degree of reflectiveness about the proper form and goals of a human life.[46]

This very evocative reading of tragic character could itself be interpreted as an aspect of Benjamin's 'praxis incarnate'. Gill's 'exemplary gestures' can easily be seen to be in dialogue with Brecht's idea of *gestus*. These 'exemplary gestures' also allow us to read the extreme actions of the tragic characters in phenomenological terms, where the emotions themselves are not seen as the abject exception, but form part of a participatory, performative trajectory. Nor are they unique. And here is a recent definition of *gestus* that could also double as an exemplary gesture:

> A gestus is a performative action which expresses a social and political attitude as distinct from a subjective or unconscious motivation. It indicates social status and a relation of the character to social and political institutions in order to draw attention to and critique those institutions rather than a character's psychological or metaphysical condition. The stance of a hungry man eating soup, shielding his bowl as though protecting it from a thief, the flourish of a bureaucrat signing official documents, or a badly-dressed man's attitude of chasing away a watchdog, each reveal the relation the character and the historical-political-economic

power structure . . . The gestus opens out the possibility of critique by explicitly turning the actor into a reader of his or her own role, standing aside from the role in order to comment on what is happening to it. This in turn provokes the spectator, who is also, by extension, refused indentification, to critique the character and events portrayed, enabling the imagination of alternative social and political worlds.[47]

This proposed way of reading particularly the extreme, horrific actions of Greek tragedy as 'exemplary gestures' also offers possibilities for acting and performance; possibilities that derive from the view that these characters are not 'individuals' to be represented and enacted through notions of emotional identification, either for the performer herself or for the audience. Gill's notions of tragic personhood also chime well with the convention of men-playing-women. There is no sense of creating a character that would rely on the conflation of the phenomenal body of the actor with the semiotic body of the role. The male *hypokrites* is called upon not to portray a particular, concrete person; rather he displays – through the Divided Self – a world-view, an allegory, more often than not through a fragmented sense of personhood. This notion of the Divided Self and the 'objective-participant' view of personhood could itself be read as parallel to that voiced by Hans-Thies Lehmann in his understanding of the tragic character in Hölderlin as dispelling any idea that 'the subject possesses self-identical status'. And this is true for both the performer and for the spectator. Could it be, however, that this view of tragic personhood could already contain within it the making of the postdramatic?

While this is indeed a speculative proposition, it is one perhaps that might prove enabling when approaching the demanding roles of Greek tragedy for the purposes of performance. For it is a tall order, one could claim especially for a female performer, to embody a role that was clearly not written for her body, but that at the same time makes a huge ethico-political interpretive claim on it. The roles especially, like Medea, Antigone, Klytemnestra, Iocasta or Agave, that deal with the politics of motherhood and reproduction prove particularly demanding for female performers, I would claim. While it is now accepted and somewhat commonplace to claim that they are not psychological roles in any Stanislavskian sense, it might also be useful to place these roles within a genealogy of performance that follows what Benjamin calls 'the little-trodden' path of theatre history through the medieval mysteries and religious dramas and leads up to Brechtian epic. Brechtian epic itself in this scheme is not unique, but transpires as a modernist reworking of a set of performance conventions that has a long and distinguished genealogy.

It could be argued that in a sense this fantastic dialogue between Greek tragic mothers – Medea in this instance – and epic mothers may itself result from the ways Brechtian aesthetics has informed late twentieth-century and contemporary performance of tragedy. For despite Brecht's proclamations, when it comes to approaching these roles for performance, epic theatre has provided an enabling vocabulary and a set of conventions that probably more than any other modernist legacy of performance has had a huge impact on the ways tragedy has been performed and adapted throughout the twentieth and twenty-first centuries. We may claim a similar context/influence on the emotional/phenomenological turn in classical studies; it, too, may result from considerable advances in the field of reception and performance. For the 'emotional' challenges that these demanding roles present were first and foremost addressed by performers and directors over the past one hundred years or so. The triangulation of actor/role/character that the tragic protagonists open up is itself an epic trope of performance, one that allows us to perhaps learn as much from Greek tragedy about epic acting as Brecht did from the Chinese performer Mei Lanfang and the theatres of South-East Asia.[48] The point made here is that performance itself asks us to rethink the ways emotion, identification and affect are mediated from particular renditions of character. Significant performances of *Medea*, for example, have helped to reconfigure our understanding of tragic and epic characters. It is as if performance is not simply the embodiment of theory, but is itself embodied theory. And Helene Weigel's rendition of the 'silent scream' is an emblematic case of how non-scripted *gestus* also helps to create embodied theory. Since the event of its initial performance it has inspired both theoretical reflection and acting tropes. For *gestus* is not meant to be reproduced, but is unique to each performer. It can, however, be quoted, as it has been since that original production of *Mother Courage*.

Whether through reciprocity, intentionally, or not at least at a level of intertexuality, reception studies has opened critical pathways that allow us to learn from the act of performance itself. Mikijirō Hira's performance of Medea in Ninagawa's celebrated production (1984) has asked critics, scholars, audiences and theatre-makers to reconsider our understanding of Medea's role. Of course, as many scholars have noted, Hira's (a male performer) and Ninagawa's rendition of the central role quotes Noh and Kabuki conventions of stylisation, but it does this, I would claim, in a manner that also brings out the epic elements in the Greek play itself. In some ways this seminal production can be seen to fuse what Brecht found enabling in Mei Lanfang's performance of the *dan* (female) characters in classical Chinese acting (Peking Opera) with Kabuki and epic tropes. For surely it is not traditional Noh or Kabuki that is being enacted but a rewriting of those conventions, similar to the ways in which Brecht rewrites the conventions of classical Chinese acting in his important essay 'Alienation Effects in Chinese Acting'. Maria Callas in Pasolini's equally important film brings to her rendition of the role her experience as an opera performer, in a way also quoting the centrality of Medea for that genre. Combined with Pasolini's idiosyncratic fusion of Marxism and Catholicism (with its own traditions of religious performance), we may also claim that there is an aspect of epic acting at work there. The particular speculative (and spectacular) perspective brought to the role through the work of the performers themselves is sometimes neglected. However, I would claim that the ways the twentieth- and twenty-first-century performers (Maria Callas, Mikijirō Hira, Melina Mercuri, Fiona Shaw, Keti Dolidze and Maude Mitchell, amongst many) have addressed Medea also brings to the fore the existing epic elements in the ways the character is written as a vehicle for performance in the original play by Euripides. Usually, when we talk about the postdramatic in contemporary performance, we refer to directors or playwrights. Equally significant, perhaps, is the role of the performer, and in this case, these towering Medeas have created roles that both revise our understanding of the classical tragic protagonist *and* also perhaps place the postdramatic within a genealogy of performance conventions.

This staged dialogue between tragic notions of personhood and epic notions of character has set out to problematise Benjamin's binary between the tragic protagonist and the epic protagonist, drawing parallels between them and confusing one of the primary oppositions of epic theatre in the ways it defines itself against tragedy. This speculative dialogue that we have sketched out might also be supported by Brecht's famous production of *The Antigone of Sophocles*, where he directly encounters – one could claim counter-rhythmically, following Hölderlin – Greek tragedy for the purposes of experimentation with epic performance. Significantly, this venture also provides the material for his first model with photographs by Ruth Berlau. Fascinating that the *Antigone-Model 1948* is the first instance of his lifelong attempt at capturing the process of performance; not a record of a specific performance, but an attempt to create a trace, a blueprint, premised on the principle of *reproducibility*, and not a simple, mechanical reproduction of performance, as his friend Benjamin would claim.

A MODEL FOR MODERN TRAGEDY

The Antigone of Sophocles was to be the first production that Brecht directed upon his return to Europe in 1947 after years of exile, the final six of which were spent in the USA. The day after his appearance before the House Un-American Activities Committee, 31 October 1947, Brecht left for Paris. His return to Europe, which he found 'shabby and impoverished', also posed the challenge of the kind of theatre appropriate for a post-war, post-fascist Europe. In a sense Brecht revisits the questions already posed by Bloch and Lukács in the 1930s about the relationship between form and content and the efficacy of 'committed art'.[49] That he chooses to do so by readdressing a text that is at once part of the classical canon and crucial to German Romanticism also needs underlining. While Brecht is working on *The Antigone of Sophocles* he is also formulating his *Short Organum for the Theatre*. These two projects need to be read in tandem. His version of *Antigone* emerges as an experimental exercise in epic theatre but as an equally experimental proposition in modern tragedy.

Of course, *The Antigone of Sophocles*, with the conspicuous, almost ironic presence of the playwright in the title, is not really based on Sophocles at all but partly follows Friedrich Hölderlin's version of 1803. Significantly, Brecht seems to skip a generation of German Hellenism (bypassing the dominant presence of Wagner and Nietzsche) to go back to Hölderlin, whose translations were ridiculed when published and had a reputation for being particularly obscure.[50] This difficulty was for Brecht part of the attraction, compounding his desired effect of distance and estrangement. In returning to Hölderlin he was performing two acts of recuperation, one for Germany (in reviving a type of classicism that wasn't tainted by Nazism) and the other for the whole of Europe (in reworking a model of tragedy for the purposes of modernity). This *Antigone* offers a platform for Brecht to reassess the role of art in the post-war era *and* to carve out a role for himself as a committed artist.

In reworking Hölderlin's translation, Brecht could be seen as elaborating on a certain German Romantic sensibility that saw in Sophocles not the lyrical, measured poet of Athenian democracy but the oriental, wild Dionysian version of the same project. Writing in the historical context of a new order, which would be republican and vital, Hölderlin was interested in making his adaptations relevant to his historical moment. David Constantine, the translator of both Hölderlin and Brecht, writes:

> That is the chief interpretative tendency in Hölderlin translations: to bring the ancient texts home in such a fashion that they will quicken hearts and minds in the torpid present. In translating like that, serving, as he thought, the present needs of his own countrymen, Hölderlin put himself ever more at risk. Always choosing the more violent word, so that the texts are stitched through with the vocabulary of excess, of madness, rage; he was also voicing those forces in his own psychology, which very soon would carry him over the edge.[51]

This fusion of the personal and the political makes Hölderlin a very intuitive reader of tragedy for Brecht. The madness, violence and rage that permeate Hölderlin's translation is, in a way, historicised (or 'rationalised', as Brecht claims) and becomes part of the political fibre of the play. Rather than reading the story in the familiar Hegelian terms of the individual against the law of the state, Brecht, following Hölderlin's lead, sees *Antigone* as a tale of destruction. He writes:

In *Antigone* the violence is explained by inadequacy. The war against Argos derives from mismanagement. Those who have been robbed have to look to robbery themselves. The undertaking exceeds the strength available. Violence splits the forces instead of welding them together; basic humanity, under too much pressure, explodes, scattering everything with it into destruction.[52]

Admittedly Brecht makes major changes and additions to Hölderlin's version: he exaggerates the role of Haemon's brother, Megareus (offstage) and disposes of the mother, Eurydice, altogether; the war with Argos gets a 'realistic' sheen and is fought over mineral wealth; Creon has total and absolute power and no rightful claim whatsoever. However, despite these attempts at 'rationalisation', I would argue that the text's main concern is with charting the 'scattering of destruction' mentioned earlier. This fascination with catastrophe that attracts Brecht to Hölderlin in the first place is, I believe, the main structuring force of the adaptation. In a sense, the whole project is about finding a form to accommodate historical catastrophe.

In turn, the role of Antigone is radically rewritten to blend with this aesthetic. Rather than presenting her moral and heroic character (Brecht's epic mothers come to mind) as the antidote to the extreme and total power of Creon, she appears to be rather more implicated in the violence she supposedly opposes. 'She ate bread baked in servitude, she sat comfortably in the shade of the strongholds of oppression. Only when the violence dealt out by the house of Oedipus rebounded on that house did she awake,' writes Brecht.[53] This reading of Antigone helps to turn her into an epic character, one that also chimes well with Gill's idea of the 'objective-participant' view of personhood. So, this 'rationalisation' does not involve a transposition of the conflict between Antigone and Creon into the terms of his own post-war present and of all the usual binaries that the play is read as enacting. Rather, this reading of Antigone presents her as inextricably linked to the power structures she is trying to resist. For Brecht, the interest of the play is not so much in showing how one system of values might triumph over the other, but how both systems are implicated in the violence of war. This reading also helps excavate the tensions in the original play between law and lawlessness, between civilisation and barbarism. Hence the emphasis placed in his production on the aesthetic of barbarism:

In modelling the set Cas [Neher] and I stumble on an ideological element of the first order. Should we place the barbaric totem poles with the horses' skulls at the back between the actors' benches, thus indicating the barbaric location of the old poem, which the actors leave in order to act (the de-totemised version?) We decide to place the acting among the totem poles, since we are still living in the state of totemic class war.

[. . .]

Antigone in its entirety belongs with the barbaric horses' skulls.[54]

His own *Antigone*, however, firmly located between the old and the new, among the totem poles, was to underline the structural, dialectical relationship between the two. Like Hölderlin before him, Brecht sees in the Greek model of tragedy not the taming, civilising *gestus* that leads to progress and civilisation, nor does he see it solely as epitomising the barbarism that results from empire and war. Rather he sees both these themes bound together, implicated in each other's narratives, like Creon and Antigone. Rather than a paean to humanism, his *Antigone* is about the violence that humanism potentially engenders. The famous 'Ode to Man', in addition to charting man's progress, becomes a catalogue of catastrophes framed by the word 'monstrous' at the start and the end of the ode. This is Hölderlin's translation (which Brecht maintains) of the term *deinon* in Sophocles. It is a notorious term that has inspired much philosophical reflection,[55] and which roughly translates as awesome, wondrous, extremely able, but also as strange, other and monstrous. Like Hölderlin, Brecht highlights this bleaker aspect of the humanism that the ode celebrates. By the end of the ode the subject of this humanism that Brecht, quoting Hölderlin, explores, becomes a stranger to himself:

> Monstrous, a lot, But nothing
> More monstrous than man.
> [. . .]
> A measure is set.
> For when he wants for an enemy
> He rises up as his own. Like the bull's
> He bows the neck of his fellowmen but these fellowmen
> Rip out his guts. When he steps forth
> He treads on his own kind, hard. By himself alone
> His belly will never be filled but he builds a wall
> Around what he owns and the wall
> Must be torn down. The roof
> Opened to the rain. Humanity
> Weighs with him not a jot. Monstrous thereby
> He becomes to himself.[56]

This reading of *deinon* as both wondrous and monstrous punctuates the whole adaptation. It informs Brecht's decision to place the horses' skulls amongst the actors and not behind them. In this way, rather than gesturing towards prehistoric ritual, these skulls become the emblems of historical violence. Although the adaptation uses ritual, and the discourse in the *Antigone-Model* is full of ritualised and medicalised language (fevered life,

Figure 5.1 Brecht-Neher, *Antigone Modellbuch 1948*, BBA. FA. 47-163.
Photo Ruth Berlau.

Figure 5.2 Brecht-Neher, *Antigone Modellbuch 1948*, BBA. FA. 47-40.
Photo Ruth Berlau.

the consumptive), this ritual is never truly conceptualised within a primitivist framework. The violence in the text and on the stage is not a reference to any quasi-anthropological, prehistoric ritual that is able to redeem a crisis-ridden humanism (and humanity). For Brecht, as he clearly states in the *Model*, his adaptation of *Antigone* is a study of state power in crisis that 'only becomes aware of its own laws of motion in a catastrophe'.[57] (The term 'crisis' is deliberately used in the Greek sense; fevered response, eruption, but also the possibility of critique.) The reading of humanism (and tragedy) proposed through this interpretation of *deinon* allows for both the wonder and the catastrophe to surface. Although the play uses the aesthetics of ritual, this ritual is never seen as prehistoric but rather as the bearer of historical catastrophe itself. The primitive, the barbarian is not something that forms part of a humanist evolutionary trajectory that we have outgrown or 'lost' and occasionally revisit in our search for experimental forms of performance ('the Greeks as the childhood of mankind', as Marx put it). For Brecht, as was the case for Walter Benjamin, it has always run parallel to the movement for progress, light, reason and civilisation, and the two cannot be structurally separated; hence the decision to place the actors amongst the skulls.

In turning to Hölderlin, Brecht is also engaging with what Françoise Dastur calls his 'speculative theory of tragedy'.[58] Hölderlin's shift from writing his own modern tragedies (*Empedocles*, 1798–80, unfinished) to translating Sophocles has been interpreted by Philippe Lacoue-Labarthe as a 'radical rupture . . . that opens onto the very root of theatre'.[59] In other words, Hölderlin approaches Sophocles after the so-called failure of his own attempts at modern tragedy in search of a 'model'. 'The "return to Sophocles" does not, for Hölderlin, mean some sort of "nostalgia for Greece". It means a return to the ground of theatricality,' as Lacoue-Labarthe claims.[60] In his essays on tragedy and 'Remarks' on Oedipus and Antigone, Hölderlin presents a version of this theatricality without which modern tragedy would be impossible. He suggests a speculative theory of tragedy as 'the metaphor of an intellectual intuition'. This use of the term 'speculative', as Dastur claims, restores to it its original Greek meaning of *theoria*, which was translated as *specto/speculatio* into Latin by Boetius. We begin to understand how Hölderlin's quest for a speculative theory of tragedy actually translates into a quest for theatricality, or a language that theorises theatricality.

In Christian theology the Greek sense of *theoria* and the original meaning of *specto* (all connected semantically with looking, scrutinising, reflecting, but also with the embodied and spatialised dimension of those original etymologies) and speculation become connected with *speculum*, the mirror. The theatrical act itself thus changes from potentially speculative to overwhelmingly spectacular. Once again we are in the familiar Platonic territory of the distorting effects of tragedy. This shift in meaning from *theoria* as a type of *speculative* thinking to *theoria* as representing a distorted image, indeed one that can only be restored by the intervention of the divine (*visio Dei*), bears all the traces of anti-theatrical philosophy. So much so that Thomas Aquinas's derivation of *theoria/speculatio* from *speculum* (rather than *specto*) can be read as echoing the master of anti-theatrical philosophy himself. In turn, the identification of things *spectacular* with distortion and corruption of the truth may account for the difficult relationship between Christianity and theatre in general.[61]

Through his encounter with the theatricality of tragedy Hölderlin is searching for both a *speculative* and a *spectacular* approach to modern tragedy; at once textual and material, metaphysical and physical. He writes in the opening of his 'Remarks on Oedipus':

> It will be good, in order to secure for today's poets, also at home, an existence in the city, to elevate poetry, also at home, given the difference of times and institutions, to the level of the *mechane* of the Ancients.
>
> When being compared with those of the Greeks, other works of art too lack reliability; at least, they have been judged until today according to the impression they produce rather than according to their lawful calculation and to the other methodical modes through which the beautiful is engendered . . .
>
> As men, we must first realize that it is something, which can be known by means (*moyen*) of its manifestation, that the way in which it is conditioned may be determined and learned. Such is the reason why – to say nothing of higher reasons – poetry is in special need of secure and characteristic delimitations.[62]

This poetics of tragedy that is at once *techne* and *mechane* shifts the critical attention from the audience to the stage, from theories of reception (*katharsis*) to theories of theatrical production and performance. It foreshadows notions of embodiment (manifestation) and also the principle of reproducibility, later to be developed by Benjamin (whose *Origin of German Tragic Drama* provides a further layer of filtering in the relationships between Brecht and Hölderlin).[63] This fascination that Hölderlin expresses for the image of the *mechane*, as we have noted above, is also in line with his notion of tragedy as 'a metaphor of an intellectual intuition', where the ideas of 'intellect' and 'intuition' are not seen as binaries and where metaphor itself is used in its primary sense of *transport*. In turn, tragedy in its significant form is interpreted as such a form of transport, a *mechane*, which acts to bridge a number of binaries: between the earthly and the divine, between the word and the body, between subject and object.

In tackling *The Antigone of Sophocles* already rewritten by Hölderlin, Brecht continues an unfinished project. We begin to understand the inclusion of Sophocles in the title. He sets out to rewrite *Antigone* as a piece of poetry *and* as an example of tragic transport. The *Antigone-Model*, produced with photographs by Berlau after the play-text, *The Antigone of Sophocles*, and significantly after the performance, could signify an attempt at such a tragic transport. Through its reliance on the principle of reproducibility (the *mechane*, as Hölderlin would have it) and the conspicuous use of photography (which Benjamin would have approved of), it emerges as a specifically modernist inflection on the idea of tragic transport.

<h3 style="text-align:center">Helene Weigel and the Door</h3>

The *Model* contains a photograph of Helene Weigel attached to a door, which she carries crucifixion-style on her back from the moment she is arrested by Creon's soldiers, from the moment the *peripeteia* begins to unravel. This is a striking image at once referring to the themes of the play but also, crucially, embodying them. The relationships between Helene Weigel the performer (in her first speaking part in ten years), the role of Antigone as tragic heroine and the theatrical object of 'the door' form an intriguing *gestus*, one whose precedent can be found in Hölderlin's caesura.

The door draws attention to the themes of the play: the *oikos* and the *polis*, home and homelessness, inside and outside the law. It is, however, a door attached to the body of the performer and also signals a relationship between actors and objects on the stage. This intricate relationship between subject and object on the stage seems to be a fundamental aspect of the Brechtian *gestus*. It is also something that will later form a very specific part of the make-up of Helene Weigel, the performer (her relationship with the cart and her money bag, for example, in *Mother Courage and Her Children*).

Unlike the image of the cross to which it also alludes, this wooden frame is never turned into a symbol in the *Model*. It never stands in for the body, which it has sublimated or sacrificed. It remains stubbornly attached to the performer as a kind of *transport* rather than substitution. Indeed, one carries the other, as the image of Weigel attached to the door proposes an interchangeability between subjects and objects on stage. Rather than presenting the door – a potent image in its own right – as the main symbol of the play, separate and distinct as a stage 'prop', this dynamic and contingent reading at once highlights the Hegelian binaries within which the play has been read, and critiques them. As a theatrical *gestus* it is also citing a particular theatrical convention, its history and its political efficacy.

In attaching Antigone to the door the *Model* cites a number of theatrical traditions: the convention that required classical tragedy to be performed at the threshold of the private and the public, the reading of the Passion of Christ as a tragedy and the medieval Mystery Cycles amongst them. In addressing these, the *Model* is also engaging with the difficult relationship that these traditions exhibit with the body of the actor. Unlike the Christian drama that turns

Figure 5.3 Brecht-Neher, *Antigone Modellbuch 1948*, BBA. FA. 47-143.
Photo Ruth Berlau.

the wooden cross into a symbol of redemption, eradicating the presence of the body in the process (although this axiom is constantly challenged in every theatrical and ritualistic re-enactment of the passion of Christ), this *gestural* drama confuses the line between actors and objects, granting neither the privilege of agency, ascension nor sublimation. However, this intermingling does not necessarily resort to primitivism, where people are reduced to inanimate things; nor is it revelling in a type of postmodern, ahistorical, ecstatic substitution of people by things. For this door is definitely a ruin. Brecht writes:

> If theatre is capable of showing the truth, then it must also be capable of making the sight of it a pleasure. How then can such a theatre be created? The difficulty about ruins is that the house has gone, but the site isn't there either. And the architects' plans, it seems, never get lost. This means that reconstruction brings back the old dens of iniquity and centres of disease. Fevered life claims to be particularly vital life; none steps so firmly as the consumptive who has lost all feeling in the soles of his feet.[64]

The door emerges as such a ruin and Weigel/Antigone as a figure of the consumptive who is nevertheless walking very firmly on her feet. Brecht's reading of the function of theatre at a 'time of reconstruction' is that of a *pharmakon* (as both poison and cure). The excavation that reconstruction implies helps to bring to the surface the centres of disease, and the moment of drama (crisis/ hypocrisis) brings together the fevered life and the vital life. As Brecht implies, life is at its most vital when it is flaring up with fever. This reading of theatre, very close to Antonin Artaud's idea of theatre as the plague, is at once ritualistic and historical. The relationship it proposes between actors and objects is an extension of this view. The relationship between Antigone and the door is not a comment on her lost humanity (her thingness) or her inability to control the world around her. Rather it points towards the materiality and the theatricality of this relationship, where, in a moment of historical catastrophe, disease and vitality, people and things, life and death become interchangeable. For Brecht, following Benjamin, this moment is also a moment of truth;[65] a truth, however, that needs to be manifested through strangeness, like the consumptive who steps firmly only 'after he has lost all feeling in the soles of his feet'.

'*Things* have a life,' says Winnie in Samuel Beckett's *Happy Days*, herself buried up to the neck in a mound.[66] In 'Helene Weigel and the door' this 'life of things' creates the main *gestus* of the *Model*, in many ways manifesting that 'counter-rhythmic rupture' that Hölderlin saw as essential to the caesura. Lacoue-Labarthe cites the few lines of speech by Hölderlin's Tiresias as the 'moment of the *caesura*':

> In both pieces [*Oedipus* and *Antigone*], it is the speeches of Tiresias which form the *caesura*.
>
> He enters the course of destiny as the custodian of the power of nature which, tragically, tears man from his own life-sphere, the mid-point of his inner life, transporting him into another world and into the eccentric sphere of the dead.[67]

Interestingly, this reworking of the caesura is not solely linguistic/poetic; it is arrived at through the encounter between the textual and the material, poetry and stage prop, actor and object. 'Helene Weigel and the door' becomes such a form of transport that enacts all the themes of the play in a manner that is at once a performance *and* a philosophical debate. This reworking of the caesura through Brecht's *gestus* posits the possibility of a 'philosophical theatre',[68] one that dramatically recasts the agonistic relationship between tragedy and philosophy.

This 'transport', as Hölderlin claims above, leads us to 'another world and into the eccentric sphere of the dead'. Crucially, this other world is not the same as the 'sphere of the dead', as the paratactic use of 'and' clearly shows. Arguably, it is the world of the stage, the in-between world, the world of mediation, where the *mechane* is exposed and theatricalised and truth potentially revealed. The 'eccentric' nature of the 'sphere of the dead' guarantees that the encounter with their world is tangible and formative. This is a reading of the stage as a site of mediation but also as a site of mourning.[69] This door becomes the rupture between the 'sphere of the dead' and the stage. It is not simply standing in for any number of doors (exile, tombstone, stage, bed, etc.) that could symbolise the themes of the play. Through its theatrical relationship with the body of the performer, it is *attempting* to embody them, as the speculative nature of this enterprise is endemic. In this sense the figure of Antigone as tragic protagonist enacts the tensions between embodiment and monumentalisation, tensions that are also thematically played out in the text. Is the performer of such a 'tragic protagonist' an *actor* (with all the notions of character and psychology that the term implies) or a *hypokrites* (a *mechane*, an acting machine)? 'Helene Weigel/Antigone and the door' does not necessarily resolve this binary, but sets to tease it out, significantly *transporting* it from the 'world of poetry' to the 'world of the stage'.

Ruth Berlau continues this transport with her photographs in the *Model*. The image needs to be read as also negotiating relationships between Brecht the director and Berlau the photographer. Is it significant that the 'gaze' is female? And is it significant that Helene Weigel is inhabiting a theatrical role that in Athenian tragedy had no female performers? In other words, how is the *Model* addressing the difficulty that tragic form has always had with the female performer?

More than a case of making the female performer visible or 'correcting' a historical form, the modern encounter with tragedy throws into crisis some of its fundamental representational economies. The convention of men playing women is endemic to tragedy and at once nods to the exclusion of women from the civic sphere and towards a male homosexual sublime.[70] The physical presence of a female performer in the role of Antigone (while important historically and politically) does not in and of itself constitute a reading of Antigone. Nor is it a case of the female performer having access to a 'real' Antigone. In many ways, the presence of the female performer highlights the role as a 'performing machine', a non-character, as a modern performer would intertexually be inhabiting a role that was written for a male *hypokrites* and is associated with a long history of female impersonation.

Interestingly, female impersonation plays a significant role in the formation of Brecht's 'V-effect', which is clearly articulated by Brecht only after his formative encounter with the Chinese *dan* (female impersonator) actor Mei Lanfang at the Writers' Conference in Moscow in 1936. Contemporary feminist performance theorists[71] have revisited this event and have criticised Brecht for exhibiting a classic Marxist 'blind spot' when it comes to gender. The tradition that he had found inspiring in its ability to separate performer from role was also one that had no female performers. Furthermore, this separability, so desirable for the activation of the V-effect, relied on a fundamental separability of female 'essence' and female 'performance'. It is fascinating to note that in the history of performance conventions the ideas of estrangement, otherness and unhomeliness are usually linked with the specific representation of the female (always performed by men). Brecht saw in Mei Lanfang's performance a fine example of his *Verfremdungseffekt*. We could say that the form performs a similar function in Athenian tragedy. In both cases the first 'thing' that is 'made strange' is the female. Read in a psychoanalytical framework, this function of impersonating the female becomes a prerequisite of tragic form in the same way that the female body (reflecting Plato's cave *and* his anti-theatricality) becomes a prerequisite of representation.[72]

Helene Weigel inhabiting the role of Antigone forms part of a huge and varied cast of female performers within modernism who rewrote theatrical conventions in order to make their presence visible as artists.[73] From naturalism's 'New Woman' to the daring experiments in modern dance (the pioneers of which were mostly women),[74] the specific representation of the female performer poses both a thematic and a formal challenge. This epic rendition of the 'New Woman' goes beyond the aesthetic and political parameters of naturalism. It views the 'woman problem' as part of the 'capitalist problem', in a tradition of philosophical reflection from Engels to Trotsky (after all, as Marx said, 'social progress can be measured exactly by the social position of the fair sex, the ugly ones included'). The work of the Russian/Soviet director Vsevolod Meyerhold and his actress wife, Zinaida Reich, is also a fine example of constructivist readings of this structural relationship between capitalism and gender oppression. Sometimes, the 'woman question' comes to stand in metaphorically and redeem 'the capitalist question', utilising the genre of classic epic and romance, in a long and distinguished literary tradition from classic epic's use of Helen of Troy to Brecht's own 'epic mothers'.[75] In this scheme of things the female protagonists of Brecht display significant attachments to 'things'; to a door in *Antigone*; to a cart in *Mother Courage*, to a 'child' in *The Caucasian Chalk Circle*; to a 'gift' from the gods in *The Good Person of Szechwan*. However, the obsession with 'things' that these roles exhibit can be seen to result from an approach that reads the female protagonist as tied up with the world around her and its history. It can also be found in the fascination with objects that we see in Heiner Müller's work (*Hamletmachine*, *Medea Material*) or in contemporary feminist performance (as the recent interface between feminist performance theory and Brechtian theory clearly indicates).[76] In both these examples, the work of Brecht is built upon but also 'supplemented', at once homage and betrayal, to paraphrase Müller. ('To use Brecht without criticising him is betrayal.')[77]

In this context, Weigel's Antigone can be read as inflecting naturalism's tradition of the 'New Woman' through an epic aesthetic that has its roots in both modernist poetic drama and the European avant-garde. In opening up to this level of experiment and critique, the epic tradition in tragedy that we have been sketching out so far is also forced to encounter another difficulty: that between Marxism and feminism. In the case of the *Model*, one could say that it is also enacted through the relationships among Weigel the performer, Berlau the photographer and Brecht the director. Weigel, the performer, reconfigures a set of conventions that historically deny her presence, and Berlau documents the event through the most modern of media, photography. The *Model* begins to emerge as a very modernist rendition of tragedy indeed, complete with 'New Woman' on and off the stage and technologies of reproduction. The figure of Brecht himself begins to fade; or rather his work – that of the playwright/adaptor/director – becomes a type of mediation, *transport*, between the stage, the lens and the book of the *Model*. The *Model* would have a similar impact, as he had hoped:

> The idea of making use of models is a clear challenge to the artists of a period that applaud nothing but what is 'original', 'incomparable', 'never been seen before', and demands what is 'unique'.[78]

In rejecting the quest for newness, Brecht turns to the oldest form of theatre available in the European canon. In doing so he is also reigniting the battle between the ancients and the moderns, ushering in a specifically modernist type of Hellenism; akin to the 'neo-classical' experiments undertaken by James Joyce, Gertrude Stein or the cubists. At the same time, he is making a contribution to a longstanding debate about the efficacy of tragedy in modernity. This contribution, it could be argued, consists mainly of the *Model* itself. The textual reworking follows Hölderlin more or less faithfully (in its attitude to language and to 'the Greeks'). The *Model*, on the other hand, comes into being through the contributions of a performer, Helene Weigel, and a photographer, Ruth Berlau. As versions of the 'New Woman' and in an amalgamation of the personal and political (which was to become a hallmark of later feminist performance), they are constitutive of the *Model* and the versions of modern tragedy it proposes.

The quest for modern tragedy is usually read within a literary history that starts with the Greeks and ends with 'high', modernist poetic drama, via the Elizabethan stage and German Romanticism. Almost invariably this approach focuses on a literary theatrical tradition and not on instances of performance or indeed on historical performance conventions. It seems that this *Model* follows what Benjamin called the 'secret smugglers' path' in theatre history (through the mysteries, through the history of performers and through baroque drama). In negotiating a relationship between tragedy and modernity, it is also raising questions of tragic form beyond the function of high verse. At the same time, it forms part of a general modernist Hellenism that views 'the Greeks' as embodied, situated and historical (the work of the Cambridge Ritualists, for example, forms part of this trend).[79]

Brecht's and Berlau's *Antigone-Model* can also be read within a literary history that seeks to rework tragic form within modernity. Rather than polarise and somewhat caricature these diverse experiments in modernist drama as either failed Christian or failed Marxist tragedies, they could be seen as negotiating different approaches to the embodiment, theatricality, reception of modern tragedy. The contribution of this particular *Model* also opens up the debate between the ancients and the moderns to the historical avant-garde. In revisiting Sophocles and Hölderlin through the incorporation of the theatrical experiments of the avant-garde, the *Antigone-Model* allows us to read the 'quest' for modern tragedy beyond its manifestations as literary drama.

This 'quest' is always shadowed by a discourse of failure. And to read the *Model* within this trajectory is to highlight its differences/contrasts but also to unravel its failures, or its attitude towards failure. In a sense failure is already inscribed in the speculative/spectacular nature of the enterprise. This is the difference between what Jameson calls Brecht's 'method' (or model, in this instance) and 'other philosophical methods or world-views'. 'Method' would appear to have a strong attachment to the 'speculative' (*theoria*). The use of the term 'method' easily translates into the ancients' *mechane*, albeit via Hölderlin. And the Brecht–Berlau *Antigone-Model 1948* can be read as such a form of transport (*mechane*), which puts forward a 'speculative concept' of modern tragedy 'by virtue of its unique form', as Jameson phrases it.[80] This 'unique form' in this instance (and, I would claim, throughout the Brechtian project) is 'profoundly related' to tragic form. This speculative failure embodies a type of negativity at once physical and metaphysical, that doesn't readily translate into quasi-existential nothingness. It relates theatrical practice to a tradition of critical philosophy (Brecht's 'philosophical theatre') and injects the Brechtian project with that 'pessimism of the intellect' that some critics believe it desperately needs. This attachment of epic theatre to tragic form that I have tried to sketch out gets an added modernist dimension through the use of photography in the *Model*.

It also posits the possibility that the failures of the avant-garde could be read as modern tragedies. The way the *Model* appears as an aesthetic object owes as much to the literary experiments of German Romanticism as to the spatial/ performative experiments of the avant-garde. As a *mechane* it can be read as inflecting on the idea of the ready-made, the discarded and used, but also utopian object. As a work of mourning the *Model* is both commemorative of the theatres of the past *and* a form of 'transport' for the theatres of the future, where the use of photography compounds the impact of commemoration/ mourning. As a model for modern tragedy it displays a profound attachment to discourses of death, in a sense rewriting the German Romantic/Idealist tradition that constantly mourns the 'death of tragedy'. The whole 'death of tragedy' thesis – one that also reads Brecht's work as part of its trajectory – comes to formally and thematically inform the *making* of the model. With a nod to German Idealism (through its radical strand, Hölderlin) but also with a keen engagement with avant-garde experiment, the *Model* emerges as Brecht's and Berlau's paradigm for the engaged work of art. That this work of art is itself a modern tragedy is significant. It challenges the impossibility of modern tragedy and the ways we as audience and/or scholars respond to tragedy; i.e. it also proposes a modern *theoria* of tragedy. This is one that is driven by a *hypocritical* imperative and displays a profound attachment to speculative and spectacular thinking. Either way, the literary/philosophical model of approaching tragedy is seriously challenged. In addressing this challenge the Brecht–Berlau *Antigone-Model 1948* also inevitably fails, but it *fails spectacularly*, or, to paraphrase Samuel Beckett, it 'fails again. Fails better.'[81]

THE AESTHETICS OF FAILURE/THE POLITICS OF ENGAGEMENT

This speculative relationship that we have been sketching out between tragedy and epic, as we see from the above example, also engages discourses of failure, which have been central in the critical reception of both the avant-garde and, importantly, the modern reception of tragedy. On the one hand the European avant-garde – and Brecht is seen to be part of this tradition – has been read as suffering a series of 'deaths' (its Nazi death, its Stalinist death and even its postmodern death-appropriation), while tragedy after George Steiner is seen as unable to respond to the demands of modernity. This critique, in its quasi-existentialist and idealist renditions (as in Steiner's famous 'death of tragedy'), sees tragedy as somehow having been consumed and unable to survive in a secular, disenchanted world. On the other hand, the quasi-materialist critique, which purports to be post-Brechtian, as voiced in the work of Augusto Boal,[82] for example, continues to misread tragedy as part and parcel of the project of the Enlightenment, its political failures and its economies of representation.

The ways we have been reading the relationships between epic and tragic in this context perhaps allow us also to revisit that political impasse that views Brechtian epic as radical and Greek tragedy as somehow part of a bourgeois aesthetic, hence inherently unable to respond to either the political or the aesthetic demands of modernity.

So when Brecht proposes: 'We know that the barbarians have their art. Let us create another,' in the aphoristic style of the manifesto, towards the middle of his *A Short Organum for the Theatre* (1947–8),[83] of course, the barbarians in this context are 'the Greeks'. For Brecht, as is the case for most of the European avant-garde, 'the Greeks' and their legacy were seen as part of the failure of the project of Enlightenment, its philosophy, its ideology and its economies of representation. His quest for a new theatre – an epic theatre, in the case of Brecht – had to be defined against the classical, Aristotelian tragic model. However, as we have seen, over the same period Brecht was working on what was to be his first production after his return to Europe from exile, *The Antigone of Sophocles*, based on a text by Hölderlin with stage designs by Caspar Neher. Ruth Berlau was to photograph the process, formulating the first of what was to become a hallmark of the Brechtian project: *the Model*. It is fascinating that while Brecht is in search of a model for epic theatre, he returns to the foundational moment of European democracy and what his friend Adorno would term the 'Dialectic of Enlightenment'. And he chooses its most beloved heroine: Antigone. In this sense the *Antigone-Model* can be read as proposition/experiment both in epic theatre and in modern tragedy.

This quest for a *model* in Brechtian thinking can be seen as at once Hellenist and quintessentially modern, especially in the ways it revives both traditional epic and classical Greek tragedy. Similar to the ways that James Joyce or Sergei Eisenstein created new generic templates for their respective genres by rewriting traditional epic, this analysis has teased out the ways that the Brechtian project undertook a similar radical approach to both traditional epic and classical tragedy. The emphasis that Brecht placed on the idea of the *model* has both a philosophical and a political imperative. Philosophically, it can be read as part of modernist experimental theatre's attempts to articulate a language of performance; an attempt to phenomenologically leave a trace or a blueprint, and not a reconstruction or reproduction. As mentioned above, Fredric Jameson claims in *Brecht and Method* that this endeavour is not simply a case of proposing a 'world-view' or reworking the *theatrum mundi* metaphor:

> It would have to be a defense profoundly related to Hegel's own case for what he called the 'speculative': namely, the way in which the very idea of a concept carries in question, at the same time as it passes judgement on worlds that have not yet raised themselves to that level. Change in Brecht would then qualify as a speculative concept of precisely that kind: a purely formal notion that implies and projects its own content by virtue of its unique form.[84]

What constitutes a 'method' rather than a philosophy, for Jameson, would have to be the very theatrical quality of the Brechtian work. The emphasis on the speculative will invariably lead, as we have seen elsewhere in this book, to the spectacular and the performative. Indeed, we may say that the 'form' that Brecht proposes strives to reconcile the speculative with the spectacular, in a gesture (or *gestus*) that embodies both critique and enactment. Hölderlin applies the similar phrase when talking about Greek tragedy. His reading of tragedy as 'a metaphor of an intellectual intuition' proposes tragedy as a speculative theory, a *theoria*. We could go so far as to claim that Hölderlin's 'metaphor of an intellectual intuition' could equally apply as a definition of epic theatre. In turn, we can trace a genealogy of the term from Hölderlin through Hegel and Benjamin to Brecht, acknowledging Brecht's debt to German Idealism. Is it, however, the same historical and political debt from which Brecht wants to vehemently disassociate himself in rewriting the term 'epic'? I would like to suggest that when Brecht rewrites this term, he infuses it with tragedy's 'intellectual intuition'. As a result, his epic theatre strives to combine the somewhat utopian aspirations of traditional epic with the speculative and spectacular modes of tragedy. This 'method' of reading epic back into tragic form could also be seen as an example of Brecht's famous strategy of 'crude' thinking.

The timing of Brecht's *Antigone* project is significant. As his first production after the Second World War in Europe, it also revisits the debates about autonomy and engagement initially articulated in the 1930s between Ernest Bloch, Georg Lukács, Walter Benjamin, Theodor Adorno and Brecht himself. In going back to the most classical figure of resistance, Antigone, Brecht's project might be read as also commenting on the concept of engaged art; however, and in the midst of the aftermath of the Second World War and while still in exile, this Antigone model is also formally experimental in the ways it fuses epic and tragic modes. In this way, perhaps, this interface between epic and tragic that we have tried to develop also revisits and even complicates the binary between autonomous and engaged art, especially in the ways it was formulated after the war by the Frankfurt School. Brecht's epic theatre was central in those debates, primarily as voiced by Adorno as somehow having failed in the all-important function of critique. And after the death of Benjamin, Brecht no longer had a champion in that particular Marxist camp. Coupled with his decision to live and work in the GDR, together with the advent of the cold war, Brechtian formal experimentation lost some of its credibility and critical edge within those original debates of the 1930s. It is interesting to note that classical tragedy too, from the opposite side of the political spectrum (as voiced by George Steiner, for example), was read as unable to speak to the atrocities of the twentieth century. This proposed way of reading tragic and epic modes of theatre, which revises both within the experiments of modernist performance, perhaps also revitalises the political efficacy of tragedy within modernity, while also stressing the formal experimentation of epic. The work of Brecht's epigone, Heiner Müller, for example, makes more sense read within this interface between tragic and epic; as does the significance of epic theatre for both late twentieth-century feminist performance and for the ways performances and adaptations of Greek tragedy, from the post-war period onwards, found in epic an enabling set of theatrical conventions that could address anxieties about their contemporary political situation.

The reflections here on the encounter between Greek tragedy and Brechtian epic in many ways address the so-called political and aesthetic failures of both traditional epic and classical tragedy. For Brecht, following Benjamin, epic is no longer part of the aesthetics of empire ('a civilization of barbarism', as Benjamin would have it); rather it is read as part of the irreverent, blasphemous, popular and oral tradition in performance that so creatively informed all of the avant-garde experiments of the period. This endeavour is parallel to the ways epic has informed the narrative and filmic experiments of modernism more broadly. At the same time, classical Greek tragedy itself is given a modernist mask and dislodged from its interpretations, primarily in the German literary theory traditions of Goethe and Schiller, which pit epic against tragic, as quintessentially 'dramatic'. This reading is not in a sense rehabilitative, trying to 'correct' a misreading of Aristotle by the tradition of German Romantic criticism; one at least initially followed by Brecht himself.[85] Rather the more speculative points raised here view these misreadings themselves as enabling and creative; what they lack in philological rigour, they more than make up for in modernist experimentation. And in this sense, Greek tragedy as much as epic theatre emerges as central for modernist performance, in its quest for both aesthetic autonomy and political engagement.

NOTES

1. See Revermann, 'Brecht and Greek Tragedy'; also see Roessler and Squiers (eds), *Philosophizing Brecht*.
2. Revermann, 'Brecht and Greek Tragedy'.
3. For an account of this trip to Moscow, see Benjamin, *Moscow Diary*. While there, Benjamin saw a production of the *Oresteia* of which he disapproved, while also exhibiting a knowledge of the trilogy: 'The director lacked any professional expertise, but possessed not even the most elementary fund of information necessary to the staging of Aeschylus. A bloodless, drawing-room Hellenism seems fully to satisfy his impoverished imagination', pp. 44–5.
4. Benjamin, *Understanding Brecht*.
5. See Eaton, *The Theatre of Meyerhold and Brecht*; also see Kleberg, *Theatre as Action*.
6. Brecht, *Brecht on Theatre*, p. 37.
7. Ibid.
8. Benjamin, *Understanding Brecht*, p. 10.
9. Brecht, *Brecht on Theatre*, pp. 33–43.
10. Plato, *The Laws*, 700 a–b.
11. For an account of the impact of the theories of Anton Mesmer (1734–1815) – mesmerism – on acting, see Goodall, *Stage Presence*, pp. 84–121.
12. Debord, *The Society of the Spectacle*. Originally published in Paris in 1967, written in the highly aphoristic style of the manifesto and part of the Situationist International, the book has been read as seeped in radical Romanticism, but I would claim that it can also be read as a Situationist reworking of the Allegory of the Cave, in the ways it reads modern subjects as slaves to the capitalist spectacle and its economies of representation. Some characteristic aphorisms: '19. THE SPECTACLE IS HEIR to all the weakness of the project of Western philosophy; 34. THE SPECTACLE is *capital* accumulated to the point where it becomes image.' This political reading of Plato may also find parallels in the

ways that Alain Badiou rewrites Plato in *Plato's Republic: A Dialogue in 16 Chapters*.

13. See Benjamin, *The Work of Art in the Age of its Technological Reproducibility*, pp. 43 (emphasis original).

14. Macintosh, McConnell, Harrison and Kenward (eds), *Epic Performances*, p. 5.

15. Eisenstein, 'Word and Image', in *The Film Sense*, pp. 3–65, p. 58.

16. For Brecht's interest in and inspiration from English Romantic poetry, see Robert Kaufman, *AURA, STILL* in Benjamin (ed.), *Walter Benjamin and Art*, pp. 121–47. Kaufman quotes Brecht: 'What about the realism of lyric poetry', p. 121, and states that Brecht had translated twenty-five stanzas from Percy Shelley's iconic poem 'The Mask of Anarchy'. Much like the misunderstanding that Brechtian aesthetics is uninterested in emotion and sentient engagement, Kaufman addresses the equally misleading idea that he was uninterested in 'aura'. He writes, 'it is no small thing to realize that in the eyes of Brecht, Benjamin, and Adorno (the very figures who in the Left tradition are so frequently said to have helped set the stage for the collapse of aesthetic distance) there really was – and there really was intended to have been – aura, still', p. 147.

17. Benjamin, 'What is Epic Theatre?' [First Version], in *Understanding Brecht*, p. 6.

18. Ibid.

19. Wiles, 'Epic Acting in Shakespeare's *Hamlet*', p. 76.

20. Benjamin, 'What is Epic Theatre?' [Second Version], in *Understanding Brecht*, p. 19.

21. Benjamin, 'What is Epic Theatre?' [First Version], pp. 11–12.

22. See Edward Said, *Musical Elaborations* (London: Chatto and Windus, 1991), where Said elaborates on the idea of the 'counter-rhythmic' as the 'contrapuntal', a musical term that he also applies to literary and cultural theory.

23. See Hölderlin, *Essays and Letters on Theory*, pp. 101–2.

24. See Lacoue-Labarthe, 'Hölderlin's Theatre', p. 130.

25. Dastur, 'Hölderlin and the Orientalisation of Greece', p. 169.

26. The difference between mechanical reproduction and 'reproducibility' as a structural/formal principle is made clearer in the recent translation of Benjamin's seminal essay of 1936; see Benjamin, *The Work of Art in the Age of Technological Reproducibility*.

27. Lehmann, *Tragedy and Dramatic Theatre*, p. 140.

28. Ibid. pp.140–1.

29. Jameson, *Brecht and Method*.

30. See Buchanan and Marks (eds), *Deleuze and Literature*.

31. Lehmann, *Tragedy and Dramatic Theatre*, p. 141.

32. Ibid.

33. Benjamin, 'What is Epic Theatre?' [Second Version], p. 17.

34. See Cairns (ed.), *A Cultural History of the Emotions in Antiquity*.

35. See Taxidou. *Tragedy, Modernity and Mourning*.

36. Benjamin, 'A Family Drama in the Epic Theatre', in *Understanding Brecht*, pp. 33–4.

37. Ibid. p. 34.

38. Ibid. p. 35.

39. See Austin, *How to Do Things with Words*.

40. See Athanasiou and Butler, *Dispossession*.

41. See Cairns, 'A Short History of Shudders'; also see Diamond, 'The Shudder of Catharsis in Twentieth-Century Performance', pp. 162–3. In both, 'shudder', horror and *phrike* are explored in relation to catharsis.

42. See Gill, *Personality in Greek Epic, Tragedy, and Philosophy*, pp. 1–20.

43. Ibid. p. 12.
44. See Revermann, 'Brecht and Greek Tragedy', p. 220, where he writes: '*His* [Brecht's] Mother Courage is the ultimate, self-interested survivor, even in a situation like this one. By contrast, Weigel as a performer – and, one might speculate, as a mother of two children aged eighteen (Barbara) and twenty-four (Stefan) at the time – felt and brought out the *emotional* necessity for Mother Courage to scream. *Her* Mother Courage: still a cunning survivor (hence the silence) – a survivor "in the flesh", with full human complexity.'
45. Diamond, 'The Shudder of Catharsis', pp. 162–3.
46. Gill, *Personality in Greek Epic, Tragedy, and Philosophy*, p. 21.
47. Antony Paraskeva, *Gestus*, entry, in Kolocotroni and Taxidou (eds), *The Edinburgh Dictionary of Modernism*, pp. 167–8.
48. See Taxidou, 'Sada Yakko, Mitchio It and Mei Lan-fang: Orientalism, Interculturalism and the Performance Event', in *Modernism and Performance: Jarry to Brecht*, pp. 118–37.
49. See Bloch et al., *Aesthetics and Politics*.
50. The translator of Hölderlin, David Constantine, notes that contemporary scholars have found more than one thousand errors in Hölderlin's versions of *Oedipus* and *Antigone*. Even if these are all random and not systematic (proposing in themselves a reading), they surely portray a consistent irreverence towards 'the Greeks'.
51. Hölderlin, *Hölderlin's Sophocles: Oedipus and Antigone*, pp. 11–12.
52. 'Texts by Brecht', in Brecht, *The Antigone of Sophocles*, p. 199.
53. Ibid. p. 217.
54. Ibid. pp. 198–9.
55. For a discussion of the philosophical debates surrounding the translations of *deinon* from Hölderlin to Heidegger (who translates the term as *unheimlich*) see Gourgouris, *Does Literature Think?*, pp. 134–7.
56. Brecht, *The Antigone of Sophocles*, pp. 17–18.
57. 'Texts by Brecht', in Brecht, *The Antigone of Sophocles*, p. 203.
58. Dastur, 'Tragedy and Speculation'.
59. Lacoue-Labarthe, 'Hölderlin's Theatre', p. 118.
60. Ibid. pp. 118–19.
61. In 'Tragedy and Speculation', pp. 78–9, Dastur writes, 'The word *speculatio* comes, of course, from *specto*, to look at, to scrunitise, and was used by Boetius to translate the Greek *theoria* into Latin. But in Christian theology the meaning was forgotten, especially by Thomas Aquinas, who derives *speculatio* from *speculum*, mirror, and relates the word of God whom we see now confusedly as "in a mirror" but whom later, that is to say, after death, we will see "face to face". *Speculation* means, therefore, partial and confused knowledge, as indirect and unclear as the image of oneself in the metal mirrors of these early times, and it is this meaning of the word that will be used by the German mystics . . . Thus speculation is connected with the *visio Dei*, the vision of the supersensible, or with what Kant calls "intellectual intuition", an intuition which is refused to finite things, which are only able to have "sensible intuition", that is, an intuition of what is already given to them through their senses.'
62. Hölderlin, *Essays and Letters on Theory*, p. 101.
63. Benjamin, *The Origin of German Tragic Drama*.
64. 'Texts by Brecht', in Brecht, *The Antigone of Sophocles*, p. 204.
65. Ibid. Brecht writes: 'But mere catastrophe is a bad teacher. One learns hunger and thirst from it, but seldom hunger for truth and thirst for knowledge. No amount of illness will turn a sick man into a physician; neither the distant view nor close inspection makes an eye-witness into an expert.'

66. Beckett, *Happy Days*, p. 40. In terms of literary history Beckett's obsession with 'thingness' has been read as deriving primarily from the experiments in anglophone poetic drama. Yeats's famous aphorism calling for actors to be probed about in barrels ('The barrels, I thought, might be on castors, so that I could shove them about with a pole when the actors required it': Yeats, *Explorations*, pp. 86–7) and Eliot's view of the stage as a physical correlative of the poet's voice (Eliot, *Poetry and Drama*) are cited as Beckett's main predecessors. However, Beckett's lineage might be more through the theatrical experiments of the historical avant-garde – where Brecht also gets his obsession with materiality and thingness – than the experiments in verse drama.

67. Lacoue-Labarthe, 'Hölderlin's Theatre', p. 130.

68. Brecht is not oblivious to the significant position occupied by German philosophy in this endeavour, as he writes as early as 1929: 'At present it is Germany, the home of philosophy, that is leading in the large-scale development of the theatre and the drama. The theatre's future is philosophical' – 'Last Stage: Oedipus', in *Brecht on Theatre*, p. 24.

69. See Taxidou, *Tragedy, Modernity and Mourning*.

70. This male homosexual sublime is punctuated by the discourses of male-to-male *philia* and *philoxenia* (hospitality), which come with their own politics and economies of exchange. For a genealogy of the politics of *philia* from Aristotle onwards see Derrida, *The Politics of Friendship*, where he writes: 'What relation does this domination maintain with the *double exclusion* we see at work in all great ethico-politico-philosophical discourses on friendship: on the one hand, the exclusion of friendship between women; on the other, the exclusion between a man and a woman? This double exclusion of the feminine in this philosophical paradigm would then confer on friendship the essential and essentially sublime figure of virile homosexuality' (p. 279). For an analysis of the function of *philia* and *philoxenia* in Athenian tragedy see Taxidou, *Tragedy, Modernity and Mourning*, pp. 64–9; pp. 119–25.

71. See Martin, 'Brecht, Feminism and Chinese Theatre', pp. 79–80. She writes: 'Brecht's emphasis on the form of Chinese acting at the expense of its interior processes, and his choice to ignore the significance of men playing women, could only have occurred because he ignored two of his own main concerns: an understanding of the historical conditions that produced traditional Chinese acting, and an inquiry into the assertion that the actor could and should quote the character played.'

72. See Copjec, *Imagine There's No Woman*, particularly the chapter entitled 'The Tomb of Perseverance: On Antigone', pp. 12–47.

73. See Farfan, *Women, Modernism and Performance*.

74. See Banes, *Dancing Women*.

75. See Smith, 'Brecht and the Mothers of Epic Theatre'.

76. See Sakellaridou, 'Feminist Theatre and the Brechtian Traditon'.

77. Müller, *Germania*, p. 133.

78. 'Texts by Brecht', in Brecht, *The Antigone of Sophocles*, p. 209.

79. See Ackerman, *The Myth and Ritual School*. For a full bibliography of the group's work see Shelley, *The Cambridge Ritualists*.

80. Jameson, *Brecht and Method*, pp. 168–9.

81. Beckett, *Worstward Ho*, p. 7: 'Ever tried. Ever failed. No matter. Try again. Fail again. Fail better.'

82. Boal, *Theatre of the Oppressed*.

83. Brecht, 'A Short Organum for the Theatre', in *Brecht on Theatre*, p. 179.

84. Jameson, *Brecht and Method*, pp. 168–9.

85. For a recent account of the revival of epic and a reinterpretation of the relationship between epic and contemporary performance, see Macintosh and McConnell, *Performing Epic or Telling Tales*. Interestingly, the authors, after delineating a formidable theoretical model that revises the opposition between 'epic' and 'dramatic' and the ways that contemporary performance engages with both, towards the end of the study also draw on the work of Mikhail Bakhtin on narrative theory; in addition, his seminal *Rabelais and His World*, originally written in the 1930s USSR, is also part of the modernist endeavour to revalorise and politicise the popular traditions of performance and storytelling (Vladimir Propp's work on Russian folk tales, for example), with his main test cases drawn from the *commedia dell'arte*. Bakhtin's work in turn can be seen as following the theatrical experiments of Vsevolod Meyerhold and Vladimir Mayakovsky.

6

AFTERWORD:
(NO) MORE MASTERPIECES

It is by repudiation, opposition, damning and cursing that the other high priest of modernist performance, Antonin Artaud, defines his project of a Theatre of Cruelty, also against Greek tragedy, and specifically *Oedipus Rex* and Sophocles. Creating 'the asphyxiating atmosphere in which we live without possible escape or remedy',[1] these masterpieces of literary tradition have weighed heavily on the bodies, souls and minds of the moderns. Even as they do so, however, Artaud's own thinking about theatre and the plague cannot really be separated from the ways this epidemic is portrayed, metaphorised and enacted as both a physical and socio-political malaise, residing both in the individual body of the king and in the body politic, in the play he loves to hate. Here is a recent verse translation of those haunting lines of the chorus's address to Oedipus by Oliver Taplin:

> You see this for yourself:
> our city's foundering, and can no longer
> keep its head above the bloody surf of death.
> The buds that should bear fruit become diseased,
> our grazing cattle-flocks become diseased:
> our women's labour-pains produce still-births.
> Detested Plague, the god who lights the fever-fires,
> has pounced upon our town,
> and drains the homes of Thebes to empty husks.[2]

And this is the same imagery that Artaud evokes in his other apocalyptic essay, 'The Theatre and the Plague'. This longstanding relationship between theatre, discourses of contagion but also of cure are at the core of the anti-theatrical tradition, and as in Plato, the main vehicle of contamination is the actor's body. Artaud writes:

> Between the victim of the plague who runs in shrieking pursuit of his visions and the actor in pursuit of his feelings; between the man who invents for himself personages he could never have imagined without the plague, creating them in the midst of an audience of corpses and delirious lunatics and the poet who inopportunely invents characters, entrusting them to a public equally inert or delirious, there are other analogies which confirm the only truths that count and locate the action of the theater like that of the plague on the level of a veritable epidemic.[3]

Let's recall once more Eleonora Duse's aphoristic epigraph to Craig's essay, 'The Actor and the Über-marionette':

> To save the Theatre, the Theatre must be destroyed, the actors and actresses must all die of the plague . . . They make art impossible.[4]

This is the same performer who may have inspired Craig in making the Black Figure of Hecuba that appears on the cover of this book.

For despite their passionate proclamations, this book has highlighted the ways that these sometimes contradictory relationships to the Greek model of theatre have helped to articulate a specifically modernist understanding of the art of the actor. The body of the actor in both the Brechtian and Artaudian legacies becomes the possibility of both damnation and critique. Greek tragedy as a result is seen as at once partaking in the discourses of the Enlightenment and in its shortcomings, in the various plagues that Artaud charts, but also as offering the possibility of a cure. And this is all the more obvious in the ways that both Brecht and Artaud, and not necessarily in opposition, have offered languages of performance for late twentieth-century and twenty-first-century stagings of classical Greek plays.

These languages of performance, through the modernist experiments in Hellenism as theatricality, have helped to alleviate the 'asphyxiating' hold of old masterpieces. They have also contributed to the notion that the event of performance is multiauthored and multivocal. Coupled with the advent of reception studies, these excursions into Hellenism as theatricality have also helped revise our general understanding and experience of the tragic. The tragic as poetics, as idea and philosophy, has been augmented by the tragic as performance event. The ancient poet and his historical relationship with the classical scholar (usually also male) has through these experiments been reworked as a new set of relationships: between actor and director; between director and scenographer; between actor and puppet; between actor and spectator. This performance imperative has taken away some of the cultural capital of the philosopher and the philologist and redistributed it to the director, the actor, the dancer and the spectator.[5] If these attempts contribute to a genealogy of the postdramatic, they can also be read as gesturing towards a theatre that is post-philosophical. At the same time, they may be read as contributing to a concept of theatricality as a theoretical, methodological and embodied trope; and the ways that this theatricality – a central trope itself of modernism and modernity – wears a Greek tragic mask have been the subject of this book.

When Artaud wrote 'The Theatre and the Plague' and Virginia Woolf wrote her evocative essay 'On Being Ill',[6] it was in the midst of the influenza outbreak that had spread throughout the world by the 1920s. The fight against disease was then, as it is now, seen as a geopolitical as well as a medical issue. Artaud witnessed his inspirational Balinese dancers at the Dutch East India Pavilion in the Parisian Colonial Exposition of 1931. This Pavilion also included a display on the fight against the bubonic plague (which had also spread around the world between 1894 and 1910) and other diseases, no doubt as part of the civilising mission.[7]

In the midst of our current pandemic, what can we learn, what can we cure by revisiting these modernists, who are in turn revisiting the Greeks? Significantly, the epidemic of the previous century was followed by great social and political upheaval. Like the plague in Athens, our present malaise is biological and bio-political, physical and spiritual. Looking at these tragedies again through modernist eyes – through the focus on failure rather than triumph, on speculation rather than success, on tragedy itself as inhabiting both the contradictions and deficits of the democratic project and the promises of the unfinished project of modernity – may help us, like Oedipus, to assume responsibility; may teach us how to mourn our dead; and, like *Oedipus at Colonus*, may urge us to rethink not only what constitutes a good life, but also a good death.

Notes

1. Artaud, 'No More Masterpieces', in *The Theatre and its Double*, pp. 74–83, p. 74.
2. Sophocles, *Four Tragedies*, pp. 15–16.
3. Artaud, 'Theatre and the Plague', in *The Theatre and its Double*, pp. 15–32, pp. 24–5.
4. Quoted in *The Mask*, vol. 1, no. 2, p. 2.
5. Rancière, *The Politics of Aesthetics*, pp. 7–15.
6. See Woolf, *On Being Ill*.
7. See Garner, 'Artaud, Germ Theory, and the Theatre of Contagion'.

BIBLIOGRAPHY

Ackerman, Alan and Martin Puchner (eds), *Against Theatre: Creative Destructions on the Modernist Stage* (Basingstoke: Palgrave Macmillan, 2006).

Ackerman, Robert, *The Myth and Ritual School: J. G. Frazer and the Cambridge Ritualists* (London and New York: Routledge, 2002).

Adorno, Theodor W., *Aesthetic Theory*, trans. and ed. Robert Hullot-Kantor (Minneapolis: University of Minnesota Press, 1998).

Adorno, Theodor W., *Notes to Literature*, trans. S. W. Nicholson, ed. Rolf Tiedemann (New York: Columbia University Press, 1991).

Albright, Daniel, 'Knowing the Dancer, Knowing the Dance', in Fiona Macintosh (ed.), *The Ancient Dancer in the Modern World* (Oxford: Oxford University Press, 2010), pp. 297–312.

Artaud, Antonin, *Œuvres Complètes. Volume VIII* (Paris: Gallimard, 1980).

Artaud, Antonin, *Selected Writings*, ed. and intro. Susan Sontag, trans. Helen Weaver (Berkeley: University of California Press, 1976).

Artaud, Antonin, *The Theatre and Its Double*, trans. Mary Caroline Richards (New York: Grove Press, 1958).

Athanasiou, Athena and Judith Butler, *Dispossession: The Performative in the Political* (Cambridge: Polity Press, 2013).

Austin, J. L., *How to Do Things with Words* (Oxford: Clarendon Press, 1975).

Ayers, David, 'H.D., Ezra Pound and Imagism', in *Modernism: A Short Introduction* (London: John Wiley & Sons, 2008), pp. 1–11.

Aymes, Sophie, 'Woodcuts and Some Words: Edward Gordon Craig's Lasting Impressions', *Image & Narrative* vol. 20, no. 4 (2019), pp. 52–68.

Badiou, Alain, *Plato's Republic: A Dialogue in 16 Chapters*, trans. Susan Spitzer and intro. Kenneth Reinhard (New York: Columbia University Press, 2013).

Badiou, Alain, *The Century*, trans. Alberto Toscano (Cambridge: Polity Press, 2007).

Bakhtin, Mikhail, *Rabelais and His World*, trans. Hélène Islowsky (Bloomington: Indiana University Press, 1968).

Banes, Sally, *Dancing Women: Female Bodies on Stage* (London and New York: Routledge, 1998).

Beard, Mary, *The Invention of Jane Harrison* (Cambridge: Harvard University Press, 2000).

Beckett, Samuel, *Happy Days* (London: Faber and Faber, 1963).

Beckett, Samuel, *Worstward Ho* (London: Calder Publishers, [1984] 1999).

Beistegui, Miguel de and Simon Sparks (eds), *Philosophy and Tragedy* (London: Routledge, 2000).

Benjamin, Andrew (ed.), *Walter Benjamin and Art* (London: Bloomsbury Publishers, 2005).

Benjamin, Walter, *Illuminations*, trans. Harry Zohn (London: Fontana Press, 1992).

Benjamin, Walter, *Moscow Diary*, ed. Gary Smith and trans. Richard Sieburth, foreword by Gershom Scholem (Cambridge, MA: Harvard University Press, 1986).

Benjamin, Walter, *The Origin of German Tragic Drama*, trans. John Osborne (London: Verso, [1928] 1998).

Benjamin, Walter, *The Work of Art in the Age of its Technological Reproducibility and Other Writings on Media*, trans. and eds Michael William Jennings, Brigid Doherty, Thomas Y. Levin and E. F. N. Jephcott (Cambridge, MA: Belknap Press of Harvard University Press, 2008).

Benjamin, Walter, *Understanding Brecht*, trans. Anna Bostock and intro. Stanley Mitchell (London and New York: Verso, 1998).

Benjamin, Walter, Marcus Bullock and Michael W. Jennings (eds), *Selected Writings Vol. 1* (Cambridge, MA: Belknap Press, Harvard University Press, [1996] 2002).

Billings, Joshua, *Genealogy of the Tragic: Greek Tragedy and German Philosophy* (Princeton: Princeton University Press, 2014).

Blair, Fredrika, *Isadora: Portrait of the Artist as a Woman* (New York: McGraw-Hill Companies, 1986).

Bloch, Ernest, George Lukács, Bertolt Brecht, Walter Benjamin and Theodor Adorno, *Aesthetics and Politics*, trans. Ronald Taylor, afterword by Fredric Jameson (London and New York: Verso, 1980).

Boal, Augusto, *Theatre of the Oppressed* (New York: Theatre Communications Group, 1993).

Brecht, Bertolt, *Brecht on Theatre*, ed. John Willet, 13th ed. (New York: Hill and Wang, 1977).

Brecht, Bertolt, *Letters 1913–1956*, ed. John Willett, trans R. Manheim (London: Methuen, 1990).

Brecht, Bertolt, *The Antigone of Sophocles – Collected Plays, Vol. 8*, ed. Tom Kuhn and David Constantine, trans. David Constantine (London: Methuen, 2003).

Browne, E. Martin, *The Making of T. S. Eliot's Plays* (Cambridge: Cambridge University Press, 1969).

Buchanan, Ian and John Marks (eds), *Deleuze and Literature* (Edinburgh: Edinburgh University Press, 2000).

Buckley, Jennifer, *Beyond Text: Theatre and Performance in Print after 1900* (Ann Arbor: University of Michigan Press, 2019).

Burrow, Colin, 'Shakespeare and Epic', in Fiona Macintosh, Justine McConnell, Stephen Harrison and Claire Kenward (eds), *Epic Performances from the Middle Ages into the Twenty-First Century* (Oxford: Oxford University Press, 2018), pp. 31–45.

Burt, Ramsay, *The Male Dancer* (London and New York: Routledge, 1995).

Butler, E. M., *The Tyranny of Greece over Germany* (Cambridge: Cambridge University Press, 1935).

Cairns, Douglas (ed.), *A Cultural History of the Emotions, Vol. 1: A Cultural History of the Emotions in Antiquity* (London: Bloomsbury, 2019).

Cairns, Douglas, 'A Short History of Shudders', in A. Chaniotis and P. Ducrey (eds), *Unveiling Emotions: Emotions in Greece and Rome II: Texts, Images, Material Culture* (Stuttgart: Steiner, 2013), pp. 85–107.

Cairns, Douglas, *Sophocles: Antigone* (London: Bloomsbury, 2016).

Cairns, Douglas, and Damien Nelis (eds), *Emotions in the Classical World: Methods, Approaches, and Directions* (Heidelberg: Franz Steiner, 2017).

Calder, William M. (ed.), *The Cambridge Ritualists Reconsidered* (Atlanta, GA: Scholars Press, 1991).

Cardullo, Bert and Robert Knopf (eds), *Theatre of the Avant-garde, 1890–1950* (New Haven: Yale University Press, 2001).

Carpentier, Martha C., *Ritual, Myth and the Modernist Text: The Influence of Jane Ellen Harrison on Joyce, Eliot, and Woolf* (Amsterdam: Gordon and Breach, 1998).

Chaniotis, Angelos, *Unveiling Emotions: Sources and Methods for the Study of Emotions in the Greek World* (Heidelberg: Franz Steiner, 2013).

Chisolm, Lawrence W., *Fenollosa: The Far East and American Culture* (New Haven: Yale University Press, 1963).

Coomaraswamy, Ananda, *The Dance of Shiva* (New Delhi: Sagar Publications, [1918] 1968).

Copjec, Joan, *Imagine There's No Woman: Ethics and Sublimation* (Cambridge, MA: MIT Press, 2002).

Cornford, Francis Macdonald, *The Origin of Attic Comedy* (London: Edward Arnold Press, 1914).

Craig, Edward Gordon, *A Living Theatre: The Gordon Craig School, the Arena Goldoni, The Mask* (Florence: School for the Art of the Theatre, 1913).

Craig, Edward Gordon (as John Balance), 'A Note on Masks', *The Mask* vol. 1, no. 2 (1908), pp. 9–12.

Craig, Edward Gordon, *A Production, Being Thirty-Two Collotype Plates of Designs Projected or Realized for The Pretenders of Henrik Ibsen Produced at the Royal Theatre, Copenhagen, 1926* (London: Humphrey Milford and Oxford University Press, 1930).

Craig, Edward Gordon, *Black Figures: 105 Reproductions with an Unpublished Essay*, ed. L. M. Newman (Wellingborough: Christopher Skelton; Chalbury, Oxford: Senecio Press, 1989).

Craig, Edward Gordon, *Books and Theatres* (London: J. M. Dent, 1925).

Craig, Edward Gordon, *Ellen Terry and Her Secret Self* (London: Sampson Low, Marston, 1931).

Craig, Edward Gordon, *Henry Irving* (New York: Longmans, Green, 1930).

Craig, Edward Gordon, *Index to the Story of My Days: Some Memoirs of Edward Gordon Craig, 1872–1907* (London: Hulton Press, 1957).

Craig, Edward Gordon, *Isadora Duncan: Sechs Bewegungsstudien von Edward Gordon Craig* (Leipzig: Insel Verlag, 1906).

Craig, Edward Gordon, *Nothing, or The Bookplate* (London: Chatto and Windus, 1925).

Craig, Edward Gordon, *On the Art of the Theatre* (London: William Heinemann, 1911).

Craig, Edward Gordon, *Scene* (London: Oxford University Press, 1923).

Craig, Edward Gordon, 'The Actor and the Übermarionette', *The Mask* vol. 1, no. 2 (1908), pp. 3–15.

Craig, Edward Gordon, *The Art of the Theatre* (Edinburgh and London: T. N. Foulis, 1905).

Craig, Edward Gordon, *The Correspondence of Edward Gordon Craig and Count Harry Kessler, 1903–1937*, ed. L. M. Newman (London: W. S. Maney for the Modern Humanities Research Association and the Institute of Germanic Studies, University of London, 1995).

Craig, Edward Gordon (ed.), *The Mask*, 12 vols. (Florence: 1908–29).

Craig, Edward Gordon, *The Theatre – Advancing* (Boston: Little, 1919).

Craig, Edward Gordon, *Towards a New Theatre: Forty Designs for Stage Scenes, with critical notes by the inventor, Edward Gordon Craig* (London: J. M. Dent, 1913).

Craig, Edward Gordon, *Woodcuts and Some Words* (London: J. M. Dent, 1924).

Crawford, Robert, *The Savage and the City in the Works of T. S. Eliot* (Oxford: Clarendon Press, 1990).

Cuda, Anthony and Ronald Schuchard (eds), *The Complete Prose of T. S. Eliot, Vol. 2: 1919–1926* (Baltimore: Johns Hopkins University Press; London: Faber and Faber, 2014).

Darwin-Cornford Papers, British Library, MS 58407, vol. 35; MS 58428, vol. 56.

Dastur, Françoise, 'Hölderlin and the Orientalisation of Greece', *Pli* 10 (2000), pp. 156–73.

Dastur, Françoise, 'Tragedy and Speculation', in M. de Beistegui and Simon Sparks (eds), *Philosophy and Tragedy* (London: Routledge, 2000), pp. 78–87.

Debord, Guy, *The Society of the Spectacle*, trans. Donald Nicholson Smith (New York: Zone Books, 1994).

Derrida, Jacques, *The Politics of Friendship*, trans. George Collins (London and New York: Verso, 2005).

Diamond, Elin, 'The Shudder of Catharsis', in Andrew Parker and Eve Kosofsky Sedgwick (eds), *Performativity and Performance* (London and New York: Routledge, 1996), pp. 152–72.

Donald, James, Anne Friedberg and Laura Marcus (eds), *Close Up, 1927–1933: Cinema and Modernism* (London: Continuum International Publishers, 1998).

Duncan, Isadora, *Art of the Dance* (New York: Theatre Arts Books, 1928).

Duncan, Isadora, *My Life* (New York: Liveright, [1928] 1996).

Eaton, Katherine Bliss, *The Theatre of Meyerhold and Brecht* (Westport, CT: Greenwood Press, 1985).

Eisenstein, Sergei, *The Film Sense*, trans. and ed. Joy Leyda (New York: Meridian Books, 1957).

Eliot, T. S., 'Classics in English', *Poetry* vol. 9, no. 2 (1916), pp. 101–4.

Eliot, T. S., 'Dramatis Personae' [1923], in *Complete Prose of T. S. Eliot, Volume 2: 1919–1926*, ed. Anthony Cuba and Ronald Schuchard (Baltimore, MD: Johns Hopkins University Press, 2014), pp. 433–7.

Eliot, T. S., 'Euripides and Professor Murray', *Selected Essays 1917–1932* (New York: Harcourt, Brace and Co, [1918] 1932), pp. 46–50.

Eliot, T. S., *Poetry and Drama* (London: Faber and Faber, [1951] 1957).

Eliot, T. S., *Selected Essays* (London: Faber and Faber, 1999).

Eliot, T. S., *Selected Prose of T. S. Eliot*, ed. Frank Kermode (New York: Harvest Books, 1975).

Eliot, T. S., *The Complete Prose of T. S. Eliot, Volume 2: 1919–1926*, ed. Anthony Cuba and Ronald Schuchard (Baltimore, MD: Johns Hopkins University Press, 2014).

Eliot, T. S., *The Letters of T. S. Eliot, Volume 4*, ed. Valerie Eliot and John Haffenden (New Haven, CT: Yale University Press, 2013).

Eliot, T. S., *The Sacred Wood* (London: Methuen, 1967).

Farfan, Penny, *Performing Queer Modernism* (Oxford: Oxford University Press, 2017).

Farfan, Penny, *Women, Modernism and Performance* (Cambridge: Cambridge University Press, 2004).

Felski, Rita (ed.), *Rethinking Tragedy* (Baltimore: The Johns Hopkins University Press, 2008).

Fischer-Lichte, Erika, *Tragedy's Endurance: Performances of Greek Tragedies and Cultural Identity in Germany since 1800* (Oxford: Oxford University Press [Classical Presences], 2017).

Foley, Helene P., *Female Acts in Greek Tragedy* (Princeton: Princeton University Press, 2001).

Frank, Adam, 'The Expansion of Setting in Gertrude Stein's Landscape Theatre', *Modernism/modernity*, vol. 3, cycle 1 (March 2018), <https://doi.org/10.26597/mod.0045> (last accessed 5 October 2020).

Franko, Mark, *Dancing Modernism/Performing Politics* (Bloomington: Indiana University Press, 1995).

Franko, Mark, *The Work of Dance: Labor, Movement and Identity in the 1930s* (Middletown, CT: Wesleyan University Press, 2002).

Friedberg, Anne, 'Introduction to *Borderline* and the POOL Group', in James Donald, Anne Friedberg and Laura Marcus (eds), *Close Up, 1927–1933: Cinema and Modernism* (London: Continuum International Publishers, 1998), pp. 212–20.

Friedman, Susan Stanford, *Penelope's Web: Gender, Modernity, H.D.'s Fiction* (Cambridge: Cambridge University Press, 1990).

Friedman, Susan Stanford, *Planetary Modernisms: Provocations on Modernity Across Time* (New York: Columbia University Press, 2017).

Friedman, Susan Stanford, *Psyche Reborn: The Emergence of H.D.* (Bloomington: Indiana University Press, 1981).

Fuchs, Elinor, *The Death of Character: Perspectives on Theater after Modernism* (Bloomington: Indiana University Press, 1996).

Garner, Stanton B., Jr, 'Artaud, Germ Theory, and the Theatre of Contagion', *Theatre Journal*, vol. 58, no. 1 (March 2006), pp. 1–14.

Gill, Christopher, *Personality in Greek Epic, Tragedy, and Philosophy* (Oxford: Clarendon Press, 1996).

Goodall, Jane, *Stage Presence* (London and New York: Routledge, 2008).

Gordon, Mel, *Dada Performance*, trans. Henry Marx (New York: PAJ Publications, 2001).

Gould, Thomas, *The Ancient Quarrel Between Poetry and Philosophy* (Princeton: Princeton University Press, 1990).

Gourgouris, Stathis, *Does Literature Think? Literature as Theory for an Antimythical Era* (Stanford: Stanford University Press, 2003).

Gregory, Eileen, *H.D. and Hellenism* (Cambridge: Cambridge University Press, 1997).

Gregory, Eileen, 'Respondent Essay: H.D. and Euripides: Ghostly Summoning', in Lynn Kozak and Miranda Hickman (eds), *The Classics in Modernist Translation* (London: Bloomsbury Publishing, 2019), pp. 120–7.

Guattari, Félix and Gilles Deleuze, *A Thousand Plateaus: Capitalism and Schizophrenia*, trans. Brian Massumi (St Paul: University of Minnesota Press, 1987).

Guattari, Félix and Gilles Deleuze, *Anti-Oedipus: Capitalism and Schizophrenia*, trans. Robert Hurley, Mark Seem and Helen R. Lane, preface by Michel Foucault (London: Bloomsbury, [1977] 2003).

Hall, Edith and Fiona Macintosh (eds), *Greek Tragedy and the British Theatre, 1660–1914* (Oxford: Oxford University Press, 2005).

Halliwell, Stephen (trans. and intro.), *Aristotle's Poetics* (London: Bloomsbury, 2013).

Halliwell, Stephen, *The Aesthetics of Mimesis: Ancient Texts and Modern Problems* (Princeton: Princeton University Press, 2002).

Hardwick, Lorna, *Reception Studies* (Oxford: Oxford University Press, 2003).

Hardwick, Lorna, 'Thinking with Classical Reception: Critical Distance, Critical Licence, Critical Amnesia?' in E. Richardson (ed.), *Classics in Extremis: The Edges of Classical Reception* (London: Bloomsbury, 2018), pp. 13–24.

Hardwick, Lorna, *Translating Words, Translating Cultures* (London: Bloomsbury, 2000).

Hardwick, Lorna and Christopher Stary (eds), *A Companion to Classical Receptions* (Oxford: Wiley-Blackwell, 2011).

Harrop, Stephe, 'Ezra Pound's *Women of Trachis*: Modernist Translations as Performance Text', *Platform: E-Journal of Theatre and Performing Arts*, vol. 3, no. 1 (Spring 2008), pp. 90–104.

Harrop, Stephe and David Wiles, 'Poetic Language and Corporeality in Translations of Greek Tragedy', *New Theatre Quarterly* vol. 24 (2008), pp. 51–64.

Hölderlin, Friedrich, *Essays and Letters on Theory*, trans. Thomas Pfau (Albany: State University of New York Press, 1988).

Hölderlin, Friedrich, *Hölderlin's Sophocles: Oedipus and Antigone*, trans. and intro. David Constantine (Bloodaxe Books, 2001).

H.D., *Bid Me to Live*, ed. C. Zilboorg (Gainsville: University Press of Florida, 2011).

H.D., *Bid Me to Live: A Madrigal* (New York: Dial, 1960).

H.D., 'Borderline: a POOL Film with Paul Robeson', in James Donald, Anne Friedberg and Laura Marcus (eds), *Close Up, 1927–1933: Cinema and Modernism* (London: Continuum International Publishers, 1998), pp. 221–35.

H.D. (trans.), *Choruses from Iphigeneia in Aulis* (London: Ballantyne, 1915).

H.D. (trans.), *Choruses from the Iphigeneia in Aulis and the Hippolytus of Euripides* (London: The Egoist Ltd., 1919).

H.D., *Collected Poems, 1912–1944*, ed. Louis L. Martz (New York: New Directions, 1983).

H.D., *End to Torment: A Memoir of Ezra Pound*, ed. N. H. Pearson and M. King (New York: New Directions, 1979).

H.D., *Helen in Egypt*, intro. Eileen Gregory (New York: New Directions, 1974).

H.D., *HERmione* (New York: New Directions, 1981).

H.D., *Hippolytus Temporizes & Ion: Adaptations of Two Plays by Euripides* (New York: New Directions, [1927] 2003).

H.D., 'Joan of Arc', in James Donald, Anne Friedberg and Laura Marcus (eds), *Close Up, 1927–1933: Cinema and Modernism* (London: Continuum International Publishers, 1998), pp. 130–3.

H.D., 'Notes on Euripides', in *Ion: A Play After Euripides* (New York: Black Swan Books, 1986).

H.D., *Notes on Euripides, Pausanius and Greek Lyric Poets* (1920), H.D. Papers, Beinecke Rare Book and Manuscript Library, Box 43: Folder 1111, Yale University.

H.D., *Notes on Thought and Vision and the Wise Sappho* (San Francisco: City Lights, 1982).

H.D., *Paint It To-day*, ed. and intro. C. Laity (New York: New York University Press, 1992).

H.D., *Palimpsest* (Carbondale: Southern Illinois University Press, [1926] 1968).

H.D., *Selected Poems*, ed. Louis L. Martz (New York: New Directions, 1988).

H.D., 'The Cinema and the Classics', in James Donald, Anne Friedberg and Laura Marcus (eds), *Close Up, 1927–1933: Cinema and Modernism* (London: Continuum International Publishers, 1998), 'I: Beauty', pp. 105–9; 'II: Restraint', pp. 110–13; 'III: The Mask and the Movietone', pp. 114–19.

H.D., *Tribute to Freud* (New York: New Directions, [1956] 2012).

H.D., *Trilogy*, intro and notes A. Barnstone (New York, New Directions, 1998).

Innes, Christopher, *Edward Gordon Craig: A Vision of Theatre* (London and New York: Routledge, 1983).

Jameson, Fredric (ed.), *Aesthetics and Politics: Theodor Adorno, Walter Benjamin, Ernst Bloch, Bertolt Brecht, Georg Lukács* (London: Verso, 2007).

Jameson, Fredric, *Brecht and Method* (London and New York: Verso, 1998).

Jelavich, Peter, *Berlin Dada* (Cambridge, MA: Harvard University Press, 2009).

Jennings, Michael, Brigid Doherty and Thomas Y. Levin (eds and trans.), *The Work of Art in the Age of Technological Reproducibility and Other Writings* (Cambridge, MA: Harvard University Press, 2008).

Jones, David E., *The Plays of T. S. Eliot* (London: Routledge & Kegan Paul, 1960).

Jones, Susan, 'Modernism and Dance: Apolline or Dionysiac', in F. Macintosh (ed.), *Ancient Dancer in the Modern World* (Oxford: Oxford University Press, 2010), pp. 313–29.

Jones, Susan, *Literature, Modernism, and Dance* (Oxford: Oxford University Press, 2013).

Jowitt, Deborah, 'Images of Isadora: The Search for Motion', *Dance Research Journal* vol. 17/18 (Autumn 1985 – Spring 1986), pp. 21–9.

Kastleman, Rebecca, Kevin Riordan and Claire Warden (eds), *Modernism on the World Stage*: special issue of *Modernism/modernity* (Baltimore: The Johns Hopkins University Press, 2019).

Kenner, Hugh, *The Invisible Poet* (London: Routledge and Kegan Paul, 1959).

Kleberg, Lars, *Theatre as Action: Soviet Russian Avant-garde Aesthetics*, trans. Charles Rougle (London: The Macmillan Press, 1993).

Kolocotroni, Vassiliki, 'Still Life: Modernism's Turn to Greece,' *Journal of Modern Literature*, vol. 35, no. 2 (2012), pp. 1–24.

Kolocotroni, Vassiliki and Olga Taxidou (eds), *The Edinburgh Dictionary of Modernism* (Edinburgh: Edinburgh University Press, 2018).

Kolocotroni, Vassiliki, Jane Goldman and Olga Taxidou (eds), *Modernism: An Anthology of Sources and Documents* (Edinburgh: Edinburgh University Press, 1998).

Koulouris, Theodore, *Hellenism and Loss in the Work of Virginia Woolf* (Farnham: Ashgate, 2011).

Kowalzig, Barbara, 'Broken Rhythms in Plato's *Laws*: Materialising Social Time in the Chorus', in Anastasia-Erasmia Peponi (ed.), *Performance and Culture in Plato's Laws* (Cambridge: Cambridge University Press, 2013), pp. 171–211.

Kozak, Lynn and Miranda Hickman (eds), *The Classics in Modernist Translation* (London: Bloomsbury Publishing, 2019).

Kuhn, Tom and Steve Giles (eds), *Brecht on Art and Politics* (London: Methuen, 2003).

Kurke, Leslie, 'Imagining Chorality: Wonder, Plato's Puppets, and Moving Statues,' in Anastasia-Erasmia Peponi (ed.), *Performance and Culture in Plato's Laws* (Cambridge: Cambridge University Press, 2013), pp. 123–70.

Lacoue-Labarthe, Philippe, 'Hölderlin's Theatre', in Miguel de Beistegui and Simon Sparks (eds), *Philosophy and Tragedy* (London: Routledge, 2000), pp. 115–35.

LaMothe, Kimerer L. '"A God Dances through Me": Isadora Duncan on Friedrich Nietzsche's Revaluation of Values,' *The Journal of Religion* vol. 85, no. 2 (April 2005), pp. 241–66.

Leach, Robert, *Makers of Modern Theatre: An Introduction* (London and New York: Routledge, 2004).

Leach, Robert, *Revolutionary Theatre* (London and New York: Routledge, 1994).

Leach, Robert, *Russian Futurist Theatre: Theory and Practice* (Edinburgh: Edinburgh University Press, 2018).

Leach, Robert, *Vsevolod Meyerhold* (Cambridge: Cambridge University Press, 1989).

Lehmann, Hans-Thies, *Postdramatic Theatre*, trans. Karen Jürs-Munby (London and New York: Routledge, 2006).

Lehmann, Hans-Thies, *Tragedy and Dramatic Theatre*, trans. Erik Butler (London and New York: Routledge, 2016).

Leonard, Miriam, *Tragic Modernities* (Cambridge, MA: Harvard University Press, 2015).

Leonard, Miriam and Joshua Billings (eds), *Tragedy and the Idea of Modernity* (Oxford: Oxford University Press, 2015).

Levin, Susan B., *The Ancient Quarrel between Poetry and Philosophy Revisited: Plato and the Greek Literary Tradition* (Oxford: Oxford University Press, 2001).

Liebregts, Peter, '"No Man Knows his Luck 'Till He's Dead": Ezra Pound's *Women of Trachis*', in *Quaderni de Palazzo Serra*, vol. 15 (2008), pp. 300–14.

Liebregts, Peter, *Translations of Greek Tragedy in the Work of Ezra Pound* (London: Bloomsbury Academic, 2019).

Macintosh, Fiona, 'From the Court to the National: The Theatrical Legacy of Gilbert Murray's Bacchae', in Christopher Stray (ed.), *Gilbert Murray Reassessed: Hellenism, Theatre, and International Politics* (Oxford: Oxford University Press, 2007), pp. 145–66.

Macintosh, Fiona and Justine McConnell, *Performing Epic or Telling Tales* (Oxford: Oxford University Press, 2020).

Macintosh, Fiona, Justine McConnell, Stephen Harrison and Claire Kenward (eds), *Epic Performances: From the Middle Ages into the Twenty-First Century* (Oxford: Oxford University Press, 2018).

Mao, Douglas (ed.), *The New Modernist Studies* (Cambridge: Cambridge University Press, online 2020, print 2022).

Marcus, Laura, *The Tenth Muse: Writing about Cinema in the Modernist Period* (Oxford: Oxford University Press, 2007).

Martin, Carol, 'Brecht, Feminism and Chinese Theatre', *The Drama Review* vol. 43, no. 4 (1999), pp. 77–85.

Miller, Tyrus, *Modernism and the Frankfurt School* (Edinburgh: Edinburgh University Press, 2014).

Müller, Heiner, *Germania*, trans. Bernard and Caroline Schütze, ed. Sylvere Lotringer (New York: Semiotext[e], 1990).

Newman, L. M., *Edward Gordon Craig, Black Figures: 105 Reproductions with an Unpublished Essay* (Wellingborough: Christopher Skelton; Chalbury, Oxford: Senecio Press, 1989).

Nietzsche, Friedrich, *The Birth of Tragedy: Out of the Spirit of Music*, trans. Susan Whiteside, intro. Michael Tanner (London: Penguin Classics, 1994).

Nietzsche, Friedrich, *Thus Spoke Zarathustra*, in *The Portable Nietzsche*, ed. and trans. Walter Kaufmann (New York: Penguin, 1959).

Nussbaum, Martha C., *The Fragility of Goodness: Luck and Ethics in Greek Tragedy and Philosophy* (Cambridge: Cambridge University Press, 1986).

Parker, Andrew and Eve Kosofsky Sedgwick (eds), *Performativity and Performance* (London and New York: Routledge, 1996).

Peponi, Anastasia-Erasmia (ed.), *Performance and Culture in Plato's Laws* (Cambridge: Cambridge University Press, 2013).

Peters, Julie Stone, 'Jane Harrison and the Savage Dionysus: Archaeological Voyages, Ritual Origins, Anthropology, and the Modern Theatre', *Modern Drama* vol. 51, no. 1 (Spring 2008), pp. 1–41.

Plato, *The Collected Dialogues*, ed. Edith Hamilton and Huntington Cairns (Princeton: Princeton University Press, 1999).

Plato, *The Laws*, trans. A. E. Taylor (London and New York: Everyman's Library, 1969).

Porter, James I., *Nietzsche and the Philology of the Future* (Stanford: Stanford University Press, 2002).

Porter, James I., *The Invention of Dionysus* (Stanford: Stanford University Press, 2000).

Potamkin, Harry A., 'The Aframerican Cinema', in James Donald, Anne Friedberg and Laura Marcus (eds), *Close Up, 1927–1933: Cinema and Modernism* (London: Cassell, 1998), pp. 65–72.

Potter, Michelle, 'Designed for Dance: The Costumes of Léon Bakst and the Art of Isadora Duncan', *Dance Chronicle* vol. 13, no. 2 (1990), pp. 154–69.

Pound, Ezra, *ABC of Reading* (London: Faber and Faber, [1934] 1951).

Pound, Ezra, *Ezra Pound: Poems and Translations*, ed. Richard Sieburth (New York: Library of America, 2003).

Pound, Ezra, *Guide to Kulchur* (London: Peter Owen, [1938] 1952).

Pound, Ezra, *Literary Essays*, ed. T. S. Eliot (London: Faber and Faber, 1954).

Pound, Ezra, *Literary Essays of Ezra Pound*, ed. T. S. Eliot (New York: New Directions, 1935).

Pound, Ezra, *Make It New* (New Haven: Yale University Press, 1935).

Pound, Ezra, *Pound/Joyce: The Letters of Ezra Pound to James Joyce, with Pound's Essays on Joyce*, ed. F. Read (New York: New Directions, 1967).

Pound, Ezra, *Selected Letters of Ezra Pound, 1907–1941*, ed. D. D. Paige (New York: New Directions, [1950] 1971).

Pound, Ezra, 'Sophokles' *Women of Trachis*: A Version by Ezra Pound', *The Hudson Review* vol. 6, no. 4 (Winter 1954), pp. 487–523.

Pound, Ezra, *The Cantos* (London: Faber and Faber, 1986).

Pound, Ezra, *The Translations of Ezra Pound*, ed. Hugh Kenner (New York: New Directions, 1970).

Pound, Ezra and Rudd Flemming, *Elektra*, ed. R. Reid (London: Faber and Faber, [1949] 1990).

Preston, Carrie, *Modernism's Mythic Pose: Gender, Genre and Solo Performance* (Oxford: Oxford University Press, 2011).

Prins, Yopie, *Ladies' Greek: Victorian Translations of Tragedy* (Princeton: Princeton University Press, 2017).

Puchner, Martin, *Poetry of the Revolution: Marx, Manifestos, and the Avant-Gardes* (Princeton: Princeton University Press, 2006).

Puchner, Martin, *The Drama of Ideas: Platonic Provocations in Theater and Philosophy* (New York: Oxford University Press, 2010).

Rancière, Jacques, *Aisthesis*, trans. Zakir Paul (London and New York: Verso, 2013).

Rancière, Jacques, 'The Archaeomodern Turn', in Michael P. Steinberg (ed.), *Walter Benjamin and the Demands of History* (Ithaca, NY: Cornell University Press, 1996), pp. 24–40.

Rancière, Jacques, *The Emancipated Spectator* (New York and London: Verso, 2011).

Rancière, Jacques, *The Politics of Aesthetics: The Distribution of the Sensible*, trans. and ed. Gabriel Rockhill (London and New York: Bloomsbury Academic, [2004] 2013).

Revermann, Martin, 'Brecht and Greek Tragedy: Re-thinking the Dialectics of Utilising the Tradition of Theatre', *German Life and Letters*, vol. 69, no. 2 (April 2016), pp. 213–32.

Roach, Joseph R., *The Player's Passion: Studies in the Science of Acting* (Ann Arbor: University of Michigan Press, 1993).

Roessler, Norman and Anthony Squiers (eds), *Philosophizing Brecht: Critical Readings on Art, Consciousness, Social Theory and Performance* (Leiden and Boston: Brill Rodopi, 2019).

Rokem, Freddie, *Philosophers and Thespians: Thinking Performance* (Stanford: Stanford University Press, 2009).

Rood, Arnold (ed.), *Gordon Craig on Movement and Dance* (London: Dance Books, 1977).

Sakellaridou, Elizabeth, 'Feminist Theatre and the Brechtian Tradition', in Antony Tatlow (ed.), *Where Extremes Meet: Rereading Brecht and Beckett, The Brecht Yearbook* 27 (Pittsburgh, PA: University of Wisconsin Press, 2002), pp. 179–98.

Schiller, Friedrich and Johann Wolfgang von Goethe, *Correspondence between Schiller and Goethe from 1794 to 1805*, trans. Liselotte Diekmann (Bern: Peter Lang, 1994).

Schopenhauer, Arthur, *On the Suffering of the World*, trans. R. J. Hollingdale (London: Penguin, 1998).

Sedgwick, Eve Kosofsky, *Touching, Feeling: Affect, Pedagogy, Performativity* (Durham, NC: Duke University Press, 2002).

Senelick, Laurence, *Gordon Craig's Moscow Hamlet: A Reconstruction* (Westport, CT: Greenwood Publishers, 1982).

Shelley, Arlen, *The Cambridge Ritualists: An Annotated Bibliography* (Metuchen, NJ and London: The Scarecrow Press, 1990).

Silk, Michael S. (ed.), *Tragedy and the Tragic: Greek Tragedy and Beyond* (Oxford: Clarendon Press, 1996).

Silk, Michael S. and J. P. Stern (eds), *Nietzsche on Tragedy* (Cambridge: Cambridge University Press, [1981] 2016).

Smith, Charles Harrison, *T. S. Eliot's Dramatic Theory and Practice: From Sweeney Agonistes to the Elder Statesman* (Princeton: Princeton University Press, 1963).

Smith, Iris, 'Brecht and the Mothers of Epic Theatre', *Theatre Journal*, vol. 43, no. 4 (1991), pp. 491–505.

Sophocles, *Four Tragedies: Oedipus the King, Aias, Philoctetes, Oedipus at Colonus*, trans. Oliver Taplin (Oxford: Oxford University Press, 2016).

Stanislavski, Constantine, *My Life in Art*, trans. J. J. Robbins (London: Routledge, [1942] 1987).

Steegmuller, Francis, *Your Isadora: The Love Story of Isadora Duncan and Gordon Craig* (New York: Pub Center Cultural Resources, 1974).

Stein, Gertrude, *A Stein Reader*, ed. and intro. Ulla E Dydo (Evanston, IL: Northwestern University Press, 1993).

Stein, Gertrude, *Doctor Faustus Lights the Lights*, in Bert Cardullo and Robert Knopf (eds), *Theatre of the Avant-garde, 1890–1950* (New Haven: Yale University Press, 2001), pp. 400–24.

Stein, Gertrude, *Last Plays and Operas*, ed. and intro. Bonnie Marranca (Baltimore, MD and London: Johns Hopkins University Press, 1995).

Stein, Gertrude, 'Plays', in Bert Cardullo and Robert Knopf (eds), *Theatre of the Avant-garde, 1890–1950* (New Haven: Yale University Press, 2001), pp. 425–40.

Steinberg, Michael P. (ed.), *Walter Benjamin and the Demands of History* (Ithaca, NY: Cornell University Press, 1996).

Stergiopoulou, Katerina, '"And a Good Job"?: Elektrifying English at St Elizabeths', *Journal of Modern Literature* vol. 39, no. 1 (Fall 2015), pp. 87–111.

Stokes, John, *Resistible Theatres: Enterprise and Experiment in the Late-Nineteenth Century* (London: Paul Elek Books Ltd, 1972).

Stray, Christopher (ed.), *Gilbert Murray Reassessed: Hellenism, Theatre, and International Politics* (Oxford: Oxford University Press, 2007).

Syros, Christine, 'Beyond Language: Ezra Pound's Translation of the Sophoclean *Elektra*', *Paideuma: Modern and Contemporary Poetry and Poetics* vol. 23, no. 2/3 (Winter and Fall 1994), pp. 107–39.

Szondi, Peter, *An Essay on the Tragic*, trans. Paul Flemming (Stanford: Stanford University Press, [1978] 2002).

Szondi, Peter, *Theory of the Modern Drama*, ed. and trans. Michael Hays (Cambridge: Cambridge University Press, 1965).

Taxidou, Olga, 'Crude Thinking: John Fuegi and Recent Brecht Criticism', *New Theatre Quarterly*, vol. 11, no. 44 (1995), pp. 381–4.

Taxidou, Olga, 'Dancer, Actor, Marionette: The Modernist Performer', *Modernism/modernity*, vol. 4, cycle 3 (October 2019), <https://doi.org/10.26597/mod.0128> (last accessed 5 October 2020).

Taxidou, Olga, *Modernism and Performance: Jarry to Brecht* (Basingstoke: Palgrave Macmillan, 2007).

Taxidou, Olga, *The Mask: A Periodical Performance by Edward Gordon Craig* (London and New York: Routledge, [1998] 2013).

Taxidou, Olga, *Tragedy, Modernity and Mourning* (Edinburgh: Edinburgh University Press, 2004).

Terry, Walter, *Isadora Duncan: Her Life, Her Art, Her Legacy* (New York: Dodd and Meade Company, 1963).

Theis, Catherine, 'Braving the Elements: H.D. and Jeffers', in Lynn Kozak and Miranda Hickman (eds), *The Classics in Modernist Translation* (London: Bloomsbury Publishing, 2019), pp. 91–105.

Venuti, Lawrence (ed.), *The Translation Studies Reader* (New York: Routledge, 2000).

Venuti, Lawrence, *The Translator's Invisibility: A History of Translation* (London: Routledge, 1995).

Walton, J. Michael, 'Craig and the Greeks', *Theatre Arts Journal* vol. 3, no. 1 (2015), pp. 23–35.

Walton, J. Michael (ed.), *Craig on Theatre* (London: Methuen, 1983).

Weber, Samuel, *Benjamin's -abilities* (Cambridge, MA: Harvard University Press, 2010).

Weber, Samuel, *Theatricality as Medium*, 4th ed. (New York: Fordham University Press, 2004).

Wilde, Oscar, *The Works of Oscar Wilde: Essays, Criticisms and Reviews* (London: Nabu Press, [1923] 2014).

Wiles, David, 'Epic Acting in Shakespeare's *Hamlet*', in Fiona Macintosh, Justine McConnell, Stephen Harrison, and Claire Kenward (eds), *Epic Performances from the Middle Ages into the Twenty-First Century* (Oxford: Oxford University Press, 2018), pp. 76–89.

Wiles, David, 'Sophoclean Diptychs: Modern Translations of Dramatic Poetry', *Arion* vol. 13, no. 1 (2005), pp. 9–26.

Wiles, David, *The Players' Advice to Hamlet: The Rhetorical Acting Method from the Renaissance to the Enlightenment* (Cambridge: Cambridge University Press, 2020).

Woolf, Virginia, *On Being Ill* [1930], intro. Hermione Lee (Middletown, CT: Wesleyan University Press/Paris Press, 2002).

Yeats, W. B., *A Vision: The Revised 1937 Edition: The Collected Works of W. B. Yeats, Vol. XIV*, ed. Catherine E. Paul and Margaret Mills Harper (New York: Scribner, 2015).

Yeats, W. B., *Explorations* (London: Macmillan, 1962).

Yeats, W. B., 'Oedipus the King' [1931], in *The Collected Works of W. B. Yeats, Volume X: Later Articles and Reviews*, ed. Colton Johnson (New York: Scribner, 2000), pp. 219–23.

Yeats, W. B., 'Plain Man's *Oedipus*' [1931], in *The Collected Works of W. B. Yeats, Volume X: Later Articles and Reviews*, ed. Colton Johnson (New York: Scribner, 2000), pp. 244–5).

Yeats, W. B., *Plays and Controversies* (London and New York: Macmillan, 1924).

Yeats, W. B., 'Preface to Sophocles', *King Oedipus: A Version for the Modern Stage* (London and New York: Macmillan & Co., 1928); also in 'Sophocles' *King Oedipus*, A Version for the Modern Stage', in R. K. Alspach (ed.), *The Variorum Edition of the Plays of W. B. Yeats* (New York: Macmillan, 1966), pp. 809–51.

Yeats, W. B., *The Collected Works of W. B. Yeats, Vol II: The Plays*, ed. David R. Clark and Rosalind E. Clark (New York: Scribner, 2001).

Yeats, W. B., 'The Irish Censorship' [1928], in *The Collected Works of W. B.*

Yeats, Volume X: Later Articles and Reviews, ed. Colton Johnson (New York: Scribner, 2000), pp. 214–18.

Yeats, W. B., *The Letters of W. B. Yeats*, ed. Allan Wade (New York: Macmillan, 1955).

Yeats, W. B., *The Writing of Sophocles' King Oedipus*, ed. D. R. Clark and J. B. McGuire (Philadelphia: The American Philosophical Society, 1989).

Zeitlin, Froma I., *Playing the Other: Gender and Society in Classical Greek Literature* (Chicago: University of Chicago Press, 1996).

INDEX

Page numbers in *italics* represent illustrations and those followed by n are notes

Printed and bound by CPI Group (UK) Ltd, Croydon, CR0 4YY

28/01/2025

01827094-0004